Culture, Curers, and Contagion

CHANDLER & SHARP PUBLICATIONS IN ANTHROPOLOGY
AND RELATED FIELDS

GENERAL EDITORS: L. L. Langness and Robert B. Edgerton

Culture, Curers, and Contagion

Readings for Medical Social Science

Selected and Edited by
NORMAN KLEIN

CALIFORNIA STATE UNIVERSITY
LOS ANGELES

Chandler & Sharp Publishers, Inc.
Novato, California

To:
*Goldie
and
Hershel*

Library of Congress Cataloging in Publication Data

Main entry under title:

Culture, curers, and contagion.

(Chandler & Sharp publications in anthropology
and related fields)
Bibliography: p.
1.   Social medicine—Addresses, essays, lectures.
2.   Medical anthropology—Addresses, essays,
lectures.   I.   Klein, Norman, 1942–
RA418.C85   362.1'08   79-10888
ISBN   O-88316-531-7

Book designed by Joe Roter
Editor: W. L. Parker
Composition by Publications Services of Marin

Contents

Acknowledgments

I would like to thank a number of friends for their assistance in the preparation of this volume. Esther Kwan-Chew, Judyann Nielsen, and Mary Riedel provided valuable service in typing portions of the manuscript as well as assisting with correspondence. I am especially grateful to Judith Terzi and Elliott Oring for their encouragement, criticism, and editorial assistance. Terzi gave willingly, Oring only under duress. Oring also suggested the title of this book, for which I owe him my thanks. Unfortunately he will assume no responsibility for any errors in it.

Culture, Curers, and Contagion

Introduction

Well-being is a human concern in all societies—in part because humans, like other life forms, are susceptible to illness. René Dubos (1959, 1965) contends that this state of affairs is axiomatic in that organisms must continually adapt (for better or worse) to their total surroundings. It would appear that perfect health is "incompatible with the process of living." Hans Selye (1956) reflects the same sentiment with his assertion that stress is endemic to life and that to realize a full life an individual *must* experience stress.

The human adjustment to life's stresses and the human concern with health are heightened by that quality which gives *Homo sapiens* its uniqueness—namely, *culture.* There is little human behavior that can be seen as truly autonomous, truly independent of culture. Even the manner and the time of rendering a belch are culturally mediated. And since culture is so important to the human condition, it is necessary to examine precisely what we are talking about when we speak of a person's culture. For present purposes it is best to adopt a position that emphasizes cognition. Culture, then, represents the way people perceive and shape their world. It is extra-somatic in the sense that humans are not born with a specific set of perceptual categories; people must *learn* how to see and interpret things. Indispensable to this learning process is the ability to conceive and use symbols. It is with this special faculty that humans are able to conceptualize and to bestow meaning as well as to express their ideas. One well-known illustration of this faculty is that only humans can distinguish between plain and holy water.

Effective communication of such human products as thoughts, ideas, innovations, and values is also basic to the concept of culture. Effective communication can be accomplished only when there is at least some sharing of behaviors, images, and ideas. If humans are indeed culture-bearing animals, they are by no means all bearers of the same culture. Part of the reason that health is a human concern may be that it can be

1

pondered. However, the perception of health differs from culture to culture as well as from individual to individual. One culture may place great emphasis on the health aspect of individuals' lives; another may deem this matter of little concern. Individuals differ similarly: witness Monsieur Argan, the main character in Molière's *Le malade imaginaire.* Argan is a hypochondriac obsessed with his "conditions." His brother Béralde, in contrast, has no patience for the doctors of his day, ridicules Argan, and considers it folly to let one's life be governed by real or imagined maladies.

Sometimes such similarities and differences between and within cultures are obvious. More often they are not. Obvious or subtle, they require us to gain an understanding of how people conceptualize the health aspect of their lives.

Health, as a category, includes a wide variety of practices, attitudes, and beliefs held by different peoples. Already mentioned was the amount of concern attributed to the state of well-being. Other facets of health range from the actual defining of illnesses, to explanations of disease causation, and the course of action to be taken in the restoration of health. In accepting the view that cultural behavior is basically individual behavior, it is not difficult to see why there is this great diversity of cultures in the world. Most fundamentally, no two individuals are exactly alike either physically or in their personal experiences. Even so, they also may share a great deal. People who have the most contact with each other, who can be described as members of the same society, will share a wide range of similar values, knowledges, and behaviors. Such people are often characterized as being members of the same culture. Incidentally, shared experience does not require direct interaction between individuals. The "simultaneous" revelations of Wallace and Darwin and of Crick and Watson and Pauling are well-known illustrations of this fact.

It should also be no surprise that people who have the least contact (direct or indirect) with each other tend to have the least in common with each other. It is logical that such differences will apply to groups of people as well. The degree of difference between interacting cultures (actually between people bearing different cultures) will vary and will depend in part on such factors as the intensity and nature of the contact.

Perceptions of health and illness differ from individual to individual and from culture to culture. Differences and similarities in such perceptions depend on a multitude of complex social, cultural, and environmental factors. People involved in the health professions in the multicultural United States are confronted with the challenge of trying to understand the implications of such differences for the provision of quality health services to their clients. The behavioral and social sciences provide insight into the complexities associated with this variation. A number of concepts and concerns central to the social sciences are emphasized in the articles and comments that follow, among them the concepts of culture, cultural relativism, ethnocentrism, and race. The comparative method provides the underlying organizational theme. It is felt that comparing and contrasting beliefs, behaviors, and institutions across national, cultural, and ethnic boundaries will result in a better understanding of problems.

There has been a tendency over the decades to isolate disciplines and attempt to describe what distinguishes one from the other. But clearly there is a great deal of overlap between fields, and it is far from my intent to further the segmentation with this collection. Attempts to distinguish between anthropology and sociology furnish a case in point, whose mutual differences and strong similarities can be illustrated. It would, for example, be naive to believe that only anthropologists use the comparative method and study folk societies while only sociologists study urban American culture and use statistical techniques. While discussion of differences as well as similarities between medical anthropology and medical sociology (and medical geography and medical psychology for that matter) might be interesting, the differences do not warrant any special concern in the context of this collection. Discipline alone did not dictate the choice of articles. Articles were selected which seemed to touch on the variety of environmental and sociocultural factors that appear important to an understanding of different peoples and their conceptions of health and curing. In addition to the general concepts previously cited, these articles specifically deal with such topics as ecology, environment, nutrition, epidemiology, folk medicine, and mental illness as well as with the effects upon health of people's religion, economics, politics, values, and world view. Also dealt with are different ways in which people have been categorized (for instance, social classes, racial groups, subcultures, ethnic collectivities) and the health beliefs of some of these peoples. All of the articles, however, reflect a basic relativist perspective. They emphasize an understanding of and sensitivity to cultural differences and people's problems and can, therefore, be applied to discussions of groups not covered in these readings.

Finally, selection of most of the articles was determined by style. I have found that students prefer to read the type of material presented in this volume. Because of the tone and nature of these articles, students not only find the subject more exciting, but also find they are better able to retain pertinent information. How can the article by André M. Tao-Kim-Hai be paraphrased without losing its essence? Clearly, effective style assists readers in remembering important concepts when it is able to transform reports or discussions into *experiences*.

The articles are drawn from a wide variety of professional journals, books, and magazines, many of which are "popular" (such as *New Yorker, Penthouse,* and *McCall's)*. For the most part they are not overtly technical, yet they make the significant points. Furthermore, this collection is intended to have an interdisciplinary flavor. The articles are by anthropologists, sociologists, nurses, physicians, freelance writers, psychologists, and chemists. The introductions to the articles are not intended merely as summaries, but as a set of guides for the reading and discussion of each section. Some of my own biases undoubtedly appear, and I must affirmatively acknowledge that some of these readings have other uses and interpretations.

Medicine in any society does not exist in a vacuum. Its form is a reflection of the cultural values and beliefs of the different peoples. This sociocultural component of medicine has, unfortunately, become increasingly cut off from its technical component. In recent years there has been an effort in the social sciences to restore the connection between these two aspects of medicine. This effort has now produced a wealth of articles and books that deal with the sociocultural aspects of health and illness. Since anthropologists first began collecting cultural data they have amassed a wide range of information on medically related topics for peoples all over the world. Likewise, sociologists have long been contributing knowledge on the social aspects of medicine. In more recent decades psychologists and psychiatrists (as well as anthropologists and sociologists) have been addressing themselves to the issues related to transcultural psychiatry. A sampling of the literature drawn from a variety of fields but relevant to the issues dealt with in this volume is offered in A Note on Readings that follows the selections and precedes the list of References.

A word about the list of References: It includes all of those cited either in the articles or in the introductions with the following exceptions. It was felt that two highly technical bibliographies could be omitted since the original articles could be easily obtained—in the articles by Ortiz de Montellano and by Mathews, Glasse, and Lindenbaum. Two articles (by Anderson and Tighe and by Snow) contained bibliographies not referred to in the body of their papers but these also are incorporated in the general list of References.

The book is divided into the following five sections: Culture and Contagion, The Ecology of Health, Patients and Practitioners, Health Care in a Pluralistic Society, and Health Belief Systems. While each has a unifying theme, no section should be considered as totally self-contained. Viewed in its totality, this collection is intended to present concepts relevant to an understanding of a variety of health beliefs and practices and should provide an important perspective in the planning and provision of health-care services in our society.

I

CULTURE AND CONTAGION

Culture influences almost all human activity. The way to walk (to strut or saunter), the way to show respect, the way to laugh—these vary from culture to culture. The appropriateness of behavior is established and defined by the bearers of a particular culture. Removed from its cultural context, customary behavior may appear bizarre or dangerous.

Social scientists have long cautioned against interpreting the actions or beliefs of other peoples by using one's own standards. This idea of *cultural relativism* permeates the anthropological and sociological literature. While the message appears simple, ethnocentric violations are common and widespread. It is, perhaps, fortunate that many misunderstandings of behavior go unnoticed and others are often minor and can be forgiven, or forgotten, or at least ignored. It is also possible, however, that resultant insults may have major consequences. On a grand scale these may include political and economic ruin for nations or governments. Of equal importance, albeit on a more proximate, individual level (and more relevant for our purposes), the product may include prolonged illness, suffering, and inappropriate health care.

There is a large body of behaviors and beliefs in each culture which does not, at first glance, appear related to issues of health. Attitudes concerning such diverse topics as food, beauty, time, and modesty can all affect people's health and their acceptance of care. It is no secret, for example, that many people in our society are reluctant to appear nude in public or private. There are numerous references in the medical literature concerning patients who did not wish to be seen nude by a practitioner of the opposite sex (or of either sex for that matter).

This variable sense of modesty is most easily illustrated at the cross-cultural level. The Botocudo woman in the Amazon who wears only facial plugs and a thin string about her waist races into the forest totally embarrassed after being enticed into giving up those plugs. The Tapirapé man in Central Brazil is clad in a thin piece of palm fiber tied snugly about his prepuce in order to insure concealment of the glans of the penis—and no self-respecting Tapirapé man would be caught with his palm down. Clearly, modesty in the United States is experienced at a point different from those described above. Nevertheless, all people are modest or can be made to feel modest in some way; we all have a modesty quotient. It is important to stress, however, that no two people have the same sense of modesty and that any general pattern for any particular culture will most certainly not apply to all members of that society. It is not diffi-cult to see that such cultural differences have profound ramifications for systems of medical treatment and health care delivery.

In all cultures there are actions that are forbidden or undesirable. To commit such an action might precipitate special behavior toward the offender, who will be seen as conta-gious and stigmatized. The notion of contagion antedates modern biological thinking and may take various forms. It may be, for example, organic, social, or ritual in origin. Contagion then is not a merely biological fact but has a social character as well. An instance of contagion seen as polluting or defiling in one culture may not be perceived as such in another. This differ-ence is illustrated in Cassel's (1955) description of the actions of a Zulu father regarding his daughter's "illness." After much discussion the father accepted that his daughter had contrac-ted tuberculosis and should be hospitalized. But then the physi-cian undid his persuasion by further explaining that the daughter's condition was contagious and that, in fact, she was a carrier. The father thereupon denied the diagnosis and refused to have his daughter hospitalized. For him to accept the physi-cian's argument would be to agree tacitly that the daughter was a malevolent person, for in this culture only a witch or sorcerer was seen to have the power of contagion.

Stigma in this case derived from the interpretation of disease transmission as explained by an outsider. A number of condi-tions in our culture carry the same sort of stigma described in the Zulu example. Venereal disease is one. Acknowledgment of infection by the spirochete may be seen as admitting that one's child (or oneself) is sexually active or, worse, promiscuous. What begins to emerge is the idea that there are "good" and "bad" diseases. And the same condition may be seen on occasion as good or bad. In our culture a pregnancy resulting from rape or incest is generally received differently from one that is the product of acceptable love. Clearly, there are proper and improper paths to a condition.

Venereal disease, leprosy, and physical deformities are obvious examples of stigmatized conditions. In such cases, where there is awareness of the feelings attached to the illness, explicit attempts are often made to deal with the special circumstances associated with conditions. Numerous problems, however, are embarrassing or are perceived as associated with negative behavior. Because such stigma is often subtle, it is most likely that no special consideration is given in designing programs to deal with such problems. A common result is that people will defer or decline treatment.

Stigma has been selected as just one of the issues that can be discussed with reference to culture and contagion since it is, in a sense, a manifestation of cultural contagion. The articles in this section relate to several other questions concerning the meaning of culture and suggest common problems and issues that require consideration.

Horace Miner illuminates some of our American values and practices. While his misexplanation is intended, his essay reveals a number of our foibles as it explores special American feelings about pain, excrement, nudity, and beauty. The reader is provided, through this pseudoanalysis of an aspect of our own culture, with a lesson in how ethnocentric and misguided we may be when looking at other cultures.

Elliott Oring hits below the belt to deal with taboo topics, raising the very important question of how we transmit the rules of behavior concerning things we prefer not to talk about. Such subjects as unconsciously patterned behavior and shared yet individual anxieties are also examined.

Proxemic systems are culturally conditioned to a great extent and human behavior is clearly affected. Edward T. Hall applies proxemic principles to the realm of health care. In American culture there is a tendency to isolate and avoid the ill even when doing so is unnecessary. This is true both in and out of the hospital setting. Efforts should be made to further determine the range and impact of such isolation. Even when isolation is necessary it may be wise to present an illusion of nonisolation and nonabandonment.

The subject of race has been a major concern of social scientists for many decades. The *New York Times* article on racial categories provides insight into how arbitrary categories can be. It also suggests the effect on people's lives of social and political policy related to racial criteria. Placing people into such categories often results in the assigning of value to the categories and not the individual people. Groups may be seen as having differing worth. One group becomes "better" than the next and may insist on differential treatment in such areas as wages, accommodations, or health care.

Death and dying are still other subjects that appear to be associated with stigma. Death as a topic is often taboo and the dying are generally avoided in American culture. My essay in this section deals, in general, with how people communicate about their feelings and it specifically appeals for caution in the routinizing of the increased awareness of and concern for the dying.

In the introduction to this book, culture was defined with an emphasis on the human ability to conceive and use symbols. The articles in this section illustrate this faculty and demonstrate the complexity and diversity of culture in the human experience. Later sections further serve to illustrate these points. Such cultural diversity, especially as related to the health dimension, adds special meaning to the "art" of medicine.

Body Ritual among the Nacirema

Horace Miner

This well-known article illustrates the concepts of culture, cultural relativism, and ethnocentrism. For years now, many unsuspecting readers have failed to identify immediately the people being described. One of the reasons for the obfuscated nature of the article is the author's substitution of anthropological jargon for descriptive terms that are more familiar to most readers. Much of the description is not really inaccurate; however, there is a lack of sound explanation and interpretation of the beliefs and actions being described. We are, additionally, being presented with a humorous view of our culture and health practices. A more baleful view of our health services is apparent in observations such as our continued seeking of painful treatment even though our teeth continue to decay. Again, what is missing is our cultural perspective and explanation of the described actions. Miner's article may be discussed at various levels; here are only a few: (1) as a parody of ethnographic description; (2) as an exemplification of the dangers of misinterpretation in cross-cultural research (and ease of misrepresentation); (3) as an illustration of etic/emic distinctions; (4) as a challenge to some of our own "natural/normal" behaviors through putting them in an unfamiliar context; and (5) as an explication of some of our nonconscious assumptions.

The anthropologist has become so familiar with the diversity of ways in which different peoples behave in similar situations that he is not apt to be surprised by even the most exotic customs. In fact, if all of the logically possible combinations of behavior have not been found somewhere in the world, he is apt to suspect that they must be present in some yet undescribed tribe. This point has, in fact, been expressed with respect to clan organization by Murdock (1949:71). In this light, the magical beliefs and practices of the Nacirema present such unusual aspects that it seems

---

Reproduced by permission of the American Anthropological Association from the *American Anthropologist,* Vol. 58, No. 3, 1956.

desirable to describe them as an example of the extremes to which human behavior can go.

Professor Linton first brought the ritual of the Nacirema to the attention of anthropologists twenty years ago (1936:326), but the culture of this people is still very poorly understood. They are a North American group living in the territory between the Canadian Cree, the Yaqui and Tarahumare of Mexico, and the Carib and Arawak of the Antilles. Little is known of their origin, although tradition states that they came from the east. According to Nacirema mythology, their nation was originated by a culture hero, Notgnihsaw, who is otherwise known for two great feats of strength—the throwing of a piece of wampum across the river Pa-To-Mac and the chopping down of a cherry tree in which the Spirit of Truth resided.

Nacirema culture is characterized by a highly developed market economy which has evolved in a rich natural habitat. While much of the people's time is devoted to economic pursuits, a large part of the fruits of these labors and a considerable portion of the day are spent in ritual activity. The focus of this activity is the human body, the appearance and health of which loom as a dominant concern in the ethos of the people. While such a concern is certainly not unusual, its ceremonial aspects and associated philosophy are unique.

The fundamental belief underlying the whole system appears to be that the human body is ugly and that its natural tendency is to debility and disease. Incarcerated in such a body, man's only hope is to avert these characteristics through the use of the powerful influences of ritual and ceremony. Every household has one or more shrines devoted to this purpose. The more powerful individuals in the society have several shrines in their houses and, in fact, the opulence of a house is often referred to in terms of the number of such ritual centers it possesses. Most houses are of wattle and daub construction, but the shrine rooms of the more wealthy are walled in stone. Poorer families imitate the rich by applying pottery plaques to their shrine walls.

While each family has at least one such shrine, the rituals associated with it are not family ceremonies but are private and secret. The rites are normally only discussed with children, and then only during the period when they are being initiated into these mysteries. I was able, however, to establish sufficient rapport with the natives to examine these shrines and to have the rituals described to me.

The focal point of the shrine is a box or chest which is built into the wall. In this chest are kept the many charms and magical potions without which no native believes he could live. These preparations are secured from a variety of specialized practitioners. The most powerful of these are the medicine men, whose assistance must be rewarded with substantial gifts. However, the medicine men do not provide the curative potions for their clients, but decide what the ingredients should be and then write them down in an ancient and secret language. This writing is understood only by the medicine men and by the herbalists who, for another gift, provide the required charm.

The charm is not disposed of after it has served its purpose, but is placed in the charm-box of the household shrine. As these magical materials are specific for certain ills, and the real or imagined maladies of the people are many, the charm-box is usually full to overflowing. The magical packets are so numerous that people forget what their purposes were and fear to use them again. While the natives are very vague on this point, we can only assume that the idea in retaining all the old magical materials is that their presence in the charm-box, before which the body rituals are conducted, will in some way protect the worshipper.

Beneath the charm-box is a small font. Each day every member of the family, in succession, enters the shrine room, bows his bead before the charm-box, mingles different sorts of holy water in the font, and proceeds with a brief rite of ablution. The holy waters are secured from the Water Temple of the community, where the priests conduct elaborate ceremonies to make the liquid ritually pure.

In the hierachy of magical practitioners, and below the medicine men in prestige, are specialists whose designation is best translated "holy-mouth-men." The Nacirema have an almost pathological horror of and fascination with the mouth, the condition of which is believed to have supernatural influence on all social relationships. Were it not for the rituals of the mouth, they believe that their teeth would fall out, their gums bleed, their jaws shrink, their friends desert them, and their lovers reject them. They also believe that a strong relationship exists between oral and moral characteristics. For example, there is a ritual ablution of the mouth for children which is supposed to improve their moral fiber.

The daily body ritual performed by everyone includes a mouth-rite. Despite the fact that these people are so punctilious about care of the mouth, this rite involves a practice which strikes the uninitiated stranger as revolting. It was reported to me that the ritual consists of inserting a small bundle of hog hairs into the mouth, along with certain magical powders, and then moving the bundle in a highly formalized series of gestures.

In addition to the private mouth-rite, the people seek out a holy-mouth-man once or twice a year. These practitioners have an impressive set of paraphernalia, consisting of a variety of augers, awls, probes, and prods. The use of these objects in the exorcism of the evils of the mouth involves almost unbelievable ritual torture of the client. The holy-mouth-man opens the client's mouth and, using the above mentioned tools, enlarges any holes which decay may have created in the teeth. Magical materials are put into these holes. If there are no naturally occurring holes in the teeth, large sections of one or more teeth are gouged out so that the supernatural substance can be applied. In the client's view, the purpose of these ministrations is to arrest decay and to draw friends. The extremely sacred and traditional character of the rite is evident in the fact that the natives return to the holy-mouth-men year after year, despite the fact that their teeth continue to decay.

It is to be hoped that, when a thorough study of the Nacirema is made, there will be careful inquiry into the personality structure of these people. One has but to watch the gleam in the eye of a holy-mouth-man, as he jabs an awl into an exposed nerve, to suspect that a certain amount of sadism is involved. If this can be established, a very interesting pattern emerges, for most of the population shows definite masochistic tendencies. It was to these that Professor Linton referred in discussing a distinctive part of the daily body ritual which is performed only by men. This part of the rite involves scraping and lacerating the surface of the face with a sharp instrument. Special women's rites are performed only four times during each lunar month, but what they lack in frequency is made up in barbarity. As part of this ceremony, women bake their heads in small ovens for about an hour. The theoretically interesting point is that what seems to be preponderantly masochistic people have developed sadistic specialists.

The medicine men have an imposing temple, or *latipso*, in every community of any size. The more elaborate ceremonies required to treat very sick patients can only be performed at this temple. These ceremonies involve not only the thaumaturge but a permanent group of vestal maidens who move sedately about the temple chambers in distinctive costume and headdress.

The *latipso* ceremonies are so harsh that it is phenomenal that a fair proportion of the really sick natives who enter the temple ever recover. Small children whose indoctrination is still incomplete have been known to resist attempts to take them to the temple because "that is where you go to die." Despite this fact, sick adults are not only willing but eager to undergo the protracted ritual purification, if they can afford to do so. No matter how ill the supplicant or how grave the emergency, the guardians of many temples will not admit a client if he cannot give a rich gift to the custodian. Even after one has gained admission and survived the ceremonies, the guardians will not permit the neophyte to leave until he makes another gift.

The supplicant entering the temple is first stripped of all his or her clothes. In every-day life the Nacirema avoids exposure of his body and its natural functions. Bathing and excretory acts are performed only in the secrecy of the household shrine, where they are ritualized as part of the body-rites. Psychological shock results from the fact that body secrecy is suddenly lost upon entry into the *latipso*. A man, whose own wife has never seen him in an excretory act, suddenly finds himself naked and assisted by a vestal maiden while he performs his natural functions into a sacred vessel.

This sort of ceremonial treatment is necessitated by the fact that the excreta are used by a diviner to ascertain the course and nature of the client's sickness. Female clients, on the other hand, find their naked bodies are subjected to the scrutiny, manipulation and prodding of the medicine men.

Few supplicants in the temple are well enough to do anything but lie on their hard beds. The daily ceremonies, like the rites of the holy-mouth-men, involve discomfort and torture. With ritual precision, the vestals awaken their miserable charges each dawn and roll them about on their beds of pain while performing ablutions, in the formal movements of which the maidens are highly trained. At other times they insert magic wands in the supplicant's mouth or force him to eat substances which are supposed to be healing. From time to time the medicine men come to their clients and jab magically treated needles into their flesh. The fact that these temple ceremonies may not cure, and may even kill the neophyte, in no way decreases the people's faith in the medicine men.

There remains one other kind of practitioner, known as a "listener." This witch-doctor has the power to exorcise the devils that lodge in the heads of people who have been bewitched. The Nacirema believe that parents bewitch their own children. Mothers are particularly suspected of putting a curse on children while teaching them the secret body rituals. The counter-magic of the witch-doctor is unusual in its lack of ritual. The patient simply tells the "listener" all his troubles and fears, beginning with the earliest difficulties he can remember. The memory displayed by the Nacirema in these exorcism sessions is truly remarkable. It is not uncommon for the patient to bemoan the rejection he felt upon being weaned as a babe, and a few individuals even see their troubles going back to the traumatic effects of their own birth.

In conclusion, mention must be made of certain practices which have their base in native esthetics but which depend upon the pervasive aversion to the natural body and its functions. There are ritual fasts to make fat people thin and ceremonial feasts to make thin people fat. Still other rites are used to make women's breasts larger if they are small, and smaller if they are large. General dissatisfaction with breast shape is symbolized in the fact that the ideal form is virutally outside the range of human variation. A few woman afflicted with almost inhuman hypermammary development are so idolized that they make a handsome living by simply going from village to village and permitting the natives to stare at them for a fee.

Reference has already been made to the fact that excretory functions are ritualized, routinized, and relegated to secrecy. Natural reproductive functions are similarly distorted. Intercourse is taboo as a topic and scheduled as an act. Efforts are made to avoid pregnancy by the use of magical materials or by limiting intercourse to certain phases of the moon. Conception is actually very infrequent. When pregnant, women dress so as to hide their condition. Parturition takes place in secret, without friends or relatives to assist, and the majority of women do not nurse their infants.

Our review of the ritual life of the Nacirema has certainly shown them to be a magic-ridden people. It is hard to understand how they have managed to exist so long under the burdens which they have imposed upon themselves. But even such exotic customs as these take on real meaning when they are viewed with the insight provided by Malinowski when he wrote (1948:70):

Looking from far and above, from our high places of safety in the developed civilization, it is easy to see all the crudity and irrelevance of magic. But without its power and guidance early man could not have mastered his practical difficulties as he has done, nor could man have advanced to the higher stages of civilization.

From Uretics to Uremics: A Contribution toward the Ethnography of Peeing

Elliott Oring

Here is an amusing article, yet it is so only in part because the author is a funny person. Humor is also derived from the choice of a subject that many people discuss only with difficulty. The action is so common that it would seem to require little discussion, yet discussion is needed. In this essay, we are given the opportunity to explore such different levels of culture as the "explicit" and "implicit." Just as the grammar of language is learned informally and at an implicit level, so is proper bathroom behavior. A number of students, having read this article, have gone home and quizzed their young male offspring and have found that even at an early age these young have become practitioners of the described behavior. It seems that children are not formally instructed in the area of what proper options remain if, for example, urinal two is occupied, yet there is conformity through adherence to unspoken rules. We are also given the opportunity to examine situations where individuals, made to feel uncomfortable, believe that their discomfort is idiosyncratic when in fact most people feel the same way. We can see that what people perceive as personal anxiety is really shared anxiety. This duality is also present in other areas of cultural behavior and may have special importance with reference to attitudes concerning health as well as to the nature of services provided. Readers interested in other uses of and attitudes toward human exudations might read Theodor Rosebury's *Life on Man* (1969), especially Chapters 9 through 12.

Other than the concern with toilet training practices inspired by psychoanalytic theory, elimination behavior has excited little anthropological interest to date. There has been a tendency to keep one's ethnographic mind above one's middle, and although social scientists have devoted full sessions at their annual meetings to the study of foodways, the investigation of the

Reprinted by permission of the author from the *California Anthropologist,* Vol. 4, Spring 1975, pp. 1–5. Copyright © 1975 by Elliott Oring.

inevitable consequences of foodways, elimination patterns, is a veritable
wasteland.

It is not surprising that elimination behavior has merited so little attention given the negative attitude our culture holds towards bodily exuviae
and exudations. Feces, urine, sperm, ear wax, mucus, spittle, sweat and
dandruff are all regarded as dirty and defiling. Only tears are exempt.
Otherwise we tend to avoid these substances when produced by others and
conceal those of our own making. The colloquial terms for such substances
are regularly employed in speech to connote negative properties and attri-
butes. *"Shithead!* Go and *piss* away your life with those *scum* you call
friends, and take that *snot* of a brother with you,"* may serve as a synoptic
if untypical example. The proverbial "shit, piss, and corruption" perhaps
states the American attitude most succinctly.

This paper will focus on only one small aspect of elimination behavior in
our culture, urination patterns in public men's rooms, but it hopes to
suggest the fertility of the entire field.

A typical peeing pattern commences, not with the physiological process
itself, but rather with the withdrawal from the social group. Such
withdrawal may require some explanation, and one must choose the appropriate terminology from the various language levels available to describe the
intended activity.

The *formal language* includes such terms as "urine," "urination," and
"micturition." They are rarely employed in casual social situations and
tend to be restricted to doctor's offices, laboratories, lectures, and educational films and pamphlets. "To piss," "to take a wicked piss," and
possibly "to take a leak," are examples of what might be called the *vulgar
language* and though employed with some regularity, their use significantly
depends upon the social composition of the group from which one is
withdrawing. If *baby language* is used by adults, women tend to employ it
more than men. Its use implies that there is something cute, childish or
humorous about the intended activity. "I've got to go do number one,"
"go tinkle," "go wee wee," "go pee," "make sissy" or "go potty" are
typical examples. *Euphemistic language* is most commonly employed. It
usually refers to the place rather than the activity to be performed, for
example: "I've got to go to the bathroom," "to the john," "to the head,"
"to the men's room" or "to the can." However, more hyperbolic
euphemisms describe activity rather than setting: "I've got to see a man
about a horse," "I'm going to walk the dog," "I'm going to use the
sandbox," "I'm going to powder my nose" (female), or "I'm going to
wash up." (See Sagarin, 1962:44–78; also Ellis, 1951:117–125.)

Bathrooms serve as loci for social activity only when such activities are
otherwise prohibited by particular circumstances. Thus soldiers may gather
in the john after lights-out or junior high school students may hang out in

the bathroom while classes are in session, but in most situations entering a public men's room implies you have come with the purpose of using one of the facilities: stalls, urinals, basins, mirror or paper supplies. When your activity is completed you are expected to depart.

Peeing is the activity primarily intended by the majority of males entering a men's room. As the facilities in a men's room are spatially separated, the committed pee-er must approach the urinals and select one of several arranged usually in a line along the wall. Though the situation most often noted by this observer involved a series of five adjacent wall urinals, many of the principles governing behavior seem applicable to a variety of other arrangements.

The principle of personal peeing space

One's personal space during urination extends one urinal to the left and right of the pee-er and therefore a minimum one-urinal distance between oneself and fellow pee-ers should be maintained whenever possible. Thus if urinal 1 is occupied, theoretically, urinals 3, 4 and 5 are available. If 3 is occupied, 1 and 5 are available. Of course, if the only unoccupied urinals are adjacent to other pee-ers, they may be selected. But if there are any isolated urinals, they must be filled before urinals adjacent to other pee-ers can be used. There are some individuals who will not violate peeing space even when the only urinals available are adjacent to other pee-ers and will wash their hands or comb their hair until the distribution of people changes sufficiently to allow them their personal space. Others will simply use the stalls when they feel their personal space cannot be guaranteed. (See Hall, 1969).

The principle of excessive dissociation

Despite the need for spacing during urination beyond that permitted by bathroom design, excessive spacing is avoided. There is a unidirectional maximum distance which should not be exceeded in the selection of a urinal. Thus, if urinal 1 is occupied, urinal 3 or 4 is subsequently selected, rather than 5. As soon as urinal 3 is occupied, however, urinal 5 becomes the necessary choice. This spacing is unidirectional with respect to the bathroom entrance. If urinal 5 is initially occupied, urinal 1 nevertheless remains a viable choice.

When all the urinals are unoccupied all urinals are theoretically available, yet only urinals 1, 2, 3, and 4 are serious considerations and then urinals 1 or 3 are selected twice as frequently as urinals 2 or 4. A possible explanation of this pattern of initial selection is that strategy-minded individuals will realize that selection of an odd numbered urinal allows for the

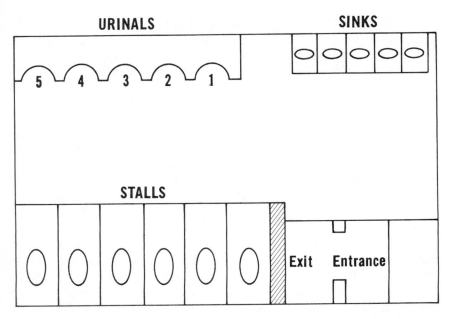

accommodation of *two* more individuals with personal peeing space, should they enter the room, whereas the initial selection of an even numbered urinal limits further accommodation to only *one.*

The state of a particular urinal will also affect selection. A "clean" urinal is preferred to one that is unflushed or covered with occasional pubic hairs. But unless the state of the urinal is so extreme as to be regarded by an individual as "unusable," and thus alter his perception of urinals available, it will only govern choice within a range of urinals that will not lead to a violation of the principle of personal peeing space. Thus, if urinal 1 is occupied, the state of the urinal may determine whether 3 or 4 is selected. All other urinals would have to be regarded as "unusable" before urinal 2 would be chosen.

The violation of the principle of personal peeing space regularly occurs in only one situation. One may stand adjacent to another pee-er, with other urinals available, only when that person is known. Conversation invariably develops between these individuals. Such conversation is often phatic and serves to demonstrate the existence of a prior social relationship rather than to convey specific information. All conversations in men's rooms are loud and can be heard by all present. There is no attempt at whispered or surreptitious communication.

During the act of peeing itself, eyes are front. One may look up, straight ahead, or slightly down (but only slightly). Looking to either side at fellow pee-ers, even though they may be more than one urinal's distance away, may be regarded as a violation of peeing space. Staring, of course, is absolutely forbidden.

The hands play a rather limited part for most pee-ers. They unzip or unbutton the fly and extract the member from its bondage within the underclothing. From that point on the hands are of little use. They are not used to hold the penis but are placed at the sides, behind the back, on the hips, in the pockets, or are rested on the flushing mechanism above the urinal. Peeing into the bowl in a stall or private bathroom requires a greater use of the hands to assure direction of the stream into the bowl rather than onto the floor. Wall urinals, however, do not require marksmanship, and thus free the hands. The hands become active again in shaking behavior and in putting the penis back. However, all this may be more a matter of individual style than adherence to a rigid set of rules.

Shaking behavior is common among most male pee-ers. It involves shaking the penis up and down several times in order to extract the last drop of urine remaining in the urethra by centrifugal force before reinserting it in one's clothing. Of course, every male knows that it is impossible to extract all the urine in this manner, and that inevitably the final drops emerge only after the penis is safely back in the pants. Nevertheless, the fact that shaking behavior is only partly successful is rarely acknowledged by individual pee-ers, though the problem is common enough and causes sufficient anxiety to produce various pieces of scatological folklore: "No matter how hard you jiggle and squeeze, the last drop always goes down to your knees," (Kira, 1966:75n62), as well as a rather excellent joke about a fellow who is sufficiently bothered by the condition to go to a physician to find out whether it can be surgically corrected.

Despite the fact that most intended pee-ers select a urinal with the best of intentions for action, the road to hell is paved with good intentions. It is not that peeing is not always what it seems to be, but rather that what it seems to be is not always peeing.

When you go in you really have to go. You don't go in just to be screwin' around. You have to go. And when you're there and all of a sudden you can't, you say, "Aw, it'll come any second now." Two seconds go by, three seconds . . . If all else fails you can fake it. You can flush the little goodie and split and no one will ever know the difference.

The fact that one is not actually urinating does not override the rules and patterns of peeing behavior. If anything, they are followed more conscientiously.

Upon leaving the men's room an ablution at the wash basin is usual though not required. The washing is often perfunctory, indicating that its value is symbolic rather than medical. It serves to signal that elimination behavior has concluded, and that the individual is now prepared to resume his previously planned activities.

These singular patterns associated with peeing in public men's rooms may be explained as the behavioral consequences of three interrelated American values: privacy, masculinity, and cool.

Since American culture regards urine and other excretions as dirty, its members are encouraged to eliminate in private from early childhood. The bathroom thus develops as the one truly private room. It is the only room which comes with a lock already on the door. The bathroom is to the home as the home is to the rest of society. It is our *sanctum sanctorum,* our ultimate refuge. For a brief period of time, in the inviolate privacy of the bathroom, we are suspended from the requirements of sociable behavior. Here we may perform our most private and most asocial acts. We may urinate, defecate, masturbate, shoot heroin, and commit suicide without criticism or interruption.

When urination is performed in the semipublic environment of the men's room, behavioral patterns attempt to maintain an illusion of privacy. Thus a sense of personal peeing space develops and is rigorously observed. This peeing space is considerably reinforced by the American male abhorrence of unmasculine behavior. Thus males must display no interest in other men, spatially or visually, particularly at a time when they have bared the organ of their sex. One must stand beyond touching distance and keep the eyes averted. To do otherwise would be to invite the suspicion of homosexual interest.

In our culture we do not entirely dissociate excretory and sexual functions. Because the penis serves double duty for elimination and sex, male urination is likely regarded as a sexual performance. Should the inadequate privacy of the men's room inhibit urination, the inability to perform is regarded as a challenge to masculinity. Rather than acknowledge excretory impotence, the would-be pee-er "fakes it" and departs with his public image intact.

The masculine image is also very much involved with particular discomfort and anxiety created by the last few drops that invariably leak out after shaking behavior is completed. Though urine itself is regarded as a defiling substance it is not the sense of pollution that is primary:

There are always a few drops that leak out after you get it back in. It always happens. You can't avoid it. You just hope that the wet spot is on the inside rather than on your pants. No one can see it there.

The fear is not that you have contaminated yourself, but that others will notice. The last few drops challenge an important aspect of the masculine image, the feeling of control. A man is supposed to control his situation, his women, and his emotions. It goes without saying that he should also be able to control his own bodily functions. With those last few drops a man has once again become a child; he has as in days long past "peed in his pants." He is no longer a man, and this knowledge he attempts to conceal for, other than effeminacy, childishness is the most severe accusation that can be directed against an American male. It is perhaps no accident that the term "sissy" connotes unmanliness but is also a reference to urine.

The last significant value affecting public peeing patterns is cool. Cool is related to the masculine image, and it dictates that the myriad of anxieties created by urinating in public are not to be acknowledged. Despite the fact that privacy is desired, if urinal 1 is occupied one does not go to 5. The principle of excessive dissociation is a function of cool. To choose urinal 5 would be to acknowledge that the individual is really uptight about his privacy or that he maximizes his peeing space because he has an inordinate fear of homosexuals or of being considered homosexual. Cool is the value that attempts to publicly deny that privacy and masculinity are bathroom issues. Because of cool, most individuals will choose a urinal adjacent to another pee-er, when no others are available, rather than opt for the privacy of a stall. Because of cool, conversations develop between pee-ers who know each other, for to remain silent is to acknowledge that special principles operate in the bathroom. To avoid conversing with people you know, you must pretend not to notice them. In many cases they will be more than happy to comply.

Basically, this paper hopes to suggest that elimination patterns are intimately linked with a culture's system of values, and that their careful investigation will prove a worthwhile effort. Needless to say, the field of ethnoelimination is wide open and will undoubtedly provide many a student with a wealth of subject matter for serious perusal. Those ethnologists who bemoan the disappearance of the field need only remember it is as near as their own bathrooms.

Proxemics: The Study of Man's Spatial Relations

Edward T. Hall

Several years ago, I encountered an examination question concerning what could be done about a situation where there were too few health facilities to serve a large population. In the facetious part of my response I suggested that one solution would be to design and provide mediocre services—fewer people would seek help and the problem of shortages would disappear. Authors such as Kunnes (1971) and the Ehrenreichs (1970) argue in a very political way that such mediocre services have, in fact, been consistently provided on a grand scale (though not with the above mentioned results). In the following article, using the health setting as a focus, Hall presents insights of a non-political nature concerning an often neglected realm of culture. We are given an opportunity to examine proxemic factors that can affect a person's well-being. People accustomed to modern medical procedures in one culture may be made to feel uncomfortable in an equally modern but different setting in another. Some clues are provided, then, about why many people might be reluctant to adopt "scientific" medicine. Proxemic considerations provide, to be sure, only part of the answer concerning acceptance and rejection of services. However, a cross-cultural examination of proxemics in medical settings might provide us with some interesting insights into the provision of services in a heterogeneous society.

There are many differences in the spatial layout of the hospital, the clinic, and the office of the private practitioner. Man's responses to these differences are not haphazard. Vincent Kling [1959] remarks that there are "happy spaces and gloomy ones." It's the anthropologist's job—using the

Reprinted through the courtesy of the New York Academy of Medicine Library from *Man's Image in Medicine and Anthropology,* Iago Galdston, ed. New York: International Universities Press, 1963 (with abridgements). Copyright © 1963, The New York Academy of Medicine.

tools of his trade—to isolate the significant variables at work, and to discover what spatial cues cause people to differentiate between "happy" and "gloomy" spaces, and how space molds behavior in various contexts.

Fixed Feature Space

Winston Churchill once observed: "We shape our buildings and later they shape us" [Kling, 1959].

Much can be discovered by observing how man uses *fixed* space in an organizational setting. Given a knowledge of the culture, it is possible to form a reasonably firm picture of the structure and function of an organization from its layout. Centrally located functions take precedence over those on the periphery; places at a maximum distance from the center are used for unimportant or low status activities, or for isolation of danger—such commonplace observations are often ignored because they seem to be so obvious.

Searles [1960] thinks that patients occupying rooms at the ends of corridors tend to do less well than patients who are more centrally located. In the same wards, he also noted that patients would put up with a disagreeable roommate, rather than be moved away from the nurses' station, which is the center of gravity of the ward. The pioneering statement on this proposition by Baker, Davies, and Sivadon describes the influence of fixed feature space on the recovery of psychiatric patients [1959].

Space and the Mental Hospital. There is a slowly accumulating body of evidence pointing to the need for a complete re-evaluation and restudy of hospital layout, taking into account cultural, as well as strictly functional factors.

In a series of penetrating papers on the relationship of architecture to the treatment of psychosis, Osmond [1957, 1959] and Izumi [1957] take vigorous exception to the conventional design of modern mental hospitals. They maintain that most are actually antitherapeutic, and tend to aggravate patients' conditions rather than to improve them. They suggest a design that will allow the patient a small place to be away—to shut himself off—from the suffering of others, a place where he can "pull himself together" from time to time. In their conception, these very small spaces radiate in a circle off slightly larger rooms, in which two to four people can interact. These, in turn, are placed around a community day room, in which larger groups can meet. The nursing staff and administrative functions form the core of this radial system.

Paralleling Osmond's thinking is Sivadon's [n.d.] highly unique approach, originated at Neuilly-sur-Marne, and currently being incorporated in a new addition being built for the Château de la Verrière at Le Mesnil-St.-Denis (Seine-et-Oise), France. This new hospital is being built according to World Health Organization plans [Baker, Davies, and Sivadon, 1959].

The entire plant uses space as a therapeutic agent. There are three "villages," arranged in a hierarchy from simple to complex. Ninety patients are housed in each village, 30 to a ward. Open spaces are used to contain the patients, rather than fences and walls. Internal space is designed so that room size can be altered by opening and closing sliding sections of the walls. This feature has much in common with the Japanese practice of opening and closing sections of the house for different occasions and moods, and for different times of the day.

An added consideration in such hospital plans is the distorted space perception of schizophrenic patients. For schizophrenics, distances are exaggerated, so that long halls make them feel small and insignificant. Weckowitz [1957], commenting on the perceptual world of the schizophrenic, describes how size-constancy becomes distorted, and the schizophrenic underestimates the size of objects seen at a distance. He therefore over-estimates distance, which puts a strain on his cybernetic mechanisms. Sivadon treats this condition by re-educating his patients in their use of space. It would be interesting to discover how normal, as well as psychotic, people in different cultures vary in their spatial perceptions.

Room Size. Hospital rooms, as currently designed, take into account virtually everything except the psychological influence of size, proportions, and outside view on the patient.[1]

For example, in a new hospital in the Washington area the rooms are so small that they barely can hold the furniture. How crowding of this type influences the patient's recovery is unknown. In another hospital (also in Washington), a private room in the surgery ward is so small that people constantly deteriorate in this room, and have to be moved. There is undoubtedly a point at which spatial economies begin to bring diminishing returns. We need to know the ideal room size for treating different conditions. We need to know the limits above and below which room size should not go.[2]

Man's tolerance of confining space and crowding is, in general, a function of time and situation [United States Navy . . . , 1959]. In this sense the consequences of bad design and crowded conditions may

---

[1]One of the few exceptions is the previously mentioned Château de la Verrière. Here, actively disturbed schizophrenic patients are given large rooms and terraces with a view, instead of restraints. The more disturbed the patient, the more space he is given. Tubular halls are avoided.

[2]A recent report of the American Institute of Architects' Committee on Hospitals and Health *(AIA Journal,* Sept., 1960) states that the average size of single rooms in American hospitals of recent date is 117 to 172 square feet of floor space. Double rooms average 157 to 210 square feet.

ultimately be less serious in hospitals than in dwellings and offices, where most people spend significant portions of their lives.

In a study I am currently conducting on space as an inducer and reliever of stress in man, office space has been examined using a variety of techniques.[3] Preliminary results indicate that office size is of crucial importance to man's comfort, productivity, and general well-being. Culture is, of course, a very significant variable that has to be taken into account, since cultures vary in the space required for the person. That is, "personal distance" as well as social distance varies from culture to culture [Calhoun, 1961].

Consequences of Crowding. The social consequences of crowding in dwelling rooms has only very recently been isolated from other factors and studies in a systematic way. The usual practice was to collect data on the number of persons or families per room or dwelling unit. It was not until Chombart de Lauwe [1959a, 1959b] calculated the number of square meters available to each individual in different situations that additional significant information became available.

His studies indicate that there are critical limits below which and above which French working-class families show the consequences of either crowding, or its opposite, which is something akin to neglect. When there is less than 8 to 10 square meters per person, social and physical disorders double. Between 8 square meters and 14 square meters per person, pathology is at a minimum. Above 14 meters, there is an increase again. Chombart de Lauwe's explanation of the latter finding is that these statistics came from upwardly mobile homes, where the parents were more interested in status symbols and getting ahead than in the family. Hence, they isolated their children in separate rooms, and did not pay enough attention to them.

It is important also to stress that 8 square meters, as a minimum, is not a constant that remains fixed. It changes in time and space, with culture and with the situation. My own observations indicate that individual distance with middle class and working class French people is much less than that for the same groups in the United States. In France, therefore, it is possible to fit more people into a given space, without their personal distances overlapping too much, than it is in the United States.

The Hospital in a Transcultural Setting. In the transfer of the fixed features of hospital designs across cultural boundaries, there is a constant danger that there will be an automatic reproduction of the familiar patterns of the donor. Failure to recognize intangibles of the other's culture is not surprising when it is considered that, even within the context of our own

---

[3]"Social Space as Bio-communication," under a grant from the United States Public Health Service.

culture, anatomy and convention are largely responsible for space allocation and layout. It is possible to measure a man, a bed, and a chair and
calculate the cost of building and maintaining a square foot of floor, but
not the cost of crowding. The data are meager on the behavioral side, and
the temptation to act on the basis of simple tangibles is strong in both the
transcultural and intracultural situation.

Sollenberger [1951–1955] provides the classic example, that of the
transmittal of a four-story hospital plant plan, *unaltered,* from the United
States to the center of China. He describes a four-story mission hospital
built on the northwest plains of China, for which literally everything had to
be packed in by animal back, including a boiler to run the heating plant.
From the very beginning, the Chinese patients disliked the hospital and
there was difficulty getting them to enter it. Because of its very great
distance from urban centers, and the difficulty of maintaining equipment, it
soon became apparent that the second-story wards were a luxury that even
the Western medical missionaries could ill afford. The hospital limped
along as a little-used, rather unpopular affair until the Chinese Communists
arrived. Then, it was torn down, brick by brick, and reassembled according
to the Chinese pattern. Instead of wards, there were small huts, separated in
space, and clustered around a clinical and administrative center. The small
huts in which the patients were housed were designed in that way so that the
families would stay with the patients and care for them.

The "family care" plan, as a matter of fact, is popular in many parts of
the world. A new hospital in El Salvador attracted considerable attention a
number of years ago because it incorporated this feature in the design of the
wards. The Salvadorians thought that the Americans (who designed the
hospital) were at last beginning to acknowledge that the culture of El
Salvador was different from their own—and not necessarily inferior.

Cultural Determinants in Crowding and Health.   Western medicine
stresses the isolation of the sick and the minimization of their contact with
the healthy. Yet, there are a number of instances, in other cultures, where
leaving the patient alone or with only a very few people around him would
signify approaching death. This pattern used to characterize the Navaho,
and undoubtedly is still extant in many of the more remote regions of the
Navaho reservation.

Traditionally, cure of the Navaho requires the presence and active
cooperation of many people. There are special ceremonial houses (fixed-
feature hogans) for curing ceremonies. Illness also provides virtually the
only occasion for everyone in these widely scattered communities to get
together. If the patient dies, however, the ground and the building immediately become contaminated. According to Navaho belief, evil spirits will
infect anyone who steps on this ground, for untold years to come. For this

reason, the white hospitals used to be avoided by the Navahos, because people died in them.

Paul [1953] reports how he and his wife, visiting a patient in a local dwelling in Guatemala, attempted to reduce the crowding in the room in order to make things more comfortable for the person they were visiting—not realizing that, as in the case of the Navaho, a lack of crowding would have been taken by the patient as a sign that death was near. Paul's example is a good one because it illustrates the fact that one never knows the significance of an action in a foreign culture in advance, even if one is a trained anthropologist, as he is.

Semi-fixed Spatial Features

The study of furniture arrangement, screens, movable partitions and the like as factors in human interactions constitutes the core of the studies that have been done on semi-fixed spatial features.

Osmond [1959] coined the terms *sociopetal* and *sociofugal* as a way of characterizing two contrasting spatial arrangements. Sociofugal space discourages human interaction and tends to keep people apart. Railroad stations, libraries, and many hospitals have their furniture set in a sociofugal mold. Sociopetal space has just the opposite effect. The small face-to-face conversational groups in the living rooms of many American houses, booths in the old-style drug store, restaurant tables and the sidewalk cafés in France and Italy are all sociopetal.

Robert Sommer [1959, 1961, 1958, 1961], in a pioneering study on the effect of space on human interaction, rearranged the furniture in a "model" ward, in which the patients had been observed to be apathetic, in spite of "bright and cheerful surroundings." As a result of these rearrangements, the number of conversations doubled, and intake of information through reading tripled. Sommer also demonstrated that apathetic patients in a large mental hospital tended to be observed in halls and corridors, where the space is sociofugal, five times more frequently than non-apathetic patients, who were constructively occupied in day rooms and shops.

The custodial nature of such hospitals, and the mechanics of house-keeping in many, tend to encourage sociofugal, isolating arrangements of furniture. Nurses do not normally arrange the chairs so that they will encourage conversation, but rather so that they will look neat and orderly. In another study, Sommer reports on the influence of seating arrangement on table conversation. Fifty observation sessions were conducted at controlled intervals of people sitting at 36x72-inch tables in a cafeteria. Side-by-side conversations were three times as frequent as face-to-face conversations (across the table). Corner-to-corner conversations were twice as frequent as the side-by-side conversations, and therefore six times as frequent as the face-to-face ones. That is, face-to-face placing at a 36-inch distance is more sociofugal than corner-to-corner placing.

There is a chance that one may feel that I imply that sociofugal arrangements are bad and sociopetal ones are good. This is not the case. There are times when each is appropriate and desirable.

It should also be noted here that *what is sociofugal for one culture may be sociopetal in another.* Americans have great difficulty carrying on conversations across a room; a few remarks, perhaps, but if the conversation is to continue they generally have to move closer together. In the mountain villages of Lebanon and Syria this is the accepted way for men to converse in the evening. They will sit on opposite sides of the room and talk across the room at each other, something that it would be virtually impossible for Americans to do. Similarly, a Chinese subject whom I interviewed a few years ago was positively tongue-tied when speaking face-to-face or at an angle, but became quite talkative when I discovered he was accustomed to a side-by-side arrangement of the furniture, and placed myself appropriately.

Dynamic Use of Space as Space in Human Transactions

In addition to the fixed and semi-fixed aspects of space, of the types described above, there is *dynamic* space, in which man actively *uses* the fixed and semi-fixed features given to him. People can be put at ease, shut up, or frozen, depending on where they place themselves in relationship to each other. A big desk is often employed to impress others, to emphasize status, or as a hiding place. The desk has other communicative functions, depending whether the man who occupies it stays fixed behind it or departs from it. Technical, consultative, or "strictly business" transactions among intimates are very often conducted across a desk or around a table. Leaving the desk and sitting away from it can be a way of staying away from business, or it can signal friendship or a personal relationship.

The Doctor and the Patient.   Sullivan [1947, 1954], one of the first to emphasize the relationship of anthropology to psychiatry, used to sit at 90 degrees to the patient because he felt that schizophrenics were embarrassed by being stared at.

Park's distinction between the "foot-of-the-bed" doctor and the "beside-the-bed" doctor is also relevant in this context.[4] The foot-of-the-bed position is a little more than six feet from the patient's head. Six feet is in the "impersonal" conversational zone. This is a strictly consultative public distance. Use of this distance by the physician communicates less

---

[4]John Parks, Dean of the Medical School of George Washington University, used these distinctions in lectures to interns and resident physicians.

interest in the patient than in his condition. Patients recognize this, but are hard put to say on what cues they base their appraisal of the doctor's attitude.

The beside-the-bed position is personal, and communicates to the patient a sense of the doctor's interest in him as a person. It is a position at which personal subjects, or those about which there is some anxiety, can be discussed. Standing versus sitting, however, is a matter of dominance. If the doctor sits, he puts himself on a more or less equal level with the patient. If he wants to elicit information about which the patient feels anxious, he may find it easier to do so seated. His bending down will also sometimes achieve the same result.

A cautionary note must be injected at this point: consistency is always desirable in communication. Tone of voice, stance, and attitude of the body communicate [Birdwhistell, 1952]. A physician who is more interested in the condition under treatment than the patient is well advised not to feign, by moving from one place to another, an interest in the patient that he does not feel.

Winick and Holt [1961], reporting on the space dynamics of group therapy, noted that many patients seemed to prefer not to sit on a sofa because they did not want to be touched by other patients. The preference for individual chairs indicated that a human being experiences his own body border, as well as a need for a "life space," in the literal sense. It appeared, however, that the strength of preference for a specific, individual space was a function of the degree of neurosis.[5]

Attempts by Winick and Holt to arrange a new therapy group in a circle led to anxiety, particularly in those members whose problems included fear of closeness to other people. They also observed that when a group wished to express anxiety, whether or not the patients or therapists were aware of their anxiety, the members would often spontaneously move their chairs into a circle. As the group addressed itself with increasing anxiety to the situation, the members drew even closer together. The circle became smaller and smaller. As anxiety diminished, the circle expanded, and the seating arrangement became more rectangular again.

As one might anticipate, the groups became freer in their use of space as their ability to cope with their hostility toward their parents and others increased. Also, the members were less insistent that "their" chairs not be used by anyone else.

Territoriality in the Mentally Ill.   For the institutionalized psychotic, laying claim to a territory is more basic than speech (in some instances). At least, it is still manifest in mute patients. Woodbury [1958] reports that

---

[5]Lawrence K. Frank's [1958] insightful and provocative treatment of life space and tactile communication is also relevant in this regard.

space was the "currency" of one of the large, seldom-visited wards in Washington, D.C.'s St. Elizabeth's Hospital. The dominant patient in the ward hierarchy had complete run of the ward; he could go anywhere. Lesser lights could move freely, but they had smaller divisions of space. No one invaded the territory of someone higher than himself in the social structure of the ward. At the bottom, there was one patient who was restricted to the bench under which he slept. This patient could not even spit in the drain hole in the middle of the ward, nor was he allowed to use the toilet. His incontinence was more a symptom of his social status in the ward than of his psychosis.

Woodbury also reports that 50 percent of the incontinent patients ceased to be incontinent when they were moved; that is, with a definite alteration in the structuring of territory, behavioral changes ensued.

Some St. Elizabeth's patients took violent exception to being touched. There was what Woodbury terms the *crise de contact* through which these patients had to pass. After this crisis, the violent fights between these patients ceased. (Lewin [1958] reported that enuresis may respond to a change in environment.)

Searles [1960], reporting on patients' spatial distortions, states that some of the patients confuse their own physical boundaries with those of the room. Davie and Freeman [1961] also comment on the "disturbed perception of the body boundaries." In an interview, Searles mentioned that he had patients who objected violently to being approached too closely during therapy.[6] One female patient would place her chair in a niche under a gable, at the maximum possible distance from the therapist (about 20 feet). As treatment progressed, she became more able to tolerate closeness: a signal of her recovery was her ability to tolerate normal interaction distances.

Anxiety and the Perception of Space.   Anxiety is a significant factor in perception, and is therefore an element to be considered in space studies. In some instances, the space itself apparently induces anxiety, which in turn distorts the perceptions, thus creating a vicious circle from which it is hard to escape. Data on spatial distortions are available for both normal and psychiatric populations.

In a study of normal subjects' responses to crowding in a bomb shelter, the walls at first appeared to "close in upon them." As they became more accustomed to the space, and anxiety diminished, the walls receded [United States Navy . . . , 1959]. Wittreich, Grace, and Radcliffe [1961] have demonstrated that man distorts his perceptions under conditions of anxiety. The greater the anxiety, the greater the distortions.

Interviews with psychiatrists in private practice failed to reveal one who

---

[6]Data collected in one of a series of interviews with physicians on proxemics in relation to psychiatric disorders.

did not use space consciously in treatment; that is, their placement of both themselves and their patients was far from haphazard. Some had a greater repertoire at their command than others. Several used space as a means of reassuring dependent patients. Another sat in his chair in such a way that his outstretched hand would be inside the patient's personal space. He noticed that as treatment progressed he was gradually able to withdraw his hand. Still another doctor put his foot against the patient's chair during treatment as a means of maintaining contact.

Summary

It is hoped that this review of proxemics will serve as an introduction to its study. My purpose has been simply to indicate who has been working in this field, and what results have been achieved. The physician, architect, biologist, psychologist, sociologist, and anthropologist all have contributions to make, each in his own specialty; I have emphasized those contributions that are of relevance to the physician and the anthropologist.

The subject is so vast in scope that I cannot help but feel frustrated concerning all that I have had to leave unsaid. However, for my anthropological colleagues, I want to summarize some of my own reasons for pursuing research in this field.

Technically, the anthropologist is drawn to the study of space for the following reasons: *(a)* it is a bio-basic, culturally modified system of behavior; *(b)* it is measurable; *(c)* as cultural systems go, it is reasonably simple; *(d)* it provides a means for comparing behavior across cultural lines in concrete terms; *(e)* it is an activity which man shares with other vertebrates, and there is a growing wealth of comparative material on related life forms; *(f)* all cultural activities occur in a spatial frame; *(g)* a great many spatial acts are so highly patterned and so automatic that they function almost totally out-of-awareness, and therefore are not subject to the kind of control and distortion that conscious words are; and *(h)* time and space are also admirably suited to multidiscipinary studies [Moholy-Nagy, 1949].

Racial Categories: South African Woman Classified Colored on Opinion of Nine Witnesses

Reuters/New York Times

This grimly humorous article demonstrates the arbitrariness of "race" as a social and biological concept. There are many excellent sources of information on the "reality" and usefulness of race and racial categories, and the interested reader is directed to works by such authors as Montagu (1964) and Wagley (1968, especially Chapter 5). Of greater interest here is a discussion of the consequences of social and political attitudes and behavior affecting different peoples, especially with regard to such matters as their self-image, health, and culture in general. An article by Cassel (1955) on the Zulu provides a good example of sociopolitical effects on the lives of an entire society. While a health team attempted to improve dietary conditions in a variety of ways, the fundamental problem can be seen as resulting from the consequences of political and economic actions taken against the people. See Scotch (1960) for more information concerning the Zulu, apartheid, and health. The United States (and most other places in the world for that matter) is not lacking in analogous cases. All this serves to echo the sentiment of Rene Dubos (1959) that many health problems can be dealt with through social reform—a lofty sentiment but, unfortunately, one easier mentioned than implemented.

PRETORIA, South Africa, Sept. 1 (Reuters)—Mrs. Annie Koekemoer, a 25-year-old housewife who was officially declared colored, or of mixed race, in spite of her white background, is the latest victim of South Africa's rigid system of race classification.

Mrs. Koekemoer recently appeared in court here on a charge of falsely declaring herself white in order to marry a white man. She was acquitted but now faces a long battle to have herself reclassified white under the Population Registration Act.

The law, enacted in 1950 and amended and tightened several times since, requires that every South African be classified according to racial group. The groups range from white through Cape Colored, Griqua, Malay, Indian, other Asian and African.

For most people, classification is easily established from parentage and acceptance in a particular society. But for borderline cases, there can be much heartbreak, often brought about by a complaint to the Interior Ministry by an unidentified person.

Mrs. Koekemoer's case is unusual, for she is continuing to live with her white husband and is thus threatened by the Immorality Act—and also because her family has been affected by classification before.

Father Lost Appeal

Her father, William Walker, was classified colored in 1963. He appealed the decision but lost. In many cases, largely because of a reluctance to register births, people do not know how they have been classified until they are adult and need official forms.

Despite Mr. Walker's classification three of his daughters were classified white and married whites. When Mrs. Koekemoer applied for an identity document in 1971, she was told she has been classified colored. An official explained that this was because of her father's race and because nine people who knew her considered her colored.

But she refused to accept the classification, and she said that when her identity card arrived she thought the code number was one used for whites.

When she answered questions for a marriage affidavit last year, she said she was white and ended up in court.

During the hearing, Dr. George Nurse, a member of the South African Institute for Medical Research, said in a sworn statement that Mrs. Koekemoer's blood contained no genetic evidence whatsoever of Negro or Khoisan—bushman or Hottentot—descent.

Worried About Son

Mrs. Koekemoer says she was reared a white and is accepted as such. Even after the court case, she says she has had no problems and has continued living with her husband, Sarel.

She is worried about her 14-month-old son: She asks, "What future will he have as a colored?" Her son is fair-haired and an Interior Ministry official in court commented, "We do not go on appearances, but the baby does look white."

Her lawyer is preparing her appeal, hoping he can repeat his success of nine years ago when he had her aunt reclassified white.

The latest Interior Ministry figures, for 1972, show that only 28 of 62 appeals were upheld by the department and that two more were upheld by the Supreme Court.

The files contain some tragic cases:

Early in 1973, a colored man had to resort to employing his daughter as a servant after she had been classified African.

A 53-year-old colored woman was told she would have to give up her foster child after he had been reclassified African. The Interior Ministry said the colored community would have rejected him if he had not been reclassified.

Variety of Changes

Because of the benefits that accrue to whites in South Africa, most applications tend to be for changes from colored to white, but there have been cases of people wanting to be reclassified the other way so they can marry or live in a particular racial group.

The 1972 record shows that changes by consent consisted of 26 colored to white, 7 white to colored, 8 Indian to Malay, 3 Malay to Indian, 2 other-colored to Indian, 11 Indian to other-colored, 2 Indian to Cape Colored, and one other-colored to Chinese.

Other-colored is a relatively new category, which one official explained contains anyone who does not otherwise fit. A colored man recently complained that five of his children had been classified colored, but that the sixth was labeled other-colored.

The system of racial classification has been attacked by Prof. Phillip Tobias, a noted anthropologist at the University of the Witwatersrand in Johannesburg, who described it as "unscientific in the extreme." He said, "Our politicians are trying to force people who do exist as real human beings into categories which do not exist as clearly defined entities."

Wake Up and Die Right: Death in the Age of Feeling

Norman Klein

Shakespeare stated it well in *As You Like It:* "All the world's a stage and all the men and women merely players." However, the playing varies with culture, even when the final message is the same. People in all societies feel grief but express it differently. We easily misread clues to people's feelings and we are influenced by factors that have different meaning in our respective cultures. Misinterpretation and stereotyping may result. Witness the following, attributed to General William C. Westmoreland, the United States Commander in Vietnam: "Well...the Oriental... doesn't put the same high price on life as does the Westerner. Life is plentiful, life is cheap in the Orient...and, uh...as the, uh, philosophy of the Orient, uh...expresses it, uh...uh...life is, uh, not important" (from *Hearts and Minds;* see Langness, 1977:1).

The following article stresses the idea that using a culture-specific routine for dealing with human needs in a pluralistic society will most surely lead to misunderstanding. It is interesting to note that the end result of even the most honest and sincere attempts to deal with multi-cultural needs may be just the reverse of what is intended. Clearly, there is danger in overroutinizing and cataloguing responses to human problems. For the providers of medical services this is a real dilemma, since a good deal of routine is required if services are to be provided at all. Clearly, the development of practical therapeutic routines should not sacrifice the flexibility necessary for the response to cultural and individual needs.

A cartoon in a recent *New Yorker* depicts a young couple discoursing at the beach with the young man stating, "I can really connect with your pain." This seems to typify a new age where personal communication is being extolled.

The general attitude today is that people should give expression to their

Elaborated with revisions, and reprinted by permission from "Is There a Right Way to Die?" by Norman Klein, in *Psychology Today,* October, 1978, copyright © 1978 Ziff-Davis Publishing Company.

sorrow and deal honestly with their feelings. Sharing such feelings appears to be no less important than experiencing them. Language has not failed us in this quest for honest expression. Statements such as "Get in touch with your feelings," "I'm getting my head together," and "I know where you're coming from" can be heard on the lips of many. To be or to have been in therapy helps but is not prerequisite for using such expressions. It is, of course, disturbing to consider that one can "hear" you without really listening and that a person can "confront his own mortality" without having the foggiest notion of what that expression might mean. In the end, many such expressions convey little meaning and actually have the opposite of the intended effect. George Steiner, who in *Language and Silence* has examined some of the implications of increased use of slogans, stock metaphors, and jargon, argues that their use impedes effective communication: "The language no longer sharpens thought but blurs it." (Steiner, 1967:96). His fears, indeed, go deeper than loss of understanding and touch on the basic issues of individual and intellectual freedom.

Language is not, however, a major concern in this paper. What is of especial interest is that our expression of the need to feel grief, to cry, and to come to grips with death smacks of an ethnocentrism that may do injustice to individuals and groups who cope differently.

As the general public converses in the language of pop psychology, many professional psychotherapists appear to be encouraging and participating in this movement. Clients are urged to "let loose" and "get in touch with their anger." Yet nowhere has it been proved convincingly that such expression has universal therapeutic value. "Feeling" and "communicating" have been promoted in this society in a way to make them seem appropriate for all. An individual's failure to show emotions is often interpreted as evidence that he or she does not experience the feelings of grief or pain. "Holding things in" comes to be seen as deviant. This attitude is reminiscent of what befalls Meursault, the hero in Albert Camus's *The Stranger*. The perpetrator of an absurd crime and victim of an even more absurd court trial, he sees himself being judged not for his crime alone, but for his failure to emote "properly" on the day of his mother's funeral. This "flaw" in his character does, in fact, influence the outcome of the trial and seals his doom.

The systematization that is being applied to dealing with emotional situations can be illustrated by examining some continuing themes in the literature on dying and bereavement. Americans are often described as being isolated from witnessing and experiencing the deaths of others (except as they are presented in the media). This isolation, we are told, is in sharp contrast to years past when exposure to such experiences was part of each individual's growing up. This change of attitudes is explained in a variety of ways. Change in the nature of the family may be implicated. Increased longevity, taken with the favored nuclear type of family, makes it more likely today that the aged and dying will not be living with their own families. Instead, the dying are more likely to be attended by specialists who are emotionally uninvolved. Likewise, the dramatic decrease in infant mortality makes it less likely that parents will experience the deaths of their own children.

Regardless of the cause of such attitudinal change, the currently expressed sentiment appears to be that isolation from death is not healthy. This proposition has never been proved, yet we are told that Americans fear and deny death (because of their lack of primary contact with it?) and that such denial, if it is total, requires "defenses which can only be destructive" (Kübler-Ross, 1969:14).

Elisabeth Kübler-Ross has become a guru of sorts on the subject of death and dying. While she presents a great quantity of valuable data and analysis on these topics, she also presents precisely the type of systematization or routinization of the dying process to which earlier allusion was made. The popular appeal of Kübler-Ross's work makes it appropriate to single out the scheme presented in her book *On Death and Dying* (1969). In that work, she presents the following five stages of a "complete" death: (1) denial; (2) anger; (3) bargaining; (4) depression; (5) acceptance. Taken alone, denial is seen to be bad, though as a temporary buffer it is good. Likewise, each stage is shown to have a transitional value; and given enough time, a patient will reach a point of acceptance. Objections to such a scheme can be made at several levels. Most important at this juncture is that five (no more, no fewer) stages are posited. "Stages" implies that there is a *normal* sequence of events. With such a scheme, both professionals and laypersons may proceed to "manage" the deaths of others (people may no longer simply die, they must have managers). It is, at the least, ironic that such a blueprint for management might aid practitioners in doing just what has incurred criticism: protecting themselves by shifting from a position emphasizing interest in the patient to one emphasizing task orientation. Imagine a "manager" assessing the course of a recent death and exclaiming that it was near perfect, perhaps a bit skimpy during the "bargaining" stage.

What Kübler-Ross presents is undoubtedly useful; even the stages have, at the very least, heuristic value. They allow for discussion and examination of people's emotional needs. They may even facilitate assisting the dying patient in dealing with those emotional needs. What is feared, however, is the danger that attends any cookbook approach to dealing with human emotions. Five stages for complete dying could eventually provide such a recipe. The ignoring of cultural differences and individual needs may be the price paid for such an approach.

A further objection to having clear-cut stages or categories has to do with definition. The nature, form, and function of responses (such as denial) to emotional distress are not altogether clear. It is possible to confuse denial, for example, with a person's or people's desire simply to avoid talking about a condition or situation. Rosenblatt, Walsh, and Jackson (1976:106) contend that "there may well be some Americans who can work through grief internally or privately, or subtly without any psychological cost." Cassem (1973) has also questioned the generally negative view of denial espoused earlier by Kübler-Ross. He argues that because denial may be constructive, it is difficult to know whether or not to break through such a response: "if a patient's relationships are good and he is not doing anything self-destructive, why object to denial? Denial can be a constructive force, enabling people to put out of mind morbid, frightening, and depressing aspects of life" (Cassem, 1973:30). With a set standard of behavior emphasizing the display of emotions, such individuals could be judged as unfeeling or uncaring.

A cross-cultural view of a subject provides a number of interesting insights easily overlooked through a study of the subject in a single culture (especially if it is one's own system being studied). A cross-cultural perspective may reveal how universal or arbitrary behaviors may be. It also serves to demonstrate how ethnocentric all peoples are. Using the Human Relations Area Files (HRAF) to examine emoting in a large number of societies, Rosenblatt, Walsh, and Jackson (1976) have provided an interesting analysis of grief and mourning that demonstrates the cross-cultural approach. It is perhaps not too surprising to learn that people throughout the world experience emotionality. What varies is the form and intensity of such emoting.

In a review of 73 societies, crying in bereavement was found to be present in 72. Only the Balinese are thought not to cry. Similarly, crying was correlated with sex for 60 societies where such differential crying could be rated. For 32 societies crying was judged to be equal for both sexes. For the remaining 28, where crying rates for males and females differed, it was the female group in every case that cried with greater frequency (Rosenblatt, Walsh, and Jackson, 1976:22). Should this distribution be taken to mean that some peoples or groups *feel* any more or less strongly than others? Rosenblatt and his colleagues point out that intensity of expression alone cannot lead to such a conclusion. The Balinese, for example, have been recorded as stating that they smile and laugh to avoid crying (1976:16). This last notion is familiar in American culture as well. From the position of the American egalitarian ideal, the 32 societies may be seen by many as healthy while the remaining 28 suffer the same malady found in the United States.

It is generally felt that males in the United States do not cry enough and many explanations are given for this malady or "fault." For example, people have been described as having female and male components, an interesting tautologous argument which assumes that crying is female rather than male and that males tend to suppress their female part and females, their maleness. What is being suggested (and not necessarily accepted), is that if we "let it all hang out" we could achieve some kind of balance and presumably emote in a uniform (and therefore egalitarian?) manner. In any case, many feel that there should be equality. But of what kind?

It was possible to measure the frequency of attempted self-injury for males and females in 32 societies (Rosenblatt, Walsh, and Jackson, 1976:24). For 18, the sexes were rated equal; for 12, females were rated as having a higher frequency. Now, if one were to argue, as has been done, that because of status women have been coerced to self-mutilate more (that they are being used as either emotion expressing or respect expressing surrogates), then we should encourage equality in mutilation. Consonant with the argument for crying, should males be encouraged to lop off finger joints in mourning with the same frequency as do females? Or should females do so as seldom as do males? I am thus suggesting that we could just as easily encourage people to control their emotions as to "let go." What emerges is that these recipes for emoting or dying are not necessarily objectively based but may reflect a species of argument involving the sale of a culture-specific ethic.

There have been few attempts to compare attitudes and responses to death and dying for different ethnic groups in the United States. A notable exception to this state of affairs is the work by Kalish and Reynolds (1976). These authors elected to compare the attitudes of Black-Americans (BA), Japanese-Americans (JA), Mexican-Americans (MA), and Anglo-Americans (AA) in Los Angeles, California. As each of these groups is found within the context of the "general American" culture, it is not surprising that they share a great number of beliefs and attitudes. (Kalish and Reynolds present cross-cultural views on more than 170 items.) At the same time, significant differences between these groups can be isolated. Explanations for such differences are necessarily complicated or unresolved and given the present limitations in space it is well to present only a few suggestions along with a taste of the available data.

Statistically significant differences between the groups may be seen in the "yes" responses to the following questions (Kalish and Reynolds, 1976:134, 206).

Would you try very hard to control the way you showed your emotions in public?
Yes: BA 79%; JA 82%; MA 64%; AA 74%; $p < .05$
Would you worry if you couldn't cry?
Yes: BA 42%; JA 42%; MA 59%; AA 42%; $p < .05$

Problems in interpretation of behavior can be illustrated through closer inspection of the Japanese-American response to the above. While the majority in each group tended to express a desire for a control of emotion in public, Japanese-Americans responded in the affirmative with the greatest frequency. This result could be seen to reinforce the commonly heard stereotype, "Orientals are stoic." This interpretation, in turn, might affect the way in which staff would evaluate and deal with friends and relatives of a dying person. The subject of Oriental stoicism has been dealt with nicely by André M. Tao-Kim-Hai in his article "Orientals Are Stoic" and is also illustrated by Kalish and Reynolds and by Payne. Kalish and Reynolds (1976:135) report that "body tension is one of the cues which Japanese-American funeral conductors observe to signal the need for a supporting hand." Payne reports that due to the reluctance of many Japanese-American women to cry out during childbirth some physicians "wonder if Japanese women feel the pain" (1970:8). Payne's interviews with Japanese-American physicians confirm this tendency to refrain from crying out but also imply a common style in expression and acknowledgment of the discomfort of labor. Among the terms these Japanese-American physicians used to describe the expressions of discomfort by the women were "wincing," "frowning," "grimacing," and "tightening of facial muscles" (1970:13).

Response to the question "Would you let yourself go and cry yourself out (in private or public)?" further complicates the notion of stoicism:

Yes: BA 63%; JA 71%; MA 88%; AA 70%; $p. < .01$

The label *stoic* appears to have been widely applied to Orientals through a lack of information or understanding about them; the very tendency to describe all Asians with a single such term demonstrates this lack. "Stoicism" is often deemed a positive attribute. Unfortunately, the attribution may turn pejorative, inasmuch as it reinforces the blatantly erroneous notion that Orientals have no feelings and are incapable of emotion. After all, how much and what type of emoting is necessary to avoid the stereotype *stoic?* Rather than clinging to such stereotypes it would be more valuable to examine such cultural values as, for Japanese-Americans, *gaman* (forbearance) and *enryo* (restraint). The real problem, then rests with the way in which the appropriate expression of emotion is defined and expected by any group of people or in any culture.

The nature of the support systems available to people in need varies from culture to culture. For each of the four groups described by Kalish and Reynolds the family was seen as an important support-providing unit (1976:107, 206).

Who would you be likely to turn to for comfort?
Family: BA 53%; JA 51%; MA 54%; AA 50%; $p < .1$

However, the boundaries of the family support system appear narrower for Black- and Anglo-Americans than for Japanese- and Mexican-Americans. In addition, for Black- and Anglo-Americans the support system is more likely to extend beyond the family to include friends and community (Kalish and Reynolds, 1976:107, 127, 168, 207).

Who would be likely to help you with such problems as preparing meals, baby-sitting, shopping, cleaning house, and things like that?
Family member: BA 50%; JA 74%; MA 65%; AA 45%
Friend: BA 42%; JA 9%; MA 14%; AA 45%
$p < .001$

While each type of support system has its strengths and weaknesses, the reaction of strangers (including hospital personnel and death managers) may be influenced by how they view the bereaved's help-seeking actions.

It should be clear that interethnic similarities and differences can be seen with regard to incidence patterns of responses to queries about dying and grief. At the same time it is very important to note that intraethnic variations exist as well. Each of the four groups mentioned above encompasses in turn a wide variety of people. This can be seen in response to attitudinal questions. In no case was there a 100% agreement by all informants in any group. Differences within a group may be based on such diverse factors as sex, age, religion, education, and degree of acculturation. Of the four groups, the Japanese-Americans appear to exhibit the greatest amount of intraethnic diversity. The Mexican-Americans exhibit the least (Kalish and Reynolds, 1976:129, 157). For Japanese-Americans the differences appear to correlate largely with generational identity. For Mexican-Americans continuity in familial relations is an important factor in the relative lack of variation. Heterogeneity of each ethnic group is, in fact, understated, since Kalish and Reynolds attempted to hold such factors as age and income relatively constant in establishing controls to facilitate relevant comparisons between the groups.

An important point about intraethnic diversity (a diversity which many people tend to overlook) is that the complexity of cultural differences prevents the formation of a blueprint for treatment. While guidelines may be offered, an emphasis on cultural awareness and flexibility in care are the really important messages.

Several years ago I heard a clergyman say, in a discussion on death and dying: "It was the most beautiful death I ever witnessed." The expression "death with dignity" was also used. Directing attention back to the five stages for a complete death, a number of questions should now be posed. Is a "beautiful" or "complete" or "dignified" death the same for the four groups described earlier? Are these even uniform within the context of any one of the groups? Does an expression such as "death with dignity" convey the same meaning (if any at all) for all peoples? For whom are these expressions really meaningful? For example, does "beautiful" or "dignified" refer to the dying person's experience or to that of the observer?

Attitudes toward death are clearly influenced by culture. Therefore, differences in attitude at the cultural and subcultural level should be expected. At the same time, the process of dying affects each individual in a personal and unique manner. It follows, then, that care must be taken not to formalize the way in which people are expected to experience dying. Kalish and Reynolds (1976:i) sum up the situation well when they state, "This era is in danger of replacing old myths and stereotypes with new myths and stereotypes, slightly more accurate and less destructive perhaps, but nonetheless not always appropriate."

It can only be hoped that the "new directions" in caring for the terminally ill and their loved ones somehow avoid the potential pitfalls of slogan and jargon in favor of a genuine understanding of the complexities of emotional experience.

II

THE ECOLOGY OF HEALTH

Every species, by definition, differs from every other. But there is something special about *Homo sapiens.* We have culture. Some would extend the possession of culture to a few other species, but it is still ours to extend since we define it. This special faculty lends new meaning to the concept of ecology. We can exploit a resource or destroy a species by design. To our knowledge, no other animal can act this way or cares to. No longer does the Natural Balance of Things look so natural. We can obliterate the whale and save the snail darter. We can allow certain microorganisms to proliferate while we attack others with a vengeance. There is nothing rational, in any absolute sense, about our decision making. We profess an egalitarian ethic, but it is an artifice. Who would raise a placard to champion the cause of the polio virus and its right to survive? *Homines sapientes* are, in fact, constantly in transaction with their environment and attempt to forge it either in a manner consistent with what they believe to be their own best interest or else in a manner that conforms to their specific notion of a "human" world. In this "human world," man believes he has fashioned the ecological system—as indeed he has in a degree, though humans may not be so totally in control as they would have themselves believe.

Disease arises within any ecological system. Since humans have such a profound impact on their physical and sociocultural environment, it is wise to look to that complicated human construct, *culture,* in order to examine both what afflicts *Homo sapiens* and lies in store for him. The study of the distribution and etiology of diseases among human groups is called *epidemiology.* Given the effect of humans on their environment and the diversity of culture in this world, it is not surprising to note that the nature of illness varies between and within populations—that culture is an important epidemiologic variable. Economics, technology, politics, social organization, religion—all these (and many more) affect the form, distribution, duration, and cause of illness for a particular society.

Clearly, humans do many things that are ultimately good for them. However, they also continue to act in ways detrimental to their ecological health. This contradiction has prompted one apparently well-known but anonymous physician to declare, "It is part of the doctor's function to make it possible for his patients to go on doing pleasant things that are bad for them—smoking too much, eating too much, drinking too much—without killing themselves any sooner than is necessary" (Dubos, 1965:414).

The articles in this section touch on a variety of ecological and epidemiological issues. In each case the human hand is seen as playing an integral part in the potential dangers faced by different societies. Arthur Levin illustrates a number of health problems associated with our penchant for urban living. We are apparently prepared to trade a degree of risk to our health for communion with a variety of animals. We seem similarly ready to exchange freedom from many forms of pollution for the excitement of city life in what appears to be deemed a fair trade.

Blake Fleetwood further expounds on the dangers of contaminating the environment (rural in this case). The desire by some companies and special-interest groups to downplay the hazards of industrial wastes at the cost of human suffering is also illustrated.

Bringing people the better life through improved technology is often accompanied by unexpected new dangers. This risk is effectively communicated by Robert Desowitz. The message is not that we should abandon new technology; it is, rather, a call for caution, since the solution to old problems often results in more difficult new problems.

The article by John Mathews and his colleagues provides a nice example of the epidemiological method. The link between health problems and cultural practices is well illustrated. People's dietary, political, religious, and social practices are seen to be responsible for the incidence and distribution of a condition hitherto elusive to explanation.

The article by Ruth Rosenbaum demonstrates the human

capacity and inventiveness to create and satisfy new desires. What Rosenbaum says about artificial flavors can be generalized and applied to discussion of such subjects as fast and convenience foods, fad diets, and pop therapies.

This section is entitled "The Ecology of Health." Why not, the reader might ask, "The Ecology of Illness" or "of Disease"? Well, "Health" does sound more elegant; it also applies to a wider range of information, allowing us not only to deal with the diseased section but also to shift the emphasis somewhat and remind ourselves that it is important to look at what makes for good health. It must be remembered that the form and function of the human animal is now, to a greater extent than ever before, a result of human design. We may opt for a short, fast life as an ideal or for one that is long and staid. We may opt for concrete (and, as one friend put it, "paint green Xs for nostalgic people to indicate the former location of trees") or for foliage. Some very important questions begin to emerge concerning human destiny. Unfortunately, there are no simple answers.

City Diseases that Can Kill You

Arthur Levin

Through the study of anthropology we know that specific cultural behaviors are arbitrary. With reference to this article, it can be stated that human attitudes toward such nonhuman animals as dogs, cats, and pigeons vary from culture to culture. The like is true for items of technology. We are clearly responsible for the mess described in this article. Dubos (1959, 1965) has stated that perfect health is "incompatible with the process of living." We seem to be developing this notion into a high art. It would seem that to correct matters should be simple, but to believe they are simple is to ignore the rational fallacy—the proposition that you need only demonstrate to people what you think they are doing wrong and they will change. Even our best friends will not listen to that kind of advice. Bates (1959) refers to the "ecological fallacy" in describing how the "natural balance" of things is complicated by the human possession of culture, which allows man to shape his world. Invariably, this shape is always something short of ideal. Finally, this article demonstrates the inadequacy of the specific-etiology model. What causes a smog death? Is it smog, bronchitis, heart failure, autos, pneumonia, the highway trust fund . . . ?

The Roman Empire declined and fell, one theory has it, because the ancients—particularly the patricians—poisoned themselves by drinking from lead goblets. Most New Yorkers do not use metal goblets.* But lead poisoning is still with us (we have even democratized it by putting the ignoble metal in our paint and gasoline). And so, too, are a few other more recently recognized health hazards.

The disease-causing agents described here are all potential threats to the

Reprinted by permission of International Creative Management. Copyright © 1974 by Arthur Levin, M.D. From *New York Magazine,* October 7, 1974, pp. 39–43.

*In recent weeks, New Yorkers were warned they may be poisoning themselves by drinking or cooking in water that has absorbed metal fragments overnight from water pipes. It is advisable to let water run when first turning on the tap for the day.

47

health of New Yorkers. All are agents which are capable of causing insidious, life-threatening illnesses—illnesses which (in case you needed to be told) are probably a good deal more common than most doctors believe.

None of these disease-causing agents can be seen, smelled, or tasted. Yet they are things to which virtually all of us—regardless of race, sex, or income—are exposed daily. They are things which, as the saying goes, you might find around the house.

Like the hapless Romans, there are doubtless plenty of other disseminated environmental diseases that, as yet, we do not know about. In the meantime, here are a few that have been identified.

Ill Temper, Heart Attacks, and Carbon Monoxide

Brian Ketcham is a husky young man with unruly brown hair and a huge beard, wearing an open-necked plaid shirt. He looks as though he should be standing on a mountain top advertising cigarettes. Instead he works for a group called Citizens for Clean Air in Manhattan, in a cavernous, ill-lit office. On the floor are a dozen cartons stuffed with scientific papers Ketcham salvaged from his last job as air pollution expert for the city's Department of Air Resources ("These are my files . . . they didn't want me to take them but I did anyway . . .").

Ketcham looks at me, his deep-set eyes steady, as he tells the carbon monoxide story.

Carbon monoxide—as the chemistry books say—is a colorless, odorless, tasteless gas. It is also probably the most dangerous surface air hazard for New Yorkers.

"The city calculated," says Ketcham, "that there should have been a 14 percent decrease in midtown in carbon monoxide levels last year." Instead, he says, levels of the gas—unlike those of other air pollutants—have actually increased. On most days, monoxide levels are well above the federally set standard of nine parts per million.

"This summer," Ketcham says, shaking his head, "there were days when levels were two or three times the Environmental Protection Agency standard."

Most monoxide comes from the exhaust pipes of cars, buses, and other vehicles. Thus, in particularly congested areas, levels may be even higher.

Stacey Moriates is an earnest, alert, intense student who is earning her Ph.D. in environmental health. When not in class she works for the Department of Air Resources measuring monoxide levels with a new portable device about the size of a small TV set. Caught in Sixth Avenue traffic one morning, Stacey decided ("just for my own curiosity") to turn on the monoxide meter.

"I measured levels of 100 parts per million," she recalls. The federal eight-hour "safe" standard is 35.

Levels of 100 may be becoming the rule for New Yorkers. Last year, in midtown Manhattan, monoxide levels during the day were above 35 some 60 to 70 percent of the time. Levels of 40 to 50 have been measured on Eighth Avenue in the garment center. Levels of 60 have been found on Lexington Avenue, 70 at the entrance to the 59th Street Bridge, and—what seems to be the record—a spectacular 217 at a toll booth at the entrance to the Midtown Tunnel.

The signs of moderate monoxide poisoning can be subtle—headaches, impaired ability to think, delayed reaction time, irritability. Schoolchildren in high monoxide areas are said to have lower reading scores. The legendary irascibility of New York cabbies has been ascribed to the gas, as have the large number of taxi accidents.

And that may not be all.

Stephen Ayres is a physician and a health consultant to the Department of Air Resources. Ayres knows as much as anyone about carbon monoxide. A few years ago it occurred to him that monoxide might have something to do with another common New York phenomenon: heart attacks.

Monoxide combines in our bloodstream with hemoglobin, the red cell pigment that ordinarily carries oxygen to the heart and other organs. Persons with coronary disease and less than normal blood flow to the heart muscles, Ayres reasoned, needed every molecule of oxygen their blood could transport. A small amount of useless carboxyhemoglobin (hemoglobin bound to carbon monoxide and thus unavailable to carry oxygen) might just be the straw, Ayres theorized, that could precipitate a full-blown heart attack.

He could be right. In one scary experiment, attacks of angina (searing chest pain due to the heart's lack of oxygen) were induced by exposing coronary patients to freeway traffic. Some patients also developed abnormal electrocardiograms. These ominous signs developed with carboxyhemoglobin levels as low as 3 per cent.

What, I asked Ayres, about the threat of monoxide in New York? Could levels of 30 to 40—levels not infrequently measured in midtown Manhattan—be a danger to the estimated 160,000 New Yorkers with coronary heart disease?

"Oh, yeah," said Ayres, matter-of-factly. "And," he adds, "we're measuring the wrong levels." Many monoxide monitoring stations, he explains, are not located at street level where concentrations are highest.

Ayres has taken blood samples from hundreds of "street level" New Yorkers. Most of us, he finds, have significant amounts of carboxyhemoglobin in our blood—the medical term is carboxyhemoglobinemia. New Yorkers engaged in mild exercise, walking around out-of-doors, have carboxyhemoglobin levels of 2 to 2½ percent. Those who smoke have higher levels, many as high as 6 percent. Among nonsmokers who have ridden a car or bus just before testing, Ayres has found sizable numbers with carboxyhemoglobin levels above 3 percent. Most policemen on the beat in high-traffic precincts have blood levels above 3 percent.

How much carboxyhemoglobin you have in your blood depends on (1) the carbon monoxide level you breathe, (2) how long you breathe it, and (3) how strenuously your body is working. A sedentary two-hour lunch during which you breathe a carbon monoxide level of 50 in a street-level *boîte* (monoxide really seeps into buildings) will give you a carboxyhemoglobin level of 3 percent. So will breathing the same gas level during a brisk hour's walk home from the office (monoxide levels don't start to fall off until seven at night). So will breathing a monoxide level of 90 while sweating over a flat tire for only 30 minutes.

"I'd like to measure people who live in these canyon apartments on crowded streets," says city air official Ed Ferrand. He has a point. A Park Avenue resident exposed to a monoxide level of 25 for several hours (not a rare occurrence) could readily build up a carboxyhemoglobin level of 3 percent.

What does all this presage for our health? Most experts agree that, unless some way to control monoxide can be found (either by controlling traffic or by lowering vehicle emission), it bodes ill for our productivity—not to mention our survival. In the meantime, all the average New Yorkers can do is try to avoid congested streets, keep to the high ground (suggested height: 50 feet above street level), and beware of strenuous exercise in places where monoxide is likely to be high. You might also try to be more understanding the next time your boss comes back from lunch and starts snapping at you. He or she might just be suffering from a mild case of carboxyhemoglobinemia. It seems to be going around.

Dogs, Sandboxes, and Toxocara

"If you were to examine the records of our hospitals," says Dr. Michael Katz, "you might find one or two cases in the last five years."

Katz, head of tropical medicine at Columbia, looks like a judge. The gray-haired physician leans back in this chair, hands together, as though pondering an indictment. Finally, he asks the question, almost rhetorically: "Have we missed any?"

Toxocariasis is one of those diseases that are easy to miss. It is a disease to which even doctors in the largest medical centers are not attuned. ("I think it's likely that many physicians simply might not think of the diagnosis.") It is a disease whose symptoms can mimic those of a dozen other problems. And, not the least, it is primarily a disease of children, who are often unable to describe their symptoms.

Toxocara is a worm. It is carried by dogs and cats, who excrete the parasite's eggs in their stools. If toxocara eggs are swallowed by humans, the eggs hatch in the intestinal tract. The larvae then burrow through the wall of the intestine and into the nearby blood vessels. Once in the bloodstream, they can migrate to virtually any body organ (the disease is sometimes called "visceral larva migrans"), often with devastating results.

Larvae swept into the lungs can cause a pneumonia—one that will not respond to the usual antibiotics. A single larva, if it plugs a blood vessel in the brain or spinal cord, can cause a stroke or sudden poliolike paralysis. Brain larvae have also been found to cause epileptic seizures, due to the reaction of the brain tissue to the foreign substance. And a similar reaction can occur in other vital organs.

"There are children in this country," says Katz, "who have their eyes enucleated [the entire eye removed] because of visceral larva migrans."

A larva carried to the eye, he explains, can cause a swelling (called a "granuloma") in the retina that may look exactly like, and be misdiagnosed as, a retinoblastoma—one of childhood's most malignant tumors.

"It's a high price to pay," Katz adds, solemnly, "for communion with dogs."

Dogs, more than cats, because they are more likely to be outdoors where children play, have been singled out as the major culprits in human toxocariasis. Dog-contaminated soil with toxocara eggs can be carried on childrens' fingers and ingested.

"I would like someone to go through Central Park," Katz says, "and sample soil in various areas . . . some sandboxes, too." A recent case of toxocariasis at Columbia, he tells me, was traced to a contaminated sandbox in Westchester—proof that the disease knows no socio-economic bounds ("even aristocratic dogs excrete in sandboxes . . ."). Katz lends me a medical article that reports that some 10 percent of London dogs were found to be toxocara carriers.

How common is the disease in New York pets—and people?

Unfortunately, no one knows for sure. Blood tests and a skin test are available. But even the human disease can still be hard to diagnose—assuming the doctor even thinks of it. "The intelligent nonhysteric guess," Katz offers, "is that the problem is worse than a casual glance would indicate—and not nearly so bad as some of the very excitable people would make it." The most recent survey I could find of New York dogs was done in 1958 by a couple of medical students who went around the city scooping up dog stools and testing the samples for toxocara eggs. The worst area: Washington Square Park, with 4 percent of all samples containing eggs. Second place: Central Park, with 2 percent.

Of course things may be different these days. (Two more medical students could perform a valuable public service by repeating the dog survey in 1974.) Katz, while he has little empathy with dog owners ("It really is a displacement . . . a cheap way of buying loyalty . . ."), suggests that pet purchasers make sure their canines are de-wormed (de-worming is now required of pet shops by the City Health Code). Sandboxes, he urges, should be covered while not in use. These precautions, plus owners abiding by what Katz calls "modest rules of civilization" (keeping dogs away from areas where children play), would go far toward minimizing the risk of toxocara.

Asbestos in the Air

"Eighty to 85 percent of all cancer," says Irving Selikoff, head of Mt. Sinai's environmental health unit, "comes from the environment."

Selikoff should know. He is probably the nation's foremost expert on environmentally related illness. Perhaps his most startling contribution has been the evidence linking mesothelioma—a particularly vicious and rapidly spreading cancer of the lungs and abdomen—with asbestos.

Over the years Selikoff has painstakingly probed the deaths of New York asbestos workers. One death in ten, he found, was from mesothelioma. Nearly half the workers died from this and other tumors. Still others died from emphysemalike lung failure.

But it's not only those who work with asbestos who are at risk. A few years ago a 30-year-old man died of mesothelioma. Investigation showed that he had never worked with asbestos. But further detective work turned up the fact that he was born in 1940, two blocks from the Brooklyn Navy Yard, where large amounts of asbestos were being used to build and renovate ships. The victim's lungs, at autopsy, were full of asbestos fibers.

This long "incubation period," says Selikoff, is characeristic of most environmentally related cancers. "What we're seeing now," he notes, "is associated with the introduction of agents twenty, 30, 40 years ago." The implication, he feels, is clear: "We are now determining the health of our children in the year 2000."

"Come in and sit down," says Arthur Langer, one of Selikoff's associates. He rushes to clear books and papers from the only other chair in the cubicle. Langer is a young, tanned, effervescent man who seems to delight in talking nonstop about the hazards around us ("I could tell you stories that'd make your hair stand on end"). As I sit down, he and a colleague are thumbing through a green softcover volume, the report of a recent government conference.

"There was a guy there," Langer recalls, almost proudly, "who yelled at me. He said, 'You goddamn eco-nuts!' "

Is it true, I ask, tentatively, that most New Yorkers have asbestos in their lungs?

"That's unfortunate," comes the unhesitating reply, "but it's true."

Once in the body, Langer explains, asbestos fibers can stay there for life. But the fibers are so tiny they can easily be missed in body tissues, even with the best light microscope. Langer uses an electron microscope in his searches ("We find them in lung, gut, pancreas, kidney, spleen, liver . . ."). Most fibers—under the electron scope they look a bit like hairpins—are found in the lungs.

This asbestos in our bodies probably comes from the air we breathe. Asbestos can be filtered from New York air (Manhattan air has the most, Staten Island the least). Large amounts of asbestos have been found near construction sites, such as the World Trade Center, even though open-air spray-fireproofing with asbestos is now illegal in New York. Vehicle brake linings also contain asbestos, and high levels are found in the air at the entrance to Midtown Tunnel—a site of frequent braking.

"C'mon," says Arthur Langer, "I'll show you something."

He opens a hall closet. Inside hangs a plastic bag on which in large dark letters someone has scrawled: ASBESTOS COAT—DO NOT OPEN.

Langer keeps me at a distance ("You've got a long life expectancy") as he exhibits a trim, light-gray garment, the collar trimmed in a dark blue. One day a young woman called the Mt. Sinai unit, asking, "Is the asbestos in my coat dangerous?" The coat, made under a now-discontinued process, was analyzed under the electron microscope.

"It was loaded," says Langer, "with asbestos."

Cancer experts once thought that there was a "threshold limit value," an amount of exposure to a cancer-producing agent which the human body could stand without developing cancer. Now they are not so sure. There may be no "safe" amount of asbestos (now used in some 3,000 products) in the human body.

Arthur Langer unfolds a huge sheet of paper. The sheet is covered with handwritten numbers. The data are from a long-time project, an analysis of the minerals in various brands of talcum powder.

"Which kind," he asks me, "do you use?"

I tell him the brand.

His finger runs rapidly down the columns on the page, slowing now and then . . . ("Nickel is very low . . . that's good"). Then the finger stops. "But it's high in tremolite."

"What's that?" I ask, not really sure I want to know.

"Asbestos."

The City Pigeon and Cryptococcus

One night, as a medical student, I recall seeing a graduate student who was brought to the emergency ward. He had been completely well, his wife said, until a few weeks before. Then he became irritable. He began to have temper fits, and at times seemed almost paranoid. He was unable to work. Finally he began to suffer from headaches and a stiffness in his neck.

With the resident on duty, I examined the man. He was deeply suspicious and uncooperative. He seemed, in fact, like a candidate for a psychiatric evaluation. There was only one thing that did not seem to fit—his stiff neck.

The resident decided to do a spinal tap. The tap was done, not without difficulty, and some spinal fluid was obtained. We put a drop on a glass slide. Under the microscope the fluid looked completely clear.

"Give me the India ink," said the resident.

On the shelf was a bottle of ordinary India ink, the kind found in artists' supply stores. The resident added a drop to the fluid on the slide. Then he again looked through the microscope.

He gestured for me to look.

No one who has seen cryptococcus fungi will ever forget them. The organisms are huge, each many times larger than the largest bacteria. They look like giant white wafers. There is something sinister about them as they float past, pale discs shimmering in inky fluid.

Cryptococcal meningitis is an uncommon disease, fortunately, since it is one of the most serious and hardest to treat forms of meningitis (our patient was one of the lucky ones who lived). But cryptococcal infection, in general, may not be uncommon.

"It's undoubtedly far more common," says infectious disease expert Donald Louria, "than previously supposed." Researchers now believe, Louria explains, that many people may be infected by the cryptococcus, but only a very few develop a life-threatening illness such as meningitis.

"Host defenses," he puts it, "are surprisingly good."

Cryptococcus is a soil fungus. In cities like New York, however, the resourceful organism has another home—pigeon droppings. A single gram of droppings (or *excreta,* as the fastidious say) can contain as many as 1 million organisms. In parts of the city where pigeons, and their excreta, are abundant (the City Hall area, for example), the fungus can be readily found.

Sometimes the fungus turns up in unexpected places.

"I took care of a Wall Street broker," says Columbia disease specialist Harold Neu, "who had his office near Trinity Church. We drew fungi out of his air conditioner . . . out of the filter."

"Pigeons," another expert explains, "like to perch on air conditioners."

But for all this, the big puzzle still remains: why do a few persons develop grave cryptococcal illness while most of us don't?

"Cryptococcus," notes Donald Armstrong, infectious disease chief at Memorial Hospital, "has a predilection for those who have some immunologic problem." An example, says Armstrong, is the patient with Hodgkin's disease—a malignancy that affects cells which aid the body in warding off infection. Kidney transplant patients on "immunosuppressive" drugs, and persons taking cortisonelike drugs are also at special risk.

Like many hospitals which care for very ill patients, Memorial has waged a constant (and losing) battle against the pigeon population.

"It's very difficult," says Armstrong, resignedly, "to get rid of pigeons."

Donald Louria agrees with the idea that only certain people are at serious hazard from the fungus. He points out, however, that more people may be at risk than previously imagined. Recently, a certain number of "normal" people with the fungal meningitis have been found to have subtle defects which prevent their body cells from attacking the invaders.

How many people have such defects? No one yet knows. Someday in the not too distant future ("This is sort of 1980-ish," predicts Louria), it should be possible to mass-test large numbers of people for immune defects, probably by means of skin tests.

In the meantime, the course of discretion would seem to be for people and pigeons to avoid one another. After researching the subject, I summarily evicted the pigeon that had habitually roosted outside my bedroom air conditioner. Then I changed the air filter. And one of these days, I'm going to have a talk with the little old lady who sprinkles birdseed in front of the building at night.

Cats, Hamburgers, and Toxoplasmosis

"Here is the center of trichinosis in the world."

Ben Kean, Cornell Medical Center's tropical medicine chief, looks as if he belongs in Panama where he began his parasitology career years ago. He has short-cropped white hair, and wears light-colored trousers. Smoking a huge cigar, Kean rambles around the office followed by a white West Highland terrier. He pulls open a drawer of Kodachromes, and hands one to me.

I hold the slide up to the light. It is a picture of the corner of Second Avenue and 85th Street.

Kean continues, as though lecturing to a somewhat retarded medical school class ("Now *why* is that the center of trichinosis?"). He hands me more slides. ("Because there, in the center of Yorkville, is this place . . . and this place . . . and this place . . .") Each slide shows a German delicatessen, long sausages hanging in the windows.

Trichinosis, Kean admits, almost sorrowfully, is less common nowadays, though sporadic cases still occur (characteristic findings: fever, muscle pains, swelling around the eyes, large numbers of eosinophil cells in the blood). But as trichinosis has receded, another meat-eater's malady has taken its place.

"Let me tell you the Christiaan Barnard story," says Kean.

A few years ago, he relates, the noted surgeon came to lecture at Cornell. The lecture was a "must" event for Cornell's medical students, many of whom crowded the dormitory snack bar that evening for a quick supper before attending. The fare was hamburgers.

"Usually," says Kean, with a wry smile, "they cook 'em by holding them up to the light. But that night they just did this"—the parasitologist kneads an imaginary hamburger in his hands.

The lecture turned out to be a big event for Kean. It provided him with a chance to study an outbreak of a disease that had fascinated him since he first misdiagnosed it in Panama 50 years earlier—toxoplasmosis.

Toxoplasmosis, like trichinosis, comes from poorly cooked meat. The parasite's cysts have been found in beef and pork. (The French, with their passion for steak tartare, and rare or "bleu" beef, experience a lot of toxoplasmosis.) Rare hamburgers, some of which are adulterated with pork, present a double hazard.

All five infected Cornell students had similar symptoms: headache, fever, muscle pains, swollen glands. Some had a rash. Kean made the diagnosis by testing them with what he calls "the most specific, most reliable biologic test in the history of medicine"—the Sabin-Feldman (Sabin of polio vaccine fame) dye test. The dye test was positive in all five students.

Toxoplasmosis is very much a New York disease. Kean has tested literally thousands of New Yorkers. Most, he says, will have the disease at some time during their lives ("At age ten, 10 percent have had it, at age twenty, 20 percent, at age 30, 30 percent . . ."). Indeed, given the huge number of rare hamburgers consumed every day, one might wonder why the disease is not universal. The probable reason is that toxoplasma are fragile organisms. One researcher found that three minutes in a frying pan would kill the cysts in pork.

The disease is probably vastly underdiagnosed by doctors. Its symptoms may easily be mistaken for flu or other viral illness. Young adults with the swollen-gland form (the most common form) are probably often misdiagnosed as having mononucleosis. Fortunately, though the disease can cause debilitating fatigue for weeks, it is usually not permanently damaging or fatal.

But it can be—in one instance.

When toxoplasmosis infects a pregnant woman (about two-thirds of all women of child-bearing age have never had it, and thus are not immune), the parasite can cross the placenta to the fetus. By the time an infected infant is born, it may have suffered irreversible damage to the brain, eyes, and other organs.

At Cornell, Kean pointed out, toxoplasmosis is now a more common cause of damaged infants than German measles. Some 100 New York babies, he guesses, will be born with the disease this year.

"All pregnant women," he warns, "should be advised to eat only well-cooked meat, and to avoid cats."

Cats?

The "cat story"—as Kean calls it—surfaced a few years ago, when a foreign researcher found that cats harbor the parasites and excrete them in their stools.

"There was a tremendous attack on me," Kean recalls, when he tried to publicize the newly found hazard in this country. Now, he notes with satisfaction, the Public Health Service has officially issued the same warning.

Toxoplasmosis in pregnancy is so serious that, if the diagnosis is made early, an abortion should be seriously considered. If the diagnosis is made late, drug treatment may be attempted (the drugs are toxic and of less than perfect efficacy).

"Or," says Kean, "you can simply not treat—just pray."

Efforts to make a vaccine for use in pregnancy are underway, but results are not expected soon. In the meantime, if pregnant, you might want to send the family cat for a vacation with friends—or at least get someone else to change the litter box. And while you're at it, you might also send that rare burger or slab of beef back for another turn on the fire.

The above hazards are all proven causes of ill health. And, while not unique to New York, they probably pose more of a problem here than in most cities. In fact—for what it's worth—New York City is now the nation's center for urban and environmental health research. The researchers are having an exciting time with all the yet to be answered questions.

Is cancer-causing vinyl chloride in plastic drinking water pipes dangerous? (Probably not.) Can children get lead poisoning from breathing vehicle exhaust? (They probably can.) Does subway air contain smog? [See the appendix.] And what about that bacteria-laden mass of sewage sludge in the Atlantic said to feed upon itself and to be advancing on the city like something from one of those Japanese-made sci-fi flicks?

The Romans may have thought *they* had problems . . .

Appendix—Steel Dust and Subway Air

In 1971, a City University of New York pre-med student somehow persuaded the Transit Authority to give him a copy of a study on subway air quality—the only such study the authority has ever done. The T.A. study showed considerable amounts of iron and steel dust—in subway air.

The T.A. study had been done in the mid-sixties. By 1971, the federal government got around to setting safe levels for air-borne particulates. By contrast with the federal safe level of 75 micrograms, the T.A. study showed levels in some subway stations as high as 1,000—levels above those defined as "Emergency."

The T.A. data also showed another potential hazard in subway air—ozone. Ozone, C.U.N.Y. professor Peter Scheiner explained to me, may be formed by electrical sparks, which occur frequently at track level. Ozone can cause anything from wheezing and chest pain to genetic damage and premature aging. It is a substance which also reacts with automobile exhaust to form a peculiar blend of irritants known as photochemical smog—the kind found in Southern California. Since subway air comes from curbside vents, it is heavily laden with vehical exhaust.

Transit officials, naturally, deny that there are many ill miasmas in their air. Former MTA Chairman Ronan, in a letter to Scheiner and others, asserted that, as far as particulates were concerned, subway air was "substantially cleaner than that of the surface streets." Ronan's letter cited no evidence to back up this assertion. Nor did the letter mention ozone or other potential air hazards.

I spoke with Dr. Louis Lanzetta, the T.A.'s medical director. Had there been any recent studies, I asked him, of subway air?

"No," Lanzetta replies, "there have not." An early 1960's survey, he noted, had shown transit workers to have less respiratory disease than postal workers. Lanzetta found the survey in a file and read me portions of it, haltingly, over the phone ("I haven't gone through this book . . . it's quite a book, to tell you the truth").

"Be kind to us," pleaded another T.A. official, as he took my name and address. Then, as though resigned, he added: "But I guess you have to tell it like it is."

The Tribe that Caught Cat Dancing

Blake Fleetwood

"My daughter grew up eating fish from this river. I grew up eating fish from this river, and so did my father and my grandfather and his father before him. It didn't seem right that the river would turn against us."

Chief Andy Keewatin of the
Grassy Narrows Indian Reserve

"I would ask for nothing else if only I could return to my former body." These words were spoken by a victim of Minamata disease (Smith and Smith, 1975). The condition was identified in 1956 and its cause proved in 1959. Yet, contamination of Minamata Bay ceased only a decade later and then only when the mercury method of production had become outmoded. For a more complete and emotional account of Minamata disease the book by Smith and Smith is highly recommended. Included is a more technical essay by Masazumi Harada and a bibliography. Minamata has perhaps become the archetype for describing the relationship between water pollution and the human condition. What has happened to the Ojibway, described below, can be added to that tale. Fleetwood's article can be used to demonstrate the relationship between the individual, economics, and health. In this case the importance of tourism and business enterprise overrode the importance of the health of local inhabitants. For more information on the Ojibway and health, see Hallowell (1963).

It started as it always does with the dancing cats. They had a glazed look in their eyes. And they started walking around in circles—two, three, four cats walking round and round in the main square of the village.

It spread to the birds, which began to fall off their perches. And probably to the bear and otter and moose, which were once plentiful in the area

---

and then suddenly disappeared. And dead fish floated atop the English-Wabigoon River.

Soon the fishermen from the Grassy Narrows and White Dog Indian reservations, which sit beside the river in Kenora, Ontario, began to complain of discomfort. They felt a tingling sensation in their fingers, a heaviness in the back of the head, a decrease in their peripheral vision. And a strange irritability permeated the rest of the people. The Indians began fighting among themselves. Killing themselves. Killing each other.

The medicine men said that the Great Spirit had put a curse on the people and that they must leave offerings in the woods to win him over. So some of the Indians left pouches of tobacco and flasks of whiskey in tree branches. But the curse did not disappear.

In 1970 Norvald Fimreite, a Norwegian biology student who was doing research for his Ph.D. at Western Ontario University, went fishing in the English-Wabigoon River. He brought some fish and birds back to the university laboratory and examined them. He found the mercury content in the fish was 50 times the accepted international level. He immediately called this to the attention of the Canadian government. A similar level of mercury discovered in the fish in the Japanese village of Minamata in 1956 had resulted in 200 deaths and crippled thousands more. At the time, it was thought to be an isolated case. Now it had reoccurred 6,000 miles away.

The Canadian government soon discovered that the Dryden Paper Company, a pulp and paper mill 60 miles north of the two Indian reserves, had dumped ten tons of mercury waste into the river over the previous eight years. They immediately banned commercial fishing in the area. But tourism is Kenora's main industry. Aside from the Indians, the only visitors to the area are tourists who come from Minneapolis and Chicago and stay at the tourist camps sprinkled along the river's edge. So the government did not want to discourage tourism completely and allowed sports fishing to go on. They put up "Fish for Fun" signs, which urged tourists to throw the fish back in the river. But the polluted fish tasted fine and so the Indians and the tourists kept fishing and eating their catch.

Barney Lamm, the owner of the Ball Lake Lodge, one of the more popular resorts in the area, was so shaken by the discovery of the mercury that he closed down his place and filed a multimillion-dollar suit against the Dryden Paper Company for destroying his business.

But the Kenora Tourist Bureau tried to quell the pollution scare. Frank Newstead, manager of the office, told visitors that the "problems were overblown." And the government turned its back on the problem.

"It came down to a question of votes," said a local politician. "The government officials just couldn't go against the lumber and tourist interests."

In the spring of 1974, Aileen Smith—who, along with her husband, W. Eugene Smith, photographed and wrote the brilliant book, *Minamata*—arrived in the Kenora area at the invitation of Barney Lamm. She was shocked at what she saw. "It was incredible how this situation parallels the situation in Japan," she said. "The same government cover-ups in favor of economic interests over human lives."

The Smiths asked a team of Japanese medical experts headed by Dr. Masazumi Harada, one of the foremost authorities on mercury pollution, to visit the Indian reserves and they came last July [1975] at their own expense.

Dr. Harada ran an extensive testing program, returned to Japan and released a report last month which concluded: "Out of 89 Indians examined, 37 displayed two or more symptoms that are found in Minamata disease patients." He emphasized that the situation was going to get much worse.

Until 1970 commercial fishing employed one-third of the Ojibway Indians and the fish from the river was their main source of food. Most of the people ate some kind of fish two or more times each day of their lives. Now Minamata disease (also called cat dancing disease or mercury poisoning) is reaching epidemic proportions among them and there is no way to stop it. It can cause deformity, nervous disorders and even death. And its effects are becoming more and more visible throughout the two tribes.

Large numbers of people have twisted mouths and twisted limbs. The rate of spontaneous abortion among pregnant women has been five times the normal rate in Canada. On the Grassy Narrows Reserve alone, there have been four babies born recently with cerebral palsy, a common occurrence among women who ingest mercury during their pregnancy.

Teachers in area schools have noticed an unusually high proportion of mental retardation among the younger children. (In Minamata, Japan, 29 percent of the babies born between 1955 and 1959 were mentally deficient.)

Previous studies of Minamata disease proved that the possibility of heart seizure increases greatly as the level of mercury in the blood increases. In 1972 an Indian fishing guide named Thomas Strong died of an apparent heart seizure. He had all the symptoms of mercury poisoning—slurred speech, shaky hands, loss of weight. No autopsy was ever performed, but his blood was tested and found to have a dangerously high mercury content. When told the the result, James Stopps, the chief of Ontario's Environmental Protection Unit, dismissed it, saying Strong's blood was "probably accidentally contaminated." But other guides have been tested and had equal levels of mercury in their blood.

Mercury poisoning causes "the Mad Hatter's disease," "a particular psychic disturbance characterized by irritability and restlessness as well as mental depression and dullness.'' Over the past year, there has been an alarming rise in the amount of violence on the two reserves.

Last fall a six-month-old baby was found floating along the shore of Grassy Lake.

In October a 16-year-old boy was shot dead in a teenage fight.

In February an eight-month-old baby boy was left outside in the snow to die of exposure and a 13-year-old boy was fatally stabbed.

In March a 30-year-old man was stabbed.

In June the body of an old man was found on the gutted dirt road that connects the reserve to Kenora, his head crushed by a rock.

In August another teenage boy was stabbed in the leg and bled to death.

In September a young girl died after being battered and left on the railroad tracks.

Before 1970, according to Marion Lamm, who lived with the Indians for more than 30 years, "You would never hear of a murder or a suicide. It wasn't in their tradition. It's just against their whole way of life."

Many of the younger, more militant Indians are pressing for vigorous action. They claim that they have had enough of what they call the "white man's slow death." Tommy Keesick, 29, the head of the Warrior Society, asked, "Does the government want 300 of our people to die before they do something about it?"

He charged that if 1,000 white citizens of Toronto were threatened as the Indians have been, the government reaction would be much more immediate.

Fred Kelly, an Indian leader in Ontario, says the government is involved in "massive political cover-up" and has withheld information from the endangered Indians. Specifically, he claims that the government took 20 tons of fish from the river several years ago and fed them to cats. Every one of the cats developed symptoms of mercury poisoning, yet the Indians were never told about the results of the test, nor were they told directly to stop eating the fish. Kelly said that the Indians deserved at a minimum a new source of food and livelihood as well as a comprehensive examination of all the Indians who were affected by the polluted fish. Dr. James Clarkson, a world-renowned expert on mercury pollution, was supposedly hired by the federal government to begin testing the Indians for mercury poisoning, but so far the government has not been willing to spend the $100 per person to do a full clinical examination of all the Indians who might be affected.

The government has refused to close down the river completely. In fact, the government of Ontario itself runs a large tourist camp on the polluted river and the managers there encourage tourists to eat the fish they catch at "shore lunches" along with their Indian guides. Dr. Clarkson has said that the fisherman who stays up there three weeks and eats fish every day "runs a very real chance of suffering permanent damage."

Dryden Paper has been strangely silent about the issue. Sometime this fall they are slated to switch over to a paper-making process that will do without mercury altogether. Nevertheless, the mercury already in the river will, according to most experts, continue to pollute the fish for a period of eight years or more.

Robert W. Billingsly, president of Reed Paper, Dryden's parent corporation, said recently that his company "had a heart," but at no time did he or anyone else attempt to communicate with the Indians whose lives they ruined, nor at any time did they try to provide an alternate source of livelihood for them. Billingsly righteously maintained that his company had "rigorously met and exceeded all government standards regarding the discharge of mercury." What he neglected to say is that before 1972 there were no government standards, and even though the company was treating its own employees for mercury poisoning in the late 1960s, it neglected to share its medical knowledge with the Indians and tourist operators who suffered because of its polluted wastes.

The Ojibway Indians "are just a fragment of what they once were," says a bush pilot who visits the area often. "They used to be strong, proud people. Now they just sit looking out into space all day. There is no purpose in their lives."

The results cannot be immediately reversed. The river that provided them jobs and food is destroyed. And the disease will only continue to spread.

"I have caught fish in this river since I was eight years old," said Chief Keewatin. "I know the fish and the animals and they know me. I can tell you each rock and bend in the river for forty miles in each direction. I know where the fish like to feed and when. These are things that were taught to me by me father, and they were taught to him by his father. Now there is no one I can teach these things to. The river, which was always a source of life to my people, is now a source of poison and death."

How the Wise Men Brought Malaria to Africa: And Other Cautionary Tales of Human Dreams and Opportunistic Mosquitos

Robert S. Desowitz

In most parts of the world, humans have increasingly set themselves apart from nature. While indeed there may be nothing wrong in so doing, certain costs may be incurred. To be sure, a price is often exacted for for whatever one does. In the three preceding articles it became apparent that social and political policy can have a tremendous impact on people's health. Once the pattern has been set, the future course of events may be dramatically affected. In this article we are able to examine dangers in not viewing the total situation in the design and implementation of developmental programs. That the interplay of economic, environmental and other cultural factors can be accompanied by ill health is also illustrated. It is important to remember that the intentions behind the development of these programs were generally good. We are further provided with an interesting interpretation of ecological balance. For example, Desowitz states that year-round exposure to malarial agents can be preferable to part-time exposure. He further provides a number of interesting examples of human ecological disasters. His view that there is sometimes little difference between results of "planned change" and the ravages of war is a distressing sentiment. For more information on "development" and disease see Hughes and Hunter (1970). A number of authors [such as Dubos (1959), Rosebury (1971), Glasser (1976), McNeill (1976), Cartwright (1972), and Zinsser (1935)] have dealt with the impact of disease on world history.

Once upon a time (but not too long ago) there lived a tribe deep within the Dark Continent. These people tilled the soil to raise crops of roots and grains, for they had little meat to lend them strength. Illness often befell

---

them, but even so, in this dry land they were not overly troubled with the fever sickness brought by the mosquito. Now in the Northern World there was a powerful republic that had compassion on these people and sent their Wise Men to relieve the mean burden of their lives. The Wise Men said, "Let them farm fish," and taught the people to make ponds and to husband a fish called tilapia.

The people learned well, and within a short time they had dug 10,000 pits and ponds. The fish flourished, but soon the people could not provide the constant labors required to feed the fish and keep the ponds free of weeds. The fish became smaller and fewer, and into these ponds and pits came the fever mosquitoes, which bred and multiplied prodigiously. The people then sickened and the children died from the fever that the medicine men from the cities called malaria. The Wise Men from the North departed, thinking how unfortunate it was that these people could not profit from their teachings. The people of the village thought it strange that Wise Men should be sent them to instruct in the ways of growing mosquitoes.

At about the same time, from 1957 to 1961, that this ecological misadventure was taking place in Kenya (for it was no fable), on the other side of the world the impoverished villagers of the Demerara River estuary in Guyana were enacting their own calamity. Striving to improve their lot by converting from subsistence farming of maize and cassava to cash-producing rice, they cleared the region for rice fields, displacing the livestock that formerly abounded in the villages. Mechanization on the roads and fields also progressed, bringing a further diminution in the numbers of domestic animals, particularly of cattle and draft oxen.

The major potential carrier of malaria in the region was the mosquito *Anopheles aquasalis,* but since subsistence agriculture created few suitable water collections for breeding, the mosquitoes were present in only modest density. The wet rice fields, however, provided an ideal larval habitat and the vector population increased rapidly. Even so, all would have been well had there been no alteration in the livestock since the genetically programmed behavior of *A. aquasalis* directs them to prefer blood meals from domestic animals rather than humans. With the disappearance of their normal food supply, however, the hungry mosquitoes turned their attention to people. Intense mosquito-man contact now enhanced malaria transmission to epidemic proportions. And so the combination of rice and tractors contrived to bring malaria to the people of the Demerara River estuary.

These two stories of ecological disaster are not isolated phenomena. In the endemic regions of the tropics, many human activities create and multiply the breeding habitats of malaria-bearing mosquitoes. Thus, in their very attempts to break from the bondage of poverty, food shortage, and ill health, third world peoples too often sow the seeds of disaster in the form of malaria.

Malaria of humans is caused by four species of a protozoan parasite of the genus *Plasmodium—P. falciparum, P. vivax, P. malariae,* and *P. ovale.* While all four species of parasites can produce debilitating illness, only *P. falciparum* is sufficiently virulent to cause death. The complicated life cycle is, in the main, the same for all species. Two hosts are required: man and a mosquito of the genus *Anopheles.* Infection in man begins with the bite of the mosquito, which injects sporozoites, microscopic threadlike forms, into the human host. The sporozoites enter liver tissue, where they divide asexually to form daughter cells. A single sporozoite may give rise to as many as 30,000 daughter cells. After a sojourn in the liver that may last from several weeks to months or even years, depending on the species and strain of parasite, the cells are released from the liver and enter the circulation, where they invade red blood cells.

Within the red blood cells the parasite grows, the nucleus divides, and in a manner analogous to the liver phase, ten to sixteen daughter cells are produced. The red cell finally bursts, freeing the daughter cells to invade new red blood cells. Since the cycle is synchronous, it causes periodically recurrent episodes of chills and fever—hallmarks of malaria infections.

Several days after the onset of the blood phase, new forms appear within the red blood cells. These sexual stages, the male and female gametocytes, undergo no further change until ingested by the feeding mosquito. A marvelously adaptive process has evolved in which the gametocytes are mature and infective to the mosquito for only a short period of the day. This period of infectivity occurs at night, matching the time that most anopheline carriers take their blood meal.

In the mosquito stomach the gametocytes are transformed into male and female gametes and fertilization occurs. The fertilized female gamete penetrates the mosquito stomach wall, coming to rest on the exterior surface where it forms a cystlike body, the oocyst. Within this cyst intense cytoplasmic reorganization and nuclear division take place, and as many as 10,000 sporozoites form. The formation of the oocyst takes seven to fourteen days, depending on temperature and other factors. Upon maturation it bursts, releasing the sporozoites, which invade the salivary glands. The mosquito can now infect a human when next it feeds.

The anopheline mosquito is the critical link in perpetuating the malaria parasite, and the nature of man-mosquito contact greatly influences the level of endemism. An important factor in this relationship is the life cycle of the mosquito in interaction with its environment. Each anopheline species has characteristic biological and behavioral traits that determine its interaction with man and other hosts. Thus, the selection for breeding water, host upon which to feed, and resting behavior are genetically controlled characteristics, which may or may not place a particular anopheline mosquito in proximity to man. In many regions of the tropics, human activities, particularly those associated with agriculture, alter the environment, producing suitable breeding sites and increasing the likelihood of human contact with malarial mosquitoes.

Of all the agricultural practices that alter the natural tropical ecosystem, rice culture is one of the most important in creating optimal conditions for malaria transmission. Rice farming requires large, open areas of water, also the preferred habitat of many of the most efficient anopheline carriers of malaria. These conditions are especially evident in new rice fields, where the young plants are placed well apart. Also, the generation time of the mosquito is accelerated in the sun-elevated temperature of the exposed water, and breeding is prolific. In addition, a relatively large body of standing water increases the humidity of the surrounding biosphere, and the higher humidity prolongs the mosquito's life. The longer a mosquito lives, the more people it bites during its lifetime.

A vicious series of events may develop beginning with the intense man-vector contact. Because rice culture is seasonal, peak densities of mosquitoes generally occur for relatively short periods. The limited transmission period prevents the development of a protective immunity. When farmers are incapacitated by malaria during the planting season, crop production suffers, leading to economic loss and food shortage.

The ecological changes described above have been excellently documented in a study carried out on Kenya's Kano Plain rice development scheme. Prior to establishment of the rice plots, the Kano Plain landscape was characterized by villages of scattered huts, maize farms interspersed with seasonal swamps and water holes in which *Pistia* plants grew. In this unmodified environment, 99 percent of the mosquito population were *Mansonia,* a nonvector of malaria, while only 1 percent were *Anopheles gambiae.* After the land was modified for rice farming, 65 percent of the mosquitoes were *A. gambiae* and 28 percent *Mansonia* (the other 7 percent were another variety). Similar alterations in mosquito populations following the introduction of rice farming have occured in such diverse areas of the world as Venezuela, Tanzania, India, Syria, and Morocco, where until 1949 the French colonial government had, for health reasons, banned rice growing.

In the tropical world the ecosystem undergoing the most rapid and extensive alteration for human purposes is the forest. These alterations have frequently resulted in an intensification of malaria, often out of all proportion to the small degree of disturbance created.

Within the intact tropical rain forest there are relatively few species of mosquitoes that transmit human malaria. Not only are there few permanent or semipermanent water collections but also the main anopheline carriers prefer sunlit breeding sites and avoid shaded conditions. But breeding conditions abound in the exposed water collections created when the forest is cleared by the farmer digging his plot of ground, by tractors and other machines used for lumbering, and by the rutted roads used to service the new settlements.

Conversely, on at least one occasion, the creation of forests has also led to problems. When the cacao industry was begun in Trinidad, a man-made forest of immortelle trees was planted to provide the shade required by cacao plants. Certain South and Central American anophelines, showing the remarkable specialization a mosquito species may have, breed exclusively in water contained in the bromeliad epiphytes of the forest gallery. When bromeliads colonized the high immortelle trees, *A. brellator* proliferated, carrying malaria to the plantation workers and their families.

In an attempt to solve their problems—overcrowded cities, land shortage, and the need for establishing a market economy—political and technical authorities in the developing countries have opened new lands to agricultural development. Such projects commonly begin with the clearing of the jungle, followed by resettlement of transmigrants and cultivation of cash crops such as cotton, tobacco, rice, and corn. But all too frequently, the ecological alterations brought about by deforestation, creation of irrigation systems, and other human activities enhance the vector population. More often than not, settlers brought into the area have had little exposure to malaria and have not acquired sufficient immunity to protect them from severe attacks. For example, within eight months of leaving nonmalarious urban centers of Java for an agricultural project in south Sulawesi, 32 percent of the settlers were stricken with malaria and the enterprise nearly collapsed.

The ability to protect the settlers by chemical control of the anopheline carrier has often been negated by prior use of agricultural insecticides such as DDT. Spraying crops to protect against the ravages of destructive insects and spraying for the control of anopheline vectors involve different and generally incompatible techniques. Where insecticide has been broadcast for crop protection, the anopheline population contracts sublethal doses that eventually render it physiologically or behaviorally resistant. Thus, by the time antimalaria measures are instituted, the avenue of mosquito control by chemical means has been closed.

Cost accounting of the economics of ecological alteration is difficult, particularly when the influence of a single factor, malaria, is traced through a complicated, interacting mosaic. One excellent exercise in ecological-economic sleuthing was carried out by the Pan American Health Organization after new lands had been opened for agricultural development in Paraguay. In the first year of the scheme, malaria seriously afflicted the settlers and the impact of the disease reduced the over-all production of cash crops—tobacco, cotton, and corn—by 36 percent. Worker efficiency, particularly during the harvest, which coincided with the height of the malaria season, was reduced by as much as 33 percent. Debilitated by malaria, the farmers devoted their limited energy to their cash crops, abandoning for subsistence all but the easily cultivated, but starchy, manioc. As a result, deterioration of their nutritional status was added to the burden of malaria.

In subsequent years there was reduced expansion of farms in the malaria-struck region. Tragically, the Paraguayan government and its advisers were aware of the health hazards, but having expended a large amount of capital on land development, it had too little left in the kitty to secure its "beachhead" by providing the infrastructure of health, education, and other social services. The Paraguayan experience has been repeated throughout the tropics.

In addition to agricultural development, third world governments have expanded electrical power resources in their attempts to promote economic development. But along with the kilowatts, rice, and fish, these giant hydro-electric and water impoundment schemes also produced malaria. The seepages and canals have provided optimal breeding habitats for malaria mosquitoes in such geographically diverse projects as the Aswan Dam in Egypt, the Kariba project in Zambia, the Lower Seyhan project in Turkey, and early in its history, the TVA scheme in the United States. On occasion, the dams and man-made lakes were not in themselves responsible for ecological change leading to intensified malaria transmission but, rather, set in motion a train of events that led to the situation. Construction of the Kalimawe Dam in Tanzania, for example, extended cultivation far beyond the original plots. This made it necessary to graze cattle, the preferred host of the local *A. gambiae,* farther from the villages. When the cows were no longer kept near houses at night, the peridomestic mosquitoes were diverted to man, and malaria transmission was intensified.

Ecological alterations have been caused not only by man's struggles toward progress but also by his conflicts; throughout the course of history the environment has been a casualty of war. This ecological havoc has often created conditions conducive to malaria transmission in both temperate and tropical regions, and epidemics of malignant malaria have victimized military personnel and civilians.

During World War II, for example, the bloody fighting near Cassino, Italy, destroyed dikes containing the rivers. Anopheline mosquitoes bred profusely in the flooded areas and bomb craters. Malaria, possibly introduced by foreign troops, occurred in its most violent form, with some villages totally infected and suffering a mortality rate of 10 percent. But it was in the Vietnam conflict that a new and devastating tactical strategy was applied—the ecosystem became a deliberate target of massive destruction. The use of aircraft-spread herbicides for the defoliation of forests and destruction of crops introduced a new dimension to the horror of war.

Scientists throughout the world were alarmed, and a number of studies were conducted to determine the consequences of defoliation.

One such study, that of the congressionally funded National Academy of Sciences committee, included an investigation of epidemiological-ecological interactions in the defoliated mangrove forest south of Saigon, a region known as the Rung Sat. This area, repeatedly sprayed with herbicide, had become a desolate, barren wasteland denuded of virtually every living tree. Studying an intact mangrove forest as a control, the NAS medical ecologists did not detect any breeding sites of anopheline mosquitoes. Other mosquitoes were abundant but the Southeast Asian mangrove ecosystem was not the kind of real estate suitable for anophelines. In the Rung Sat, however, the mosquito population consisted largely of *A. sinensis* and *A. lesteri*. Malaria was endemic throughout the region.

Again, rice seems to have been the final ecological culprit. As people were deprived of their main livelihood from woodcutting, they turned to rice culture in the less saline areas of the dead mangrove. The rice fields provided ideal breeding sites for the two anopheline species.

In Vietnam the main foci of malaria are found in the montane forests, the vectors being *A. maculatus,* breeding in exposed hillside streams, and *A. balabacensis,* living in sunlit standing collections of water. Removal of the forest's shade cover created new breeding sites for these mosquitoes. At the time of the NAS study in Vietnam the temperature of the war was too hot to permit on-the-ground study, but when the study group flew over the deforested mountain areas, they saw a landscape typically colonized by these two efficient vectors. Notably, American soldiers fighting in the Vietnam highland forests were severely afflicted by malaria, with the attack rate in some units as high as 53 cases per 1,000 troops per day.

Paradoxically and cruelly, in the absence of an effective control program, a community's welfare and stability often depend on continuous, intense exposure to malaria. Under these conditions, as in the agricultural villages of Africa and Southeast Asia, malaria accounts for high infant mortality; some 40 percent or more of the children under the age of five may die of the infection. Those who survive, however, develop a protective immunity, and adults, the productive segment of the community, remain relatively free of the pernicious clinical manifestations of the infection. Usually, the high infant mortality is compensated by a high birthrate, and so a population equilibrium is achieved in which the workers are sufficiently healthy to provide the community's food requirements.

The relatively slow acquisition of functional immunity to malaria and its concomitant cost in infant life have led to several disasters of good intent and have presented new moral dilemmas for discomfited public health workers. The Western and Western-trained health professionals have held, by tradition and education, the philosophy of the importance of individual human life and the right of every member of the community to good health. The heroic efforts begun in the mid-1950s to realize global eradication of malaria were rooted in this moral premise. But where these control programs were successful in the developing tropical countries, population numbers increased rapidly, while technical-agricultural resources to accommodate the burgeoning community lagged sadly behind. Following a successful control scheme in Guyana, infant mortality was reduced to one-third its former rate; in one study group, a sugar plantation village, the population rose from the precontrol level of 66,000 in 1957 to 110,000 in 1966. Some students of public health, as well as health officials, are now beginning to question the wisdom of instituting such measures as malaria control unless they are accompanied by effective population control programs or by expansion of resources to feed, clothe, educate, and house the increased population.

The disasters of good intent are related to malaria's tendency to return several years after a successful mosquito control program. During this period the mosquito populations have once again returned to former density, and the human population's collective immunity has waned. Wherever it recurs under these circumstances, malaria is explosive and clinically severe.

It is doubtful whether progress for the peoples of the developing world, as we define progress, can be achieved unless malaria and other diseases draining their intellectual and physical energies can be brought under control. Yet the enterprises of progress contribute, with monotonous regularity, to the deterioration of health. What is now required is a holistic approach. Engineers, agronomists, epidemiologists, economists, ecologists, demographers, cultural anthropologists, and political leaders must all contribute to the planning, execution, and evaluation processes. In this way, malaria and many other diseases can be reduced to a manageable state if not actually eradicated. Human needs demand it; human intelligence and ingenuity must be turned to achieving a degree of progress, rather than disaster, for the peoples of the third world.

Kuru and Cannibalism

John D. Mathews, Robert Glasse,
Shirley Lindenbaum

To discover something fundamental is always exciting. James Watson (1968), in *The Double Helix,* is able to convey effectively the drama of such a moment. Triumphant solutions to epidemiological mysteries are no less exciting. Berton Roueché (1947) has, in fact, presented such material in detective-story form. Clearly, many medical mysteries remain. We know, for instance, that multiple sclerosis is many times more prevalent in the northern latitudes than in the southern, yet the reasons for such a differential incidence eludes us. With regard to multiple sclerosis, epidemiological studies have suggested that both acquired and inherited factors may be at play (Nelson, 1973; NDES, 1976). Through epidemiological research, other conditions are more fully understood even though the final verdict is not yet in. One such example from the anthropological literature is pibloktoq (more commonly referred to as arctic hysteria). Foulks (1972) presents a variety of arguments that have been posited regarding pibloktoq in which an examination of cultural and ecological factors leads toward an understanding of the condition. The following article deals with another condition that was poorly understood until recently. Stanley Garn (1962), for example, discussed the state of research on this condition known as kuru. With regard to transmission of the disease all environmental factors had been studied (food, body paints, and even campfire smoke) and proved negative, allowing the conclusion that heredity held the total answer. Apparently food was not studied carefully enough. In this selection, the authors provide a good deal of sociocultural material in explaining incidence patterns of the disease. Cannibalism is implicated as the vehicle responsible for transmission of the disease agent and this provides an opportunity for further discussion of cultural relativism. The case of kuru presents a nice epidemiological analysis of a disease that is related to a practice often considered exotic, bizarre, or even barbaric (all value-laden terms) by a great number of people in the world. While the cultural-relativist limits of some readers may be

Reprinted by permission of the authors and *The Lancet,* Vol. 2, No. 7567, August 24, 1968, pp. 449–452. Footnotes deleted.

breached in this instance (cultural relativism can have its limits), it is important to point out that a good number of articles in this reader describe beliefs, practices, and conditions found in the United States that could be viewed as equally bizarre and exotic. After all, we are well prepared to accept a certain degree of psychiatric imperialism, city-related diseases, mercury poisoning, and abritrary labelling. Such facts appear to make good sense to us.

Summary. Evaluation of the available evidence supports the hypothesis that cannibalism of kuru victims was responsible for the epidemic spread of kuru through the Fore and their immediate neighbours with whom they intermarry. Clinical disease ensues 4–20 years after ingestion of poorly cooked tissues containing the transmissible agent. The rarity of kuru in men suggests that horizontal transmission of the agent other than by cannibalism is rare, or that it causes kuru of a much longer incubation period. New data suggest that genetic factors are not of major importance in the determination of host susceptibility. Since other cannibal peoples in New Guinea do not suffer from kuru, the kurugenic agent itself may be the unique factor in the aetiology of the disease. Unless vertical transmission to give kuru from mother to offspring or horizontal transmission of an extended incubation period can continue in the absence of cannibalism, kuru should disappear within the next few decades, by which time most people still carrying the agent will have died from kuru.

Introduction

Kuru is a neurological disorder found among the Fore and adjacent peoples with whom they intermarry in the Eastern Highlands of New Guinea; it has been seen in adult women and in young people of either sex. To account for the rarity of kuru in adult males, Bennett et al. postulated that kuru was determined genetically as a dominant trait in females but as a recessive trait in males. In the light of evidence for the recent epidemic spread of kuru, and for the transmission and passage of kuru to chimpanzees by inoculation of kuru-tissue suspensions, purely genetic theories of kuru aetiology have had to be abandoned. However, one must still account for the fact that adult males rarely get kuru. One of us (J.D.M.) has suggested that there are two mechanisms of transmission of the kurugenic agent viz., horizontal transmission causing kuru in adult women only, and vertical transmission from mother to offspring, causing kuru in children or young adults. This interpretation is compatible with recent epidemiological data.

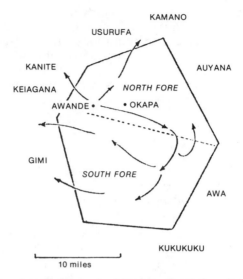

Fig. I—Schematic map showing Fore and neighbouring linguistic regions.

Arrows indicate the main parts of kuru spread from Awande. The Kukukuku have no tradition of intermarriage with the Fore, no tradition of cannibalism and no kuru. Kuru occurs among the Fore, Gimi, Keiagana, Kanite, Usurufa, and Kamano peoples who have a tradition of cannibalism and intermarriage, but the incidence of kuru decreases with the distance from the focus in the South Fore.

Evidence

The possible importance of cannibalism in aetiology of kuru has been the subject of speculation for some time. Cannibalism may have had a fundamental role in spreading the virus-like kurugenic agent through the community. Before the suppression of cannibalism in the 1950s people in the Fore region (fig. 1) ate their own dead kinsfolk for gastronomic reasons, and also to show respect for the dead. It was customary for women and young children to be the main cannibals. Older boys and men rarely took part in these meals, particularly if the victim had been a woman and had died from kuru. Horizontal transmission of kuru could have depended directly on the eating of incompletely cooked human kuru tissue by women, and vertical transmission, in part at least, could have been due to the consumption of kuru material by young children sharing human flesh with their mothers. Experiments to determine the tissue distribution and heat stability of the kuru agent are in progress. By analogy with the properties of the scrapie agent, one might expect the kuru agent to withstand usual Fore cooking procedures without complete inactivation, especially since water boils at less than 95 °C in much of the Fore area due to the altitude. Most of

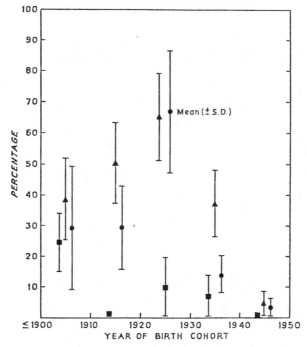

Fig. 2—Risk of kuru, by birth cohort, for particular female relatives of propositi in genealogies ascertained in low-incidence kuru areas.

Risks plotted are the means of values calculated from (a) the percentage of each birth cohort actually reported to have died from kuru, and (b) the percentage calculated from the same data using actuarial methods to allow for the effect of deaths from causes other than kuru at earlier ages.

▲ Mothers, sisters, and daughters of kuru index cases (deceased 1957–66) ascertained in low-incidence areas—viz., Keiagana, Kanite, Gimi, and North Fore.

● Wives of brothers of the same kuru index cases.

■ Mothers, sisters, and daughters of living control propositi ascertained at random in kuru-prone villages of Keiagana and Kanite (1966).

the circumstantial evidence of links between the ethnography of cannibalism and the epidemiology of kuru is summarised in the table.

There are, in addition, consistent ethnological accounts of the first kuru cases in certain villages. Consumption of the body of the first victim was said to have been followed 4–8 years later by a crop of secondary cases among those who ate the first victim.

Fig. 2 shows new data bearing on the high risk of kuru in sisters-in-law of kuru index cases from low-incidence kuru areas (see table, item 12). The average risk of kuru in these wives of brothers of index cases is consistently much higher (41% for birth cohorts 1910–30) than the risk in female relatives of control indexes randomly ascertained in kuru-prone villages (average risk 12%); the risk in females genetically related to the kuru index

Summary of Ethnographic and Epidemiological Evidence Linking Cannibalism and Kuru Transmission

Item	Epidemiological or genealogical observation	Ethnographic explanation	Comments or deductions
1	Kuru is a familial disease	Cannibalism was a matter of kinship; certain dead relatives were eaten for gastronomic reasons, or to show respect. Enemies occasionally eaten too	Familial aggregation of disease does not necessarily indicate genetic determination
2	Kuru is common in women, but rare in adult males (horizontal transmission)	Cannibalism by adult males was rare, especially in the South Fore; they avoided female flesh and male kuru victims. Women commonly ate kuru victims, and more often consumed brain and visceral material than did men	Adult males were likely to consume little of kurugenic agent, and it is possible that only high titre brain and visceral tissues would consistently transmit the disease after cooking (see text)
3	Kuru presents in the children of women who die from the disease (vertical transmission)	Young children often shared at cannibal feasts with their mothers	Vertical transmission to children could be just a special case of horizontal transmission by cannibalism, but a more biological type of vertical transmission is possible, perhaps to give kuru of longer incubation period (see text)
4	Kuru is more common in the South Fore than in the North Fore	There was more resistance to the eating of kuru victims in the North Fore	Early reactions to the appearance of the disease gave way to the widespread belief that kuru was due to sorcery
5	Initially, the kuru epidemic spread slowly from village to village, sometimes with a latent period of 5 years or more	At first there was some reluctance to eat kuru dead even in the South Fore	Incubation period likely to be up to 5 years or more; agent unlikely to spread readily other than by cannibalism, or if it does, unlikely to cause either immunity or kuru
6	The first kuru victims in any place were often women who had come as wives from a previously affected village	Such immigrant wives would be likely to eat kuru victims in the home village either before marriage or on a return visit	
7	Kuru could spread into a previously affected village if an emigrant wife developed kuru elsewhere	Maternal kin (in the home village usually) had rights in the body after death	One can account for the tempo or "explosive nature" of the epidemic by postulating that 3–6 secondary cases followed 4–10 years after each preliminary case

No.			
8	An explosive kuru epidemic had developed in the South Fore by the 1940s and 1950s	Consumption of kuru dead had become more general and many females were likely to eat each victim	
9	Villages affected later in the kuru epidemic tend to have a lower incidence of the disease	Cannibalism was suppressed at an early stage of the local epidemic	Low incidence due to limited opportunities for kuru cannibalism
10	There is a decreased incidence of kuru across linguistic and cultural boundaries	There is less intermarriage and shared cannibalism across such boundaries	Could also be due to the importance of genetic factors in predisposing to kuru
11	There was no kuru amongst the Awa women unless they married into Fore villages	The Awa were probably not cannibals, but Awa wives in Fore villages could have taken part in kuru cannibalism	Suggests that genetic factors are of little importance in determining the relative incidence of kuru in the area
12	In low-incidence areas, the risk of kuru in wives of brothers of kuru index cases is higher than the risk for relatives of control propositi, and is almost as high as that for mothers, sisters and daughters of the same kuru cases (see fig. 2)	The victim's mothers, sisters, daughters, and brothers' wives were likely to have had similar opportunities for kuru cannibalism	As for item 11
13	Since about 1960 there has been a general decline in the incidence of kuru, along with a definite increase in the average age of people dying from kuru. There have been no kuru deaths in anyone born since about 1954	Cannibalism was largely suppressed in the 1950s due to the activities of administration and mission personnel	Transmission of the kurugenic agent (at least to give kuru of a shorter incubation period) may have ceased with the suppression of cannibalism. Ex hypothesis, most cases of kuru seen now must have been incubating the disease for 10–12 years or more; the increase in the average age of victim reflects the ageing of cohorts exposed 10 or more years ago
14	The Gimi have yet to show such a significant decline in kuru incidence, and hitherto there has been no increase in the age of kuru victims	Cannibalism probably persisted for longer among the Gimi	
15	The youngest kuru victims currently observed come from isolated hamlets	Cannibalism was probably practiced for longer in these places	Surreptitious cannibalism was harder to detect in the Gimi and other isolated areas
16	Several men over 40 years of age have been seen with kuru recently and rare cases of kuru in old men have been reported by native informants	Adult men have occasionally eaten kuru victims; in South Fore those of fighting age were most likely to abstain	The disease in middle-aged men could represent kuru of long incubation period following vertical transmission in the 1920s, or it could be due to occasional kuru cannibalism by the men. The disease in old men is almost certainly due to the latter

cases was not much higher (51%) than the risk cited above for females related by marriage only (41%). It is improbable that this distribution of risks could have a purely genetic explanation, even after allowance is made for the high frequency of cousin marriage.

The hypothesis of the transmission of a rare pathogenic agent by cannibalism thus accounts for the limitation of kuru to the Fore and their immediate neighbours, the familial patterns of kuru incidence, and the sparing of adult males. An alternative hypothesis, that kuru develops in a genetically unique host after contact with a recently introduced transmissible agent which may be otherwise innocuous, is less attractive, since any simple genetic theory of host susceptibility cannot explain the apparent absence of horizontal transmission to men. Blood-group data and ethnographic studies of migration do not fully support the postulate of massive genetic drift previously advanced to account for the evolution of a host genotype unique to the Fore region. A priori, a unique transmissible agent seems more likely than the wide dissemination of a unique host genotype (although if lysogeny were proved in mammals, the distinction between these two possibilities could become blurred).

The data from the table and fig. 2 accord with the view that genetic factors are less important than the environmental factor of kuru cannibalism in determining individual risk. If there is a necessary host genotype, it must be present in 50–80% of people even in the lower incidence kuru areas (about 80% of South Fore women in birth cohorts 1901–1930 were potential kuru victims, and well over 50% did in fact die from kuru). This is not to deny the possibility that genetic factors might be of importance in determining susceptibility after transmission of the agent other than by cannibalism, or in determining the incubation period of the disease.

Transmissibility of Kuru Agent

Gajdusek et al. have initiated experiments to determine if kuru is transmissible to chimpanzees by the oral route. No animal has yet developed kuru after oral administration of kuru brain suspension, but the longest incubation period yet recorded is only 14 months. Argument by analogy with the scrapie system suggests that the incubation period of kuru by the oral route could be 4 years or more, even in chimpanzees; and incubation periods of 10–38 months in chimpanzees inoculated by the intracerebral route accord with this suggestion. Ethnographic and epidemiological data suggest that human kuru has an incubation period of at least 4 years, with a significant number of cases developing the disease after more than 10 or 20 years. If the kurugenic agent is ever transmitted horizontally to man other than by cannibalism, the sparing of adult males suggests that it could not cause kuru unless the incubation period was at least 20–30 years. Seasonal factors, perhaps nutritional, may be important in precipitating the onset of clinical kuru in those incubating the disease. Kuru probably developed at Awande in the North Fore as early as 1900, but the disease did not reach epidemic proportions until it spread to the South Fore, where kuru cannibalism became prevalent. To solve the paradox of the first kuru case, one might suppose that the kurugenic agent arose de novo in the Fore area from human, animal, or viral genetic material, and that its continued existence was ensured by cannibalism. The adoption of cannibalism by the Fore probably antedates the origins of kuru, and it is interesting to speculate that the change to cannibalism may have facilitated the origin and survival of the kurugenic agent. Once several people carrying the agent had been eaten, there would be little chance of its extinction; "blind passages" (passage to new host without disease in previous host) could have selected a faster replicating form of the agent. If, as seems likely, horizontal transmission did not occur readily except by cannibalism, there would be every reason to expect rapid selection for maximum pathogenicity. The analogy with scrapie is interesting. Natural vertical transmission of scrapie seems to be common, and horizontal transmission occurs much less often. Experimental scrapie is transmissible by inoculation and by mouth, and it can pass from mother to offspring, probably in utero. The exact pathways of natural transmission are still obscure. For kuru the consumption of brain could have facilitated selection for maximum neurotropism, and perhaps have had a less specific "adjuvant" action. The shorter average incubation period deduced for kuru in the high-incidence area of the South Fore accords with the general postulate that pathogenicity of the agent might increase following multiple serial passage by cannibalism.

Conclusion

An open problem is posed by the group of cases which are presumed due to vertical transmission. Cannibalism by young children may be the sole explanation for this group of cases, but there could have been transmission by other routes, to children from mothers who had previously acquired the agent by cannibalism. If maternal transmission of the agent is continuing, it cannot cause kuru with an incubation period of less than about 15 years, since virtually no person born in the Fore area since 1954 has yet developed kuru.

If all kuru transmission ceased in the 1950s, when cannibalism was suppressed, then the decline in kuru incidence will be rapid; each new crop of cases will be progressively older, and the preponderance of kuru in females will continue. If kuru is maintained by passage from mother to offspring, or even by horizontal transmission without cannibalism, then the incidence of kuru will decline more slowly, and the cases will tend to become more equally distributed between the sexes, with an age range from 15–20 years upwards.

Today the Strawberry, Tomorrow...

Ruth Rosenbaum

Scientists have apparently been experimenting with and progressing in the development of a "clean bean" *(Newsweek,* 1973). At the same time there is discussion of the very real problem of hospital-induced malnutrition in surgical patients (Hill, *et al.,* 1977). Clearly there are different foci and priorities in research regarding food and nutrition, and these differences result in part from the encouragement received from different funding agencies. The following selection allows for discussion about technological "progress" and a possible direction that our culture may be taking. Some would argue that danger is indicated, that we are headed for a more "plastic" or artificial lifestyle (is there any other kind?) and that we should take heed of frequent discoveries of the carcinogenic nature of substances which are regularly used with foods (such as Red Dye Number 2). Others might argue that the risks are negligible when one considers that the new developments are on the wave of the future that will offer a variety of conveniences in food preparation and production. Are these new developments dangerous or are they simply the price of progress? Researchers claim to be able to construct a strawberry that is better than the real thing.

They call them creative flavorists. In the entire world there are only 13 great creative flavorists and no more than 150 others who have what it takes to be considered part of their select society. Shielded from the public eye, these high priests of the multimillion-dollar flavor industry invoke the chemical elements and create from them the counterfeit flavors that are in three-quarters of the products on our supermarket shelves.

Advertisements in food industry journals boast of their masterpieces: fake chocolate flavor that tastes and smells just like "the dark expensive stuff made from imported South American cocoa beans"; synthetic chicken flavor that *"feels* more like chicken than any other chicken flavor you have ever tasted"; "right-off-the-bush" imitation strawberry flavor; imitation coconut flavor that "tastes more like coconuts than coconuts"; three species of artificial potato flavor—"European Bintje, green earthy Idaho and popular King Edward." . . . Though nature still clutches a few last secrets (the flavor and odor of fresh-baked bread and fresh-ground coffee are the most elusive), it cannot be long before the remaining untouched edibles are transformed by the alchemical powers that be.

Flavorists have even managed to go beyond nature with their artificial *canned* tomato and *canned* tomato paste flavors that give people the tinny taste they have become accustomed to. And their artificial fruit flavors infused with "burnt or scorched nuances" match the effect that processing has on the real thing.

But more than simply replicating all natural and industrial tastes within our experience, flavorists will soon be able to create primal taste-experiences and provide an individual with flavor landmarks from cradle, or even pre-cradle, to grave.

Researchers are investigating the possibility of actually flavoring the amniotic fluid; they have found that if a pregnant woman is fed especially well-flavored food, the fetus knows and will consume more of the fluid.

At International Flavors and Fragrances, Inc. (IFF—the largest international flavor seller, based in New York), flavorists had perfected an artificial human breast-milk flavor as early as 1968. How did they do it? "We brought some mothers into the lab, squeezed the milk from them and then managed to simulate it," a flavorist fondly recalls. IFF also invests in Masters and Johnson's Reproductive Biology Research Center. "It can't hurt to know what we can do to improve man's sexual urge," said one IFF researcher.

Even death has been conquered. A flavorist at Norda, Inc., another large New York-based flavor house, successfully reproduced the odor of a cadaver, although flies put to the test seemed to prefer an artificial strawberry aroma.

Heavy steel doors guard the entrance to the flavorists' laboratories. Inside, the old guard of herbal extracts, essential oils and flower absolutes from all over the world are being pushed aside on vast shelves by hundreds of bottles of wood- and petroleum-derived chemicals. Powerful odors pervade the long corridors, changing outside each laboratory: air pockets of cheddar cheese, maple, onion and garlic, fried hamburger, brown gravy. . . . Magical changes, as there is not a telltale sign of the sites of creation, no steaming vials, no bubbling test tubes, just rows of unanimated bottles of multicolored powders and liquids.

The formulas conceived in these labs are locked away and guarded with greatest care and expense. Even flavorists within the same company may be denied access to one another's formulas. There is talk of secret labs in remote mountainous regions. According to one flavorist I spoke to, kidnapping has become a real menace in the industry. He dares not tell his wife and children even the names of the food manufacturers his company sells its flavors to, so they will have nothing to say to potential extortionists.

The center of artificial intrigue and creation is the New York-New Jersey area, where most of the handful of companies that account for nearly all U.S. flavor sales are based. These include Fritzsche-Dodge & Olcott Inc., IFF, Givaudan Corp., Firmenich, Inc., Norda, Inc., Monsanto Flavor/Essence Inc., H. Kohnstamm & Co., Felton International, Inc., and Ungerer & Co. Major exceptions are McCormick Industrial Flavor Division in Maryland, and Warner-Jenkinson in St. Louis, Mo.

Each day these companies send out drums containing up to 50 gallons of precious formula (hand-mixed by employees who often know only code names for the chemicals they combine) not only to U.S. food manufacturers but to companies in almost every country of the world.

Cutthroat competition among flavor houses has forced executives to seek out, bid for, and woo top creative flavorists who can conjure unique tastes for their customers' products. One New Jersey company with a newly formed flavor division managed to attract a master flavorist who had previously worked at IFF. "It was like the culmination of a two-year romance," the president told me proudly.

Romanticism is the core of the flavorist's profession. To "capture in a formula the essence of what I perceive with my own nose and tongue," is how one flavorist describes his ambition. Another calls God his "toughest competitor."

As I went from flavor lab to flavor lab, I found that they practice a distinctive art form with its own romantic aesthetic, and that they are themselves the gourmet chefs of the world of convenience foods.

People in the industry compare flavorists equally to sculptors, composers, painters and writers ("Shakespeare created great literature, we create great flavors," runs one ad), but the spirit of flavor creation seems closest to that of music composition. Even the vocabularies of the two arts converge at several points. The "note" is the basic unit of flavor vocabulary, and the desk at which the flavorist creates his chemical harmonies is called a "console."

No bigger than an average office desk, the console has several tiers of shelves above it, placing at the flavorist's fingertips the chemicals he considers most essential. (Chemicals used in flavors are called "flavomatics.")

Let's say a flavorist wants to create an artificial strawberry flavor. First he has to have the "notes" of a real strawberry clear in his mind. Every flavorist will perceive them differently, but the "dominant notes" in strawberry that almost everyone agrees on are the the "straw or hay notes," "sour notes," a "sweet green note," "ester notes" and "green butter notes," as well as "rose effects" and a "decidedly balsamic character." These vary according to the kind of product the flavor is destined for. With strawberry preserves, for example, the flavorist will play up the "rose and honey notes" and cool it on the "butter-balsam." For taffy candy, he'd tone down the "green notes." Once at his console, the flavorist's fingers fly to the flavomatics he knows, through years of experience, to yield basic strawberry notes.

Then one by one he chooses others, blending, smelling, tasting, adding a bit more of one, smelling and tasting again, trying another, refining the flavor each time until it is complete—with "supporting notes," "background notes" and "interest notes" as well as the basics.

In all, there are about 2,000 raw materials for the flavorist to choose from, each one with several characteristic notes. As the flavorist composes at his console, he must be able to envision how the notes of each material he adds will "sound" with every other note in the final flavor composition. (All materials have to be chemically attuned as well.) Flavor creation requires a great deal of delicacy. A change in a single ingredient at the ratio of a few parts per million in the final product could result in "off-flavors," or could even make the difference between the product's tasting like sweat or like coconut.

The number of ingredients in an artificial flavor varies from 25 to 100 or more, depending on the flavorist's style.

"With some of these newfangled mixed fruit and punch flavors, my colleagues'll use 200, even 300 ingredients. I personally prefer to keep things simpler," said one flavorist.

As with strawberry, each particular flavor has a few indispensable notes. Normal milk, for example, has a "minute note of the body odor of the cow" and a slight "feedy note." You won't find beer or honey without their "horsey notes," nor apple without its "pip note." "Tingle notes," as in mint and anise, go into mouthwash and toothpaste flavors.

In my efforts to find out about the chemical concertos many of us consume at every meal, I came across a sinister unruly underworld of flavor notes, the minor key of the flavomatic scale.

"Oily Tonka-bean undertones" find their way into nut, cheese, vanilla and caramel flavors, and "sweat-like notes" into imitation rum, chocolate, pecan and butterscotch flavors. A flavomatic with "tarry-repulsive" and "choking" notes is used in making artificial cheese, coffee, chocolate, grapefruit and nut flavors. "Gassy notes" crop up in fruit, wine, brandy and nut flavors.

And there it was—the "fecal note." The chemical that brings us this note is commonly called skatole—appropriately like scatology and skata ("shit" in Greek)—and is used in cheese, fruit and nut flavors. One author writes, "The use of skatole in flavors may come as a surprise to some perfumers who find it hard to believe that we can 'eat' this odor."

"Overripe bass notes," "fresh metallic topnotes," "piercing apricot-like notes," "ethereal winey overtones"—the beat goes on as the flavorist, alone at his console, orchestrates everything into final flavor harmony.

"I am known in the industry as the creator of strawberry," says C. Strawberry, a senior flavorist at an important New Jersey flavor house who prefers that his real name remain confidential. His strawberry is called a "classic"; it is in every kind of pink-flavored food or drink you can imagine, and it has made millions for his company.

But ask C. Strawberry how *he* feels about it. "I'm not satisfied. It's still not what I have in mind. Strawberry has been my pet flavor since I was a child, and I want to examine it more, delve into it, see what makes it flash."

The technique of examining a flavor when he first began, over 30 years ago, and of examining one today are as different as "making fire with flint or making it with a match," says Mr. Strawberry. In the flint era, it first took a ton of strawberry, say, to get a half-pound of extractive of strawberry. The flavorist then had to separate out as many of the chemical constituents as possible through traditional chemical analysis (he might have obtained 10 or 12 for all his trouble) and then sniff for clues to the chemicals that yielded flavor notes.

Now, with the gas liquid chromatographer (GLC) that was used in most U.S. flavor companies by the early sixties, he can inject 5 millionths of a liter of strawberry oil into the GLC and, within minutes, obtain a long chart with a series of peaks that can be used to identify about 200 of the chemical constituents of the oil. Of these, the flavorist may be able to find 50 or 60 that contribute to natural strawberry flavor and that give him a broader range of definite "notes" from which to compose his flavors.

Flavorists don't hesitate to tell you what a tremendous aid the GLC has been to them, as long as you know who's still boss. And they make sure you know.

"I don't know how many times I've had to correct that thing," one said in mock exasperation. "You see, it confuses structurally similar chemicals, but if *I* go over and put my nose to the exhaust board, I can distinguish them as they separate out." No, flavorists do not feel technology is anywhere ready to replace them. What does worry them is that a new breed of flavorist, with undue respect for machinery and not much romantic motivation, may eventually degrade the profession.

J. J. Broderick, manager of H. Kohnstamm & Co.'s flavor division in New York City and author of *The Apricot—A Disappearing Art?* seemed sincerely concerned as he spoke about the problem: "What will happen to the industry if there are no more flavorists who know how to rely on their own creativity and sense of perception? No flavor has ever been created from 100 percent technical know-how.''

"You have these young men coming from all these universities and centers of education and so forth; well, they have a lot of knowledge of instruments, but so many of them have no imagination." C. Strawberry's tone was sad and a little scornful. "What they have yet to realize is that this is a very slow-going profession. Even now with the instruments, it takes a lifetime to really get to know all the raw materials and to get close enough to nature to be able to emulate her creations. You see, no instrument can ever achieve what a human nose and tongue can achieve.''

The Monsanto Flavor Library in Montvale, New Jersey. A large room filled with tall cases, several shelves high, with rows four and five deep of brown-tinted glass bottles, each containing an achievement of the human nose and tongue.

"You just have to smell our watermelon. That's my favorite. Let's see. I think it's in the 8000's.''

I follow my guide, Joe Jacobs, head of Monsanto's Flavor Application Laboratories, to the sixth aisle, where he begins looking among the early 8000's, reading off the selections.

"Lemon special, Formosan mushroom, celery, guava, bacon . . .'' It's like being in an uncatalogued bookstore where you can find *Twelfth Night* next to *Helter Skelter* and you never know what to expect next. ". . . Deer tongue, blackberry, cherry tobacco, black pepper . . .'' Still no watermelon.

Mr. Jacobs calls an invisible librarian and asks for help. A few seconds later we hear, from beyond the last set of shelves, perhaps from an adjacent room: "Try #8794 and #8999.'' First 8999, Imitation Watermelon. Joe unscrews the bottle and waves it in front of my nose. Perfect—watermelon at the reddest part, far from the rind. Next to this, Imitation Watermelon #8794 is very disappointing—a vague fruity sweet-sour odor, probably used in hard candies.

We move through the stacks, stopping in almost every aisle, spending the lunch hour sniffing whatever looks good—imitation ham and beef flavors, barbecue sauce flavors, three kinds of artificial mushroom flavor, imitation Yago Sant'gria, butter, sour cream, green pepper, boiled milk, Parmesan cheese, white wine, and mango flavors. All these were satisfying, but what I really recommend is their Cucumber #7035— the artificial odor itself carries the impression of crunchiness, moisture and seeds, as well as real cucumber flavor.

For dessert I order artificial cheesecake flavor. A quick call to the librarian, who calls back "6002,'' and in seconds I have it before my nose.

One-quarter of the 11,000 flavors in Monsanto's library were created in the past eight years; so were approximately one-quarter of the 103,000 flavor formulas (dating from 1920) in the library of Fritzsche-Dodge & Olcott, one of the leading U.S. flavor companies. Most of the new stock is synthetic in these and other companies equally prolific.

Synthetic flavors were first widely used in the U.S. about 1880. They were mostly imported from Germany—imitation pear, cherry, melon, mulberry, quince, apricot, rum, and cognac flavors used to replace part of the natural flavor in food, wines, and brandies. When World War I brought a stop to the importation of these delights, the U.S. began to cultivate its own garden, then mostly overrun with natural flavors.

From this time until almost 1960, fruit flavors, vanilla, maple and imitation spices (mostly developed during World War II) were the only synthetic produce. Not only that, the flavors were used either to add a dimension to a food with an unrelated flavor (artificial vanilla flavor used in making chocolate), or they were used to give a cheap boost to the natural flavor, as in ice cream or beverages. But except for certain classes of foods, like gelatin desserts and hard candy, artificial flavors were not used to replace totally the natural, nor to give a food its fundamental taste.

In the early sixties, however, flavorists armed with new flavor chemicals and with a mandate from the food manufacturers stormed the barnyard, the sea, the orchards, supplanting the first set of creations with their own. One company now offers 41 varieties of imitation meat and meat gravy flavors. There is an artificial "gulf-fresh shrimp" flavor, imitation tuna fish, scallop and crab flavors, and an all-round "crustacean flavor." What is significant is that more and more of the flavors are being used to replace entirely the real things. Soon the hamburger will not simply be helped, it will be relieved of all duties, dismissed completely. There already are meat-like products made from vegetable protein and artificial flavoring, and there are many more flavors waiting in the aisles of flavor company libraries for the proper product to come along. If manufacturers manage to mold a chicken shape from vegetable protein, they can dress it immediately with imitation chicken breast flavor, chicken fat flavor, chicken skin flavor and basic chicken flavor.

Fruit flavors have reached such a state of perfection that food manufacturers have been inspired to come up with totally artificial dried apricots and artificial "chopped strawberries" used in muffin mixes, both complete with flavor, aroma, and texture of the real thing.

I was impressed to learn that it is often the flavorist himself who instills his flavor with texture, or, as they call it, "mouthfeel" (or "how it chews"). They can bring to life whole families of flavors, each member having a different "bite." A chocolate flavor, say, could come in five different mouthfeels, ranging from a pulpy sauce to "a crispy bit typified by a crouton."

The vegetable patch was nature's last stronghold against the flavorists' advances. Not until the late sixties did the imitations begin to sprout. Tomato was first, followed by potato (baked and French fried), green bean, celery, parsley, pea, cucumber, carrot and mushroom. Most of these, with tomato the main exception, are not yet good enough to replace a natural flavor completely and may simply add "vegetable interest" to dressings, dips and sauces. (Even Monsanto cucumber flavor that smelled so perfect is probably only capable of "enhancing cucumber character.")

But serious forays into vegetable territory began only within the last decade; there is not much doubt about what will happen in the next.

Having watched its army of artists triumph over almost every individual edible creation, the flavor industry was ripe for an assault on nature itself.

Earlier, in the fifties, companies would talk of their flavor conquests somewhat apologetically, embarrassed. "We are proud to announce our new improved cherry flavor; of course it is still no match for Mother Nature's," a company bulletin read.

In the early sixties, there was open boast of the flavorist's knowledge of nature and his ability to duplicate her. Everybody was doing it; there was no point in maintaining Victorian modesty. Still, Mother Nature was respected as *the* standard of excellence. Just a few years later, however, the campaign began subtly, and the quality of her flavors was to be cast in doubt, maybe forever.

I first suspected foul play when, in the journals of the same companies that only ten years earlier were eating humble pie, I found whole articles devoted to character assassination. A pear, for example, is described as "temperamental, demanding to be picked while it hangs still imperfectly colored upon the tree"; otherwise it is "tasteless and gritty." No such problems with *synthetic* pear flavor.

Then the digs began to appear in ads. "Mother Nature is fickle," one says. "Profuse with her blessings one day, then turns on a flood, drought or blight the next." Why put up with these humiliations when a constant synthetic can give you "flavor that nature envies"? Another company points out that its artificial tomato flavors don't "leak, bruise or take up space." Above the comment is a picture of some fat, dented, overripe tomatoes made by you-know-who.

You see, nature only reminds of Eden, synthetic flavors actually bring it to you. No death, no change, no fickleness. So if you want "foreign particles, shell fragments, molds, off-flavors and shriveled pieces"—go ahead, eat real nuts instead of new nutmeat substitutes that come in four flavors: pecan, black walnut, English walnut and almond.

In fact, the very idea of eating certain of nature's creations is enough to make you shudder. A recent IFF annual report warns its shareholders that "natural foods" are "a wild mixture of substances created by plants or organisms for completely different non-food purposes—their survival and reproduction," and that they "came to be consumed by humans at their own risk." W. C. Fields was more succinct—"Don't drink the water, fish fuck in it."

Although flavorists have become instruments of the industry's Faustian ambitions, they are themselves very likable characters, still in love with their work and driven by their own gentler ambitions.

"My cherry flavor is better than the natural, and without a single cocoa bean I make a chocolate flavor, so exquisite, so beautiful . . ." As Shlomo Reiss speaks, his wife, sitting next to him, watches him admiringly, nodding occasionally at me as if to reassure me that, as incredible as it seems, what he says is true.

Chief and only senior flavorist at Ungerer & Co.'s labs in New Jersey, Mr. Reiss began his career 40 years ago at the age of 15. His appealing accent derives from German, Polish and Ukrainian, the languages of his childhood.

"When I can go back to the bottle that has, say, my raspberry flavor in it—my raspberry is perfect—when I can go back to the bottle, sniff the flavor, taste it and honestly say, 'Ah, *this* is beautiful,' the pleasure at that moment is . . ." Mr. Reiss pauses, looking out ahead of him, imagining, then continues: ". . . It is indescribable." Mrs. Reiss nods.

Since the time I met my first flavorist, I had been wondering how the Grecian-urn existence they lead on the job might affect them. What happens to creators when they descend from the land of perfect raspberries to the coarser, shadowy place where we live and eat? Do they suffer for artistic hubris? Until I spoke with the Reisses, I got only abstract, noncommittal comments: "Well, my wife says I'm difficult to live with, so I guess I must be"; or, "You know, with an artistic job, you don't have much free time."

When I asked Mr. Reiss if his job had any unexpected effect on his life, this time his wife nodded *before* he spoke. "I used to enjoy eating everything, but shortly after I started working, I began to criticize and reject all kinds of food. Nothing seemed good enough, and if the taste was not exactly as I thought it should be, I just wouldn't eat it."

"I had to learn not to cry," Mrs. Reiss said matter-of-factly. "I would make something special—it could have taken me hours—and then he would come home, sniff it and if it was not to his liking he wouldn't touch it."

Since this apparently happened several times a week, I wondered how Mr. Reiss had survived all these years. When I mentioned this, they looked at each other for a moment, resigned and affectionate, and then Mr. Reiss' eyes glazed over, trance-like, and in a devout tone only equalled when he talks about his indescribable flavors, he said, "The best dish—that can only be," his eyes brighten another degree, "rye bread—fresh from the bakery."

Mrs. Reiss smiled at me, nodding, but with a slight nervous restraint, as if she's known him to eulogize for hours.

"With butter—while it's still hot, just baked, ahhh, or with a clove of garlic . . . Have you ever tried it that way? Or even plain, as long as it's still warm . . ."

Several minutes later Mrs. Reiss speaks. "Now if he doesn't like what I make, I just let him eat his rye bread and I don't get too upset."

The Reisses' friends can't afford to get upset either. When Mr. Reiss comes to dinner, the first thing the hostess does is to pass the plate of food in front of his nose, and if he shakes his head no, she removes the plate and says not a word. Mrs. Reiss insists that they have not lost any friends over food. "He has such a good sense of humor, so he tells jokes while they eat to compensate."

"It's time to come back to natural flavor. Remember the real taste of luscious golden apricots or ripe juicy pineapples? Your customers do—And they are asking for real flavor. They want ingredients that are natural."

Ralph Nader breaking into the flavor biz?

The *National Enquirer* of the food industry?

It's actually from an ad by H. Kohnstamm & Co. in a 1972 issue of *Food Technology,* amidst rave reviews of artificial breakthroughs and articles warning against natural foods.

Flavor people are furious at the big food manufacturers for trying to capitalize on consumer and health food movements. "Instead of using their advertising power to assure people that there is nothing unsafe about artificial food additives, they come out with their own line of natural cereals and what-have-you. It's bound to make people wonder what's wrong with the other 80 percent of their food," one flavor researcher complained.

They are furious, but since they are not at the top of the food chain, survival means catering to the food manufacturing monopolies. So flavor companies now are pushing their natural flavors, as well as synthetic, hoping the ill wind will soon blow over.

If it doesn't, it could be the flavorist who suffers most, since his work is most dependent on the use of synthetic materials. Asking a great flavorist to create natural flavors is like asking a great painter to paint by number.

"They're no fun, no challenge. Making a natural flavor is basically an engineering job," one creative flavorist said.

Most flavor people try to downplay the force of the natural counter-revolution and to appear confident and unthreatened.

"Lower- and middle-class Americans—they're the main market for artificially flavored products, and they couldn't give a damn if a package says 'artificial' or 'natural.' " But apparently, the dam has already given. The industry's paranoia and fear of unfavorable public judgment are phenomenal.

To gain entry to some companies I had to go through a long clearance process, which involved speaking and writing to several people assuring them that my objective was not to stir the fires of the artificial-natural debate (which, in fact, it wasn't). At a few industrial fortresses, when I finally arrived, I was asked outright if I was a vegetarian, if I bought health foods, if I was a friend of Ralph Nader's. It got to the point where, if someone walked toward me, I expected to be frisked for sunflower seeds.

There seemed to be no way *not* to stir fires.

I called an executive at IFF to ask about "mouthfeel," and the first thing he said was, "I hope you're going to make it clear to everyone that this desire for 'natural' foods [pronounce 'natural' with a sneer on the first syllable] is downright stupid."

I innocently asked a flavorist what percent of raw materials used today is synthetic and what percent is natural. Immediately he started in: "First, let's get one thing straight—there is nothing bad about synthetic food additives. We are all made of chemicals, and all our food is made of chemicals. This 'no artificial anything,' 'no chemicals used' business is absolutely ridiculous. Let's face it—a chemical is a chemical is a chemical."

During lunch with three flavorists, one of them mentioned something about a flavorist getting ulcers. Quickly a second followed with, "If some of us do get ulcers, I can assure you it's only because of the tension involved every day in our work. The chemicals we work with are ABSOLUTELY safe. Every single one of them is on the government's GRAS list. G-R-A-S. Generally Recognized As Safe."

So what's everyone getting so upset about?

To its critics, the Generally Recognized As Safe (GRAS) list is generally recognized as suspect. Created in 1958 as part of the Food Additives Amendment, all substances listed on it have the privilege of unrestricted use in foods.

James Turner, author of *The Chemical Feast* (Ralph Nader's Study Group Report on the FDA), offers evidence that many of the substances have yet to proved safe, that the FDA composed the list haphazardly, neglecting the stipulations it had itself set up. From what many critics say, it seems that some GRAS-listed chemicals should already have been sent to Flavomatic Heaven, by way of the Delaney Clause. (This clause, also part of the 1958 Food Additives Amendment, requires the banning of any additive that causes cancer when ingested by animal or man.) Other GRAS or regulated additives (the latter allowed in food only in certain specified amounts) may, critics fear, be teratogenic (causing birth defects) or mutagenic (causing gene damage). Even though those additives are used at very low levels in food, the argument is that cancer and mutagenesis are more likely to be caused by long-range daily exposure to tiny amounts of hazardous substances than by single or occasional large doses.

Dangerous chemicals remain in our food, critics say, because the various food industries supervise the FDA rather than vice-versa, as it should be. In the case of the flavor industry, its powerful lobbying force in Washington, the Flavor and Extract Manufacturing Association (FEMA), has had its own GRAS list since 1961. It now lists 1,476 substances, over 300 of which are not on the FDA list. The FEMA list is subject to FDA scrutiny but apparently is not often subjected to this scrutiny. According to one FDA official, decisions about flavoring additives are left pretty much up to the FEMA's hand-picked, high-paid panel of experts. "There are only one or two people on our [FDA] staff who are involved with the flavor industry," he said.

One of industry's main defenses against its critics is the benefit-risk concept. One flavorist asked indignantly, "How can people expect us to ward off starvation in this world [by trying to flavor algae, bacteria, manure and other cheap but unpalatable sources of protein] and yet expect that everything we use will be 100 percent safe 100 percent of the time?"

Flavorists present themselves as live evidence of the safety of the chemicals they use. "Look at me," one said. "Before all the regulations came about, I used to taste every single compound that came into the fragrance or the flavor division to see if it could be used in a flavor, and I'm fine."

The various pacts and sects, the ins and outs of chemicals on the GRAS list—these are, in the long run, of little consequence to the flavorist sitting at his console, taking upon himself the mysteries of flavor. It is just the Third Day of artificial flavor creation—a long time before the creators rest, or are laid to rest by their critics. And tremendous forces, favorable to continuing creation, have aligned.

Food manufacturers now spend more for artificial flavoring than for any other group of synthetic food additives (including preservatives, stabilizers, colors, thickeners, anti-oxidants, etc.). The sales value of food, beverages and tobacco containing synthetic flavors, in the U.S. alone, is close to $80 billion per year. (This is a conservative estimate based on figures obtained from IFF.) Unless you religiously buy all your food from health food stores or raise it yourself, and unless you refrain from smoking and drinking most liqueurs, fruit brandies and even some wines, you have assimilated the gospel of the new artificial order.

Synthetic flavors have created desires that they alone can fulfill. Take vanilla: if high cost were not a problem and we could have all the vanilla grown in the world, it would not be enough to satisfy the vanilla-cravings of Americans.

As an increasing number of Mother Nature's flavors fade from the marketplace because of high cost or scarcity, flavor companies are not waiting to see if we can wean ourselves and do without, or with less of them. They have already come up with addictive new flavor archetypes that will reign even if nature's become more accessible again. One company touts a cherry flavor that is typical of "neither the raw nor the processed cherry, nor of any special variety of cherries." This kind of flavor may be the key to addiction—"If you can't pin it down, you won't put it down," I was told.

Some flavorists look forward gleefully to the gradual elimination of their major competition. "In 20 years," one said, "I'll bet you that only 5 percent of the people will have tasted fresh strawberry, so whether we like it or not, we people in the flavor industry will really be defining what the next generation thinks is strawberry. And the same goes for a lot of other foods that will soon be out of the average consumer's reach." Under the guise of democratizing taste experiences—making everything available to everyone—the flavor industry will dictate more and more eating habits that can only be supported by its artificial flavors.

Americans have the most "educated" tastes so far, but people in nearly every country of the world are being gradually mouthwashed. Firmenich, Inc. in Princeton, N.J. (known in the industry for its fruit and peanut butter flavors), has over 90 companies and agencies world-wide. In 1972, 60 percent of IFF's sales were outside the U.S.; 75 percent is projected for 1982. They have discovered a great market in countries where the economic outlook is bleakest. An IFF executive cheerfully reports that "the poorer the malnutritioned are, the more likely they are to spend a disproportionate amount of whatever they have . . . on some simple luxury," like a flavored drink or smoke.

They call it the "Titanic Syndrome." If the boat is going down, you blow all your money on what seems most attractive at the moment. Also, lax or nonexistent food additive and labeling laws in many of these countries make it very easy on the flavor company.

While flavorists study the food preferences of poorer cultures so they can create seductive flavors for their last "rites," they positively confront the problem of starvation by trying to flavor inexpensive protein sources with the tastes each population is used to.

"What we want to do is get the chicken feathers back to the chickens," an IFFer told me. It sounded like a quote from a sequel to *Animal Farm* until he explained. Flavorists are working on a flavor to be added to recycled chicken feathers (very high in protein) so that they can be used as animal feed, leaving the grain for people.

Firestone Tire and Rubber Co. discovered a few years ago that a very nutritious strain of yeast grows magically on discarded rubber tires. (Enter: deus ex flavor company to make the yeast taste good.)

The roles that the flavorist may be called on to play in the next several decades are limitless. Each idea being researched now holds in itself incredible possibilities. Like the idea that the fetus is sensitive to the flavor of the amniotic fluid. When your great-grandchild is born, the type of flavoring given to his mother may be marked on his birth certificate along with his sex and blood type; e.g., Boysenberry L-243. Later in life, if the child has problems that a large chocolate-flavored ice cream soda won't solve, rather than submit himself to the psychoanalytical cult leaders of his time, he will simply go to one of many buildings filled with warm padded rooms, pay a single fee and enter the room filled with Boysenberry L-243 aroma for instant return to the womb.

Postscript—Barnyard Tastes

Flavorists have to meet the demands of the farm population: horses prefer fruit notes in their feed; cows would rather have a cocoa-y flavor spruced with "milk and wintergreen notes"; and chickens go for a "smoky note."

Dogs know what they want: putrid "dead fish notes" with an aroma so strong they could roll in it. But their masters make satisfying dogs one of the flavorists' greatest, still unfulfilled challenges. They are working on a way to include these notes along with some other ingredient that would mask their offensiveness to human nostrils.

A flavor for dog food is tested by as many as 150 panelists before it goes to a dog-food manufacturer. Over a period of several days, each dog is given two bowls of food—one flavored, one unflavored—and about a half-hour to eat. After that, what remains in each bowl, and on the floor around it, is collected and put into two separate bags. These are then weighed, the lightest bag indicating the food of the dog's choice.

The greatest pitfall in these tests is "paw prejudice." Some dogs are either right- or left-pawed and may lunge indiscriminately for the bowl placed on their favored side, regardless of the dignity of the test situation. To compensate, tests are conducted over an even number of days, the position of the bowls being switched each day so that results are objective.

All breeds have equally discriminating tastes—except beagles. "They'll eat whatever is put in front of them—you can't learn anything from a beagle," one researcher said.

III

PATIENTS AND PRACTITIONERS

Examining the social structural relationships between inter-acting people lends insight into the problems of providing services to different groups. Social differences have an impact on the ways health-care programs are designed, delivered, and received. Understanding the attitudes and behavior of patients is a prerequisite to effective care of the ill. For example, the status accorded to practitioners by their clients differs from culture to culture. The way illness is defined differs as well. However, optimum care requires more than the understanding of the patients' position. It is necessary also to consider the beliefs and attitudes of "curers" toward patients as well as toward other curers.

Social structural and role disparity are, perhaps, most obvious between practitioners and patients. It is rare for physicians and patients to enter a relationship on an equal footing. The patient is the one seeking assistance and in most instances is in a dependent, subordinate position. In approaching each other, the patient and practitioner bring with them different orientations. There are numerous ways in which such different orientations manifest themselves. Upon being hospitalized, for example, a patient must learn to assume a new role and —perhaps more difficult—to adopt a new culture. The status of such a patient has changed from Special (at home) to Ordinary (in the hospital). The patient, then, is required to adapt to situations that seem unusual. He or she is, for a time, an outsider. For the practitioner, the institutional insider, nothing unusual is happening: most situations are merely routine. These stances influence the expectations of all participants. The patient may expect special treatment for what he or she sees as a special problem. The practitioner, on the other hand, sees a rather ordinary condition and may expect immediate cooperation and compliance. Most people fall into or appear to fall into the appropriate roles. Occasionally implicit or explicit negotiations to accept each other's framework do break down and patients or staff get labeled as "bad" (or worse).

The relations between staff are often ambiguous. There are conflicts in such areas as responsibility, power, and prestige. A practitioner, whose primary concern is patient care, may move into an administrator role that may conflict with his therapeutic responsibilities. Most often, the relationship between doctors and nurses is the one cited as a locus for conflict. Not only is this relationship fraught with ambivalence, but in addition the relationship between staff within similar domains—nurse/nurse specialist, general practitioner/specialist—is accompanied by potential conflict. It is not difficult to see then how patient/practitioner differences and staff differences, taken with the newness of the hospital setting, may engender special problems for the patient. In effect, a patient must often cope with anxieties produced by the medical regime in addition to those directly associated with the presenting illness.

Good communication between all those involved in an illness episode is central to achievement of optimum care. It is not surprising that language reflects precisely the scope of potential misunderstanding. The medical world has long recognized the need for bilingual personnel in many communities. Where such staff is available many organizations rest easy, believing all their problems have been solved. This assessment of the communication difficulties, however, is naive. Such a view ignores all that we know about sociocultural dynamics. There is no reason to believe, for example, that Spanish-speaking staff and Spanish-speaking patients will necessarily understand each other's needs any more than comparable English-speaking parties. Though a most important initial step will have been taken, is it enough?

Ineffective or inappropriate language often fashions acceptance and rejection of proffered treatment. Special interest has recently focused on the subject of the "noncompliant patient." Communication holds a partial key to this problem. Failure to understand most certainly affects the amount of confidence and faith that an ill person will have in the ministrations of the health professional. It furthermore impedes the practical application of medical knowledge.

The articles in this section illustrate the social dynamics of the patient/practitioner interaction and its influence on the nature of health care. Ozzie Simmons describes how a people's culture influences the way in which problems are deemed important. Social class provides the focus as Simmons stresses the role of society in shaping the nature of the medical approach.

Julius Roth emphasizes how social hierarchies are reinforced by the trappings of a society. His article also serves to illustrate how numerous ritualized medical procedures may have little to do with medical scientific fact.

The succeeding three articles deal with communications problems at different levels of interaction. The introductory excerpt from the article by Julian Samora and his collaborators serves well to demonstrate the problems in communication between people speaking the "same" language who come from different backgrounds. All people have specialized vocabularies. This fact is not immediately evident, however, and more often surfaces in subtle ways. Lois Pratt and her colleagues stress the practitioner's difficulty and apparent inability to correctly assess the patients' level of medical knowledge. This disability appears to be present in assessments of patients from all social backgrounds. Joan Lynaugh and Barbara Bates demonstrate that language usage varies for people with medical training but with different goal orientations. Such usage tends to reflect and reinforce status differences as well as role and task boundaries. Yet at the same time these differences and boundaries are not clearly delineated. Disharmony, dissatisfaction, and depression can result, especially in the light of the changes taking place in the health professions.

Richard Ballad's interview with Thomas Szasz illustrates some basic conflicts between society and the individual. The article points to the important issue of who defines illness and has the power to enforce decisions. Szasz confronts the very complex topic of societal versus individual rights and freedoms.

The relationship between the patient and practitioner is a very special one. People seek counsel with practitioners for a multitude of reasons. The practitioners' perception of those who seek counsel differs reciprocally. The confrontation involves a dynamic that is additional to and sometimes overrides the presenting medical complaint. All parties should be cognizant of the fact that practitioners do not merely treat illness—they treat people.

Implications of Social Class for Public Health

Ozzie G. Simmons

Anthropologists spend a good deal of time looking at disparate cultures and lauding the importance of a cross-cultural evaluation of problems. Though not so intended, this focus might detract from an interest in variations within a culture. The detraction would be unfortunate, as the cross-cultural approach can be used to emphasize the importance of such differences. Differences between cultures and within a culture are based upon the same premises, and Simmons's article serves to illustrate the significance of being aware of this issue. We are presented with some very important questions concerning the possible influence of the values held by health practitioners in their interaction with clients. The implications of imposing middle-class values (or any other set of values, for that matter) on the recipients of services become all too clear. A number of articles in this collection further demonstrate this point. The discussion of attitudes toward polio and tuberculosis, taken with the epidemiological facts, provides further insight into the interrelationship of politics, economics, and disease. Readers wishing to pursue the subject of class differences between patient and practitioner will encounter a formidable literature and should, perhaps, begin with a reading of Hollingshead and Redlich's classic work *Social Class and Mental Illness* (1958.)

This paper[1] will consider three areas in which social class and status have important implications for public health: (1) The differential distribution of disease and consequent evaluations of appropriate foci of public-health interest and activity; (2) The functioning of interpersonal relations within the health team and between team and public; (3) The congruence between

Reproduced by permission of the Society for Applied Anthropology from *Human Organization,* Vol. 16, No. 3, 1957. Copyright 1958 by the Society for Applied Anthropology.

[1]Revised version of a paper read at the 1955 annual meeting of the American Anthropological Association, Boston, Mass.

public-health precepts and felt needs of the public at whom these precepts are directed.

For present purposes, "status" and "class" will be employed as generic terms, the former to refer simply to rank, or relative position in a status hierarchy, and the latter to refer to a group of individuals who occupy a broadly similar position in a status hierarchy. When the term "class status" is used, it refers to membership in a given stratum of a status hierarchy, whether this stratum be a statistical aggregate or a real group. When class value differences are discussed in terms of middle-class and lower-class, the reference is to modal types which higher and lower status people may manifest in different degrees; it does not necessarily follow that all higher status people adhere to the middle-class modal type, and all lower status people to the other. Presumably, many members of both these strata may not incorporate the corresponding class values and may deviate from the modal type in other respects. It may be noted that the character of modal types is determined by common economic and power situations and cultural experiences, which offer more or less similar life chances or opportunities. In discussing interpersonal relations, the primary focus will be on the ways in which orientations to relative status affect the functioning of a given relationship. In discussing congruence and divergence between public-health precepts and felt needs of the public, the primary focus will be on modal subcultural types.

I

Like the social welfare movement, the public-health movement has been conceived and implemented primarily by middle-class people, and directed primarily at lower-class people. As in most social movements, the public-health movement was mainly activated by motives of social uplift and self-protection. The conclusion, in 1830, that if cholera were not stamped out it might move from the slums to within the middle-class gates led to a sudden increase in interest in public health both in Europe and the United States. According to Shryock, "Fear now combined with humanitarianism to demand investigations, cleanups, and general sanitary reform" [Shryock, 1947].

Public health has traditionally focused on the control of the mass diseases which, by and large, have had their greatest incidence and prevalence among the lower-classes, as, e.g., smallpox, typhus, typhoid, the nutritional deficiency disorders, and tuberculosis. With increasing control of these diseases, new mass diseases, such as the cardiovascular disorders and poliomyelitis, have claimed not only the attention of public-health personnel but have excited great public interest among our higher status groups as well, as currently reflected in the great annual fund-raising drives.[2] Taking as a specific case the contrast between polio and tuberculosis, we find that when the treatments for the latter were developed, professional interest far exceeded public interest; yet, when the Salk polio vaccine was developed, public interest far exceeded professional, and Salk became a national hero. There is an inverse correlation between degree of public interest and incidences connected with these two diseases. Polio rates are relatively low compared to those of other mass diseases, and tuberculosis rates continue relatively high.[3]

This striking difference between polio and tuberculosis may be regarded in large part as a function of class distributions and perceptions of disease.[4] Tuberculosis, like many of the older mass diseases, is primarily identified with lack of personal and environmental hygiene, poverty, overcrowding, and malnutrition, but in the case of polio, as in that of the cardiovascular ailments, no such identification has been established. In fact, there is some evidence to indicate that higher polio rates are to be found among those who enjoy quite the opposite set of conditions.[5] Tuberculosis and polio are

---

[2]The writer is indebted to Dr. Edward Wellin for suggesting this instance of class differentials in disease, and in particular for bringing out the significance of the contrast between tuberculosis and polio.

[3]National figures for three sample years are as follows (from the Massachusetts Bureau of Health Information):

Year	Poliomyelitis		Tuberculosis	
	Cases	Deaths	Cases	Deaths
1940	9,804	1,026	102,984	60,428
1945	13,624	1,186	114,931	52,916
1950	33,330	1,686	121,742	33,633

[4]The role of class factors in these contrasting public reactions seems clear, but obviously there are always other variables associated with specific diseases that play some part as well. In the case of tuberculosis and polio, there may be, e.g., differences in dramatic impact and publicity. Polio has physically visible after-effects, although this must be compared with the social visibility associated with tuberculosis. Also, any disease, like polio, that tends to victimize children in disproportionately large numbers seems to excite more public reaction. However, in view of the great overlap in age between those who contract the two diseases, it is difficult to say what part this factor may actually play in determining public attitudes. Although comparable information for tuberculosis is lacking, the importance of class factors in evaluating polio is borne out by Deasy's findings regarding participation in the 1954 polio vaccine field trials, namely that upper status mothers were much more likely to have taken previous precautions against the disease, knew more about the trials, and demonstrated a higher awareness of the disease entity itself. See Leila C. Deasy [1956].

[5]Paffenbarger and Watt [1953], in their epidemiological study of polio in South Texas, report that "groups of individuals living under better economic circumstances with the many associated 'advantages' of greater personal cleanliness, less crowding, better food, and less association with verminous insects may suffer a significantly higher attack rate to the paralytic disease and suggests that . . . for the United States [this] is somehow related to an improved standard of living."

both public threats, but the crucial difference here seems to be that tuberculosis is pretty well confined to our lower status groups, while polio is within the middle-class gates.

II

The practice of public health is carried on within two main interpersonal relations systems, the intrateam and team-public systems. Participants in either system may be members of the same or different societies, but in either case, class, as it refers to subcultural differences, may add an important dimension. Although there has been some research on interpersonal relations in the practice of clinical medicine and psychiatry, investigations in the public-health field have scarcely yet gone beyond impressions and casual observations. We will consider here only a few of the possibilities in intrateam relations in the intercultural situation, and in team-public relations in the intercultural situation.

The most common instance of public-health teams where members belong to different societies is to be found in technical assistance programs in "underdeveloped" countries. In this intercultural situation, class considerations can minimize or enhance major cultural differences that obtain between team members. With regard to class factors that serve to reduce cultural differences, it has been noted that class cultures tend to go beyond societal boundaries. As Saunders has pointed out, an upper-class Mexican American may feel more at ease with an upper status Anglo American than with a lower-class Mexican American in a situation involving some degree of intimacy, since their awareness of cultural group distinctions is minimized, even though it may not be entirely superseded, by their social class identification [Saunders, 1954]. In Latin America, upper-class groups in different countries, due to similar positions of dominance, possession of power and wealth, and the common experience of travel and education in Europe and America, tend to have value systems which not only approximate those of higher status Americans, but are more similar to each other than to those of lower-class Latin Americans in their respective countries.

With regard to the role of class factors in enhancing cultural differences among team members, it may be that, despite the cross-societal bond, tensions will be engendered, e.g., between Americans and their local collaborators because of failure of the American to understand and acknowledge what may often be substantial differences in status between the two relative to their own class hierarchies. Thus, in contrast to the American, who will only in the rare case be descended from a top status family and have held a high-level position in his own country, local collaborators are likely to be members of ruling class families and to occupy high-ranking positions in their government's ministry of health. Americans, by virtue of their tendency to play down class differences, as well as of pronounced ethnocentric tendencies, are not likely to manifest overtly the degree of respect for their collaborators which the latter may expect as their due. For the same reasons, they are likely to reject or ignore the subordinating and deference devices traditionally used by upper-class people in conducting their relations with lower status people in those countries where status differences are generally explicitly acknowledged and taken for granted. One of the most pervasive grievances nursed by upper-class people abroad with respect to Americans concerns the latter's treatment of servants as near-equals by giving them the same food, paying them "too much," and so on.

Ideally, the doctor's role in the therapeutic relationship focuses on his performance of a technical specialty, on his impartially serving the patient's health needs independently of whether he likes the patient as a person, and on his obligation to give priority to the patient's well-being over his own personal interests. This ideal seems to hold across the board in most Western societies [see Marriott, 1955]. This role definition is calculated to inspire trust, respect, and confidence between doctor and patient, and thus insure cooperation. In practice, however, it seems that the ideal is seldom approximated in professional-patient relationships, and that it is precisely in the doctor-patient relationship where it is least likely to be achieved.

Studies in intracultural situations, both here and in other societies, indicate a tendency for class considerations to overshadow therapeutic considerations in the professional-patient relationship. It appears that the degree to which the qualities ideally defined as essential to the therapeutic relationship, namely mutual trust, respect, and cooperation, will be present in a given professional-patient relationship varies inversely with the amount of social distance. Conversely, the greater the social distance, the less likely that participants will perceive each other in terms of the ideal type roles of professional and patient, and the more likely that they will perceive each other in terms of their social class status in the larger society.

The therapeutic relationship should function at its optimum where professional and patient are of the same class status. Studies of the psychotherapeutic relationship in this country indicate that the patients who most nearly approach the therapist's status are accorded the best treatment and the most sympathy [see Grey, 1949; also Redlich, Hollingshead, and Bellis, 1955]. In the public-health context, it is possible that, although professionals may deem it easier to relate to patients who are of the same class status, higher status patients may reject the health worker not because of his class status as such but because they perceive his attempts to serve them at all as identifying them with lower status people typically served by public health, and thus regard him as a threat to their social position. In a Peruvian village, an auxiliary health worker was rejected by higher status people because "she was perceived as equating them with the unwashed and uneducated poor" [Wellin, 1955]. In Chile, nurses in a health center were extremely reluctant to approach middle-class families in their sectors because they anticipated a poor reception [Simmons, 1953].

In public health, where the typical case is that of higher status professional and lower status patient, the available evidence indicates that doctors and patients do not "get along" as well as do nurses and patients, but this need not mean that the respective class statuses of doctor, nurse, and patient are the sole or even principal factors in determining the difference in quality of doctor-patient and nurse-patient relations. Such factors as differences in professional training and expected role performances must also be weighed [Simmons, 1955].

In attempting to specify the varying roles that class perceptions and values may play in the functioning of professional-patient relations, it would be worthwhile to investigate whether status considerations loom larger for the professional or for the patient. In Regionville, e.g., there was considerable feeling on the part of the lower status people that physicians did not want them as patients [Koos, 1954]. On the other side, some of the factors that influence professionals to inject status considerations into their relations with patients may be related to the professional's orientations to upward mobility. In Colombia, e.g., the cities have been flooded by rural immigrants who no longer classify themselves according to the traditional status system. As a result of the competition to rise socially, individuals with some small position of authority press their weight on others to force a recognition of their status. Thus, doctors and nurses in the Colombian government health centers are often overbearing in their treatment of the public [Erasmus, 1952].

III

To the extent that it may be characterized as a social movement, public health has inevitably incorporated the dominant middle-class values of our society, primarily those that stem from the "Protestant ethic" core.[6] It follows that public-health precepts are formulated in terms of these values, and applied on the assumption that they are universally meaningful and desirable. However, class differences may set substantial limits to the degree

---

[6]This refers to public health not only in the United States but in all areas that have been importantly influenced by the British and American varieties of public health.

of congruence possible between these precepts and the felt needs of a lower-class public.[7] We may ask: (1) To what extent do public-health workers apply their middle-class norms in working with lower status groups? (2) Are lower-class norms significantly different in those areas where middle-class norms are imposed? (3) If there are such points of difference, how relevant are they for the effective functioning of public-health activities?

Lower status families are beset by greater economic insecurity than higher status families, and their "scientific" knowledge about modern medicine is apparently less extensive than that of higher status people, but beyond these reality factors, classes also vary in their behavioral characteristics and value orientations.

In view of the prominent public-health emphasis on personal and environmental hygiene, possible class differences in the importance attached to cleanliness is an area that readily comes to mind. For middle-class people, cleanliness is not simply a matter of keeping clean but also an index to the morals and virtues of the individual. It has been frequently observed that middle-class valuations of cleanliness approach compulsive proportions, and that lower status people are much more casual in this matter. It is possible that the stress placed on cleanliness in health education and other public-health activities far overshoots any felt needs in this area on the part of lower status people.

Middle-class norms place great emphasis on the ability to defer gratifications in the interest of long-run goals. Readiness to sacrifice the present for some possible gain in the future may not be nearly so pervasive a pattern among lower status people, who may accord priority to immediate rewards. This suggests some questions with regard to the public-health emphasis on prevention. Is acceptance of the value of prevention contingent upon ability to defer gratification, and, if so, do lower-class norms in this area set limits to such acceptance? Are lower status people as willing, as higher status people may be, to inconvenience themselves by adoption now of practices aimed at avoiding possible consequences in the future?

Middle-class norms accord high value to rationality, as it refers to use of foresight, deliberate planning, and allocation of resources in the most efficient way.[8] This again places an emphasis on future time orientations that may not be particularly meaningful to lower status people. However,

---

[7]In preparation of this section, the writer is indebted for suggestions to an address by Dr. Walter B. Miller entitled "Social Class: Its Influence on Health Behavior," delivered at the October, 1955 meeting of the Massachusetts Public Health Association.

[8]This and the following formulation of middle-class norms were suggested by a summary description of middle-class standards in Albert Cohen [1955:89–90].

public-health teachings assume that this value does hold for lower status people when they emphasize the development of regular health habits and the expenditure of the domestic budget in ways best calculated to insure a balanced diet for the family.

Middle-class norms prescribe a strong sense of individual responsibility, which sets a high premium on resourcefulness and self-reliance. This value is frequently built into public-health goals. For example, the principal objective of health education is often expressed as the "inculcation in each individual of a sense of responsibility for his own health." This ideal pattern of individual responsibility can be contrasted with one of reciprocity, particularly within the family, that seems more characteristic of lower-class norms. The lower status individual may be much less likely to think that responsibility for his well-being rests solely with himself, and more likely to think that if something does happen, the kin group will see him through.

An individual's definitions of and responses to health and illness have import for a wide range of public-health problems, and these are usually class-linked. Throughout Latin America, e.g., lower status groups adhere to a vigorously functioning medical tradition which health workers and other medical people do not share [see Erasmus 1952; Foster 1952; Simmons 1955a]. The gulf is in part maintained by the health worker's rejection of this folk medicine tradition as "superstition," and in part by the fact that lower status people reserve for folk medicine a wide variety of illnesses defined as inaccessible to scientific medicine because doctors do not "know" them and therefore cannot cure them.

Finally, we may briefly consider class differences in child training patterns as these are relevant for public health. Middle-class socialization patterns tend to be consistently organized in accordance with the middle-class emphases on effort and achievement, which are thought to be good in themselves or good because they are instrumental to long-run goals, and, as a consequence, the middle-class child is subjected to considerable close supervision and control [see Green, 1946]. On the other hand, lower-class socialization patterns are relatively easy-going, and allow the child much more latitude with respect to eating, sleeping, cleanliness, dress, work, school, and play. Lower status parents may be much more rigid about obedience, but the imposition of authority is usually arbitrary and inconsistent. Maternal and child health programs are considered to be one of the most crucial in any large-scale public-health effort, and the mother is generally regarded as the most strategic person to reach in health education. Much of the education of lower status mothers seems to be based on the premise that the latter are as motivated in controlling and molding their children as are higher status mothers, and if this is not actually the case, it would mean that these teachings stand relatively less chance of being implemented. Moreover, if lower-class socialization is so likely to be governed by the child's own inclinations, his parents' convenience, and fortuitous circumstances, it is probable that the health worker must cope with much greater variation in practices than he may be aware of.

IV

This discussion has considered three areas in which social class has important implications for public health. Social class differences are associated with the differential distribution of disease and consequent definitions of appropriate foci of public-health interest and activity, with variations in quality of interpersonal relations and the health team and between the team and the public it serves, and with divergences in goals and perceptions between the health worker and his client.

By virtue of the fact that the situation of action in the public-health field typically involves the higher status practitioner and lower status patient, class differences in realistic conditions, value orientations, and behavioral characteristics may have a substantial role to play in determining the outcome of public-health programs. Acceptance or rejection of the goods and services that public health has to offer in large part depends upon how these are perceived by the recipient. Such perceptions vary with one's class membership, and attempts to change them are likely to collide with the individual's investment in his group affiliations. A social class constitutes a membership group, and promoting and maintaining one's acceptance by the group calls for conformity with the perceptions and behavior deemed correct and desirable by the group, whether it be in relation to health and illness or anything else.

Ritual and Magic in the Control of Contagion

Julius A. Roth

This article presents a light-hearted view of the hospital social order. Roth's discussion of utilization rates of protective garments allows for an examination of status relationships. Of interest is the fact that utilization and nonutilization do not seem to be related to the number and intimacy of contact hours with patients. It seems, rather, to correlate with the amount of knowledge the garment wearer has about the condition. This correlation provides further information on social status in the hospital setting. Roth comments that patterns of using protective clothing allow one to conclude that the tubercle bacillus is active only during working hours. His observation raises questions concerning the importance of faith and suggestion in the therapeutic process as well as consideration of Margaret Mead's (1955) notion of "cultural baggage." Faith in the power of doctors and their apparent concern for the patient is suggested to the consumer by physicians' seeming disregard for their own safety and inherent ability to resist illness. These suggestions to the patient are demonstrated and reinforced by such actions as the physicians' nonutilization of protective clothing. Mead's "cultural baggage" can refer to paraphernalia that have no scientific utility but which might have a positive therapeutic effect because of traditional use. Excess baggage, then, refers to items of culture that can be shed in providing services to peoples who do not make these traditional associations. Ironically, excess baggage is so familiar to the bearer that it may not be easy to identify. In *The Mind Game,* E. Fuller Torrey (1972) pursues this topic and presents a cross-cultural view of this phenomenon (especially in his discussion of the "Edifice Complex") and in so doing, provides further insight into the ritual and magic within our own health system.

Reprinted by permission of the author and the American Sociological Association from the *American Sociological Review,* Vol. 22, 1957, pp. 310–314. Copyright © 1957 by the American Sociological Society.

Tuberculosis is a contagious disease. But just how contagious is it? In what ways and under what circumstances is it likely to be transmitted from one person to another? And what procedures are most effective for preventing its transmission? The answers to these questions are quite uncertain and TB specialists show considerable disagreement in the details of the manner in which they deal with these problems. These uncertainties leave the way open for ritualized procedures that often depend more on convenience and ease of administration that on rationally deduced probabilities. They also leave the way open for irrational practices that can properly be called "magic."

Protecting the Outside World

In one Veterans Administration hospital, occupational therapy products are routinely sterilized by exposure to ultra-violet light before being sent out. (Patients sometimes by-pass this procedure by giving their OT products to their visitors to take out.) Books are sometimes sterilized before being sent out, sometimes not. Other articles mailed by patients may or may not be sterilized depending largely upon whether or not the patient requests it. Letters are never sterilized. The inconsistency of these procedures is not lost on the workers. One volunteer worker held up a package she was mailing for a patient and said: "Now, I can mail this without sterilizing it, but if someone wants to send home some OT work, I have to sterilize it before I can mail it for him. It doesn't make any sense."

The fact that sterilization is carried out by volunteer workers under the direction of the Special Services Division is in itself an indication that it is regarded as an auxiliary rather than an essential activity of the hospital. The extent to which sterilization procedures are a matter of convenience is shown by the reply of a volunteer worker when questioned about sterilizing books to be returned to outside libraries: "Anytime you want a book sterilized before it's sent out, just let me know and we'll do it for you. Of course, we probably wouldn't be able to do it shortly before Christmas, because that lamp will be in constant use for sterilizing OT work that the men are sending out as presents."

Money regularly passes out of the hospital without sterilization. Patients give money to volunteer shoppers, the newsman, canteen, and postal workers. These people put the money into pocket, purse, or money box, and pass it on to others without raising any questions about the possibility of spreading the disease. Quite often money changes hands quickly after being taken from the patients. The volunteer shoppers, for example, take the patients' orders and money, go directly from the hospital to town to do the shopping so that the orders may be brought to the patients the same day.

In the stores, the money passes into cash registers and pockets and is handed on to other customers as change—all within a period of a few hours. The danger of transmitting tubercle bacilli by money is probably very slight, but it is certainly many times greater than the chance of spreading the disease through books and OT products, which spend at least a day or two in transit through the mails.[1]

An even more striking example of inconsistency is shown in the policy toward visitors. Visitors are not required to wear any protective clothing, not even masks, and none of them ever do. The same is true of entertainers and members of service and veterans organizations who play games with the patients or bring them gifts. Some patients have positive sputum, so that a visitor probably runs a much greater risk of taking viable bacilli into his body than does the person who handles money, books, or OT products of a patient after a period of several hours or several days. However, TB hospitals have a tradition of permitting persons without protective clothing to visit patients, and to break such a tradition would almost certainly bring strong protests from patients and their families and would in any case be evaded by many people.

In Wisconsin the legislature prohibits public libraries and state-controlled institutions from lending books to patients in TB hospitals.[2] But the law says nothing about the protection of visitors or about other articles, which can be brought in and taken out by visitors, volunteer workers, members of service organizations, and patients themselves (when they go out on pass). The Chief of Special Services refused to guarantee the sterilization of books from outside libraries because he was afraid he might violate a law. This same man has direct control over entertainers and members of service organizations who come into the hospital, and he does not require these people to wear protective clothing nor does he try to control all the games, musical instruments, and other articles they bring into and carry out of the hospital.

In summary, the devices for protection against the spread of the disease outside the hospital are controlled largely by tradition, convenience, and adherence to legal technicalities rather than to rational estimates of the chances of transmission of tubercle bacilli. The limited efforts at preventing the transmission of the disease are concentrated chiefly in those areas where the chances of transmission are probably the least.

---

[1] There has been very little careful bacteriological investigation of possible transmission of TB in such "life situations." What has been done suggests that the tubercle bacilli are unlikely to be transmitted under the circumstances described.

[2] In Illinois, where there is no such law, public libraries freely lend books to TB hospital patients.

TABLE 1. Wearing of Protective Clothing by Nursing Personnel
in Veterans Administration Hospital

	Times Entered Room	Percentages Wearing		
		Cap	Gown	Mask
Nurses	56	100	57	75
Attendants	200	100	72	90

Rank and Protective Clothing

A number of procedures are designed to protect the employees and patients within the hospital from spreading TB. One method, which has come into prominence in recent years, is the use of protective clothing —masks, gowns, and hair coverings—which the hospital personnel are supposed to wear when they come into contact with the patients or their effects. However, this protective clothing is often not worn. There is a definite relationship between the degree to which it is worn and the rank of the employee.

I recorded the wearing of surgical cap, gown, and mask by the nursing personnel of a VA hospital when entering a patients' room over a four-day period. The results are shown in Table 1.

More detailed records were made of the use of protective clothing when entering patients' rooms in a state hospital that had a more complex nursing hierarchy. The record was made on ten different days, plus additional days for doctors and professional nurses in order to increase their very small number. The records were made on three different wards with different sets of personnel and were always for complete days to avoid the selective influence of certain work shifts or kinds of ward duties. Results are given in Table 2. The two instances of a doctor wearing cap and mask on recorded

TABLE 2. Wearing of Protective Clothing by Doctors
and Nursing Personnel in State Hospital

	Times Entered Room	Percentages Wearing		
		Cap	Gown	Mask
Doctors	47	5	0	5
Professional nurses	100	24	18	14
Practical nurses	121	86	45	46
Aides	142	94	80	72
Students	97	100	100	100

TABLE 3. Wearing of Protective Clothing by State Hospital Nursing Personnel While Carrying Out Given Functions*

	Times Entered Room	Percentages Wearing		
		Cap	Gown	Mask
Take temperatures				
Professional nurses	26	19	54	46
Practical nurses	24	79	63	71
Students	6	100	100	100
Dispense medications				
Professional nurses	7	28	14	0
Practical nurses	15	87	40	40
Students	5	100	100	100
Talk to patients when not performing a duty				
Professional nurses	11	18	0	0
Practical nurses	31	87	26	23
Aides	29	86	52	55
Students	5	100	100	100
Bring in food trays				
Practical nurses	10	100	80	80
Aides	21	100	100	81
Students	20	100	100	100
Collect food trays				
Practical nurses	9	67	67	67
Aides	17	94	100	94
Students	14	100	100	100
Serve drinking water				
Practical nurses	10	80	40	60
Aides	11	100	82	73
Students	3	100	100	100

Distribute towels or linen				
Professional nurses	2	0	0	0
Practical nurses	6	100	67	67
Aides	12	100	100	83
Students	9	100	100	100

Adjust blinds or windows				
Professional nurses	3	33	33	0
Practical nurses	4	75	25	25
Aides	14	93	72	72
Students	7	100	100	100

Distribute mail				
Professional nurses	5	0	0	0
Practical nurses	3	67	0	0
Aides	6	83	33	33

Give out supplies (tissues, tissue bags, etc.)				
Practical nurses	11	82	73	91
Aides	9	100	89	100
Students	3	100	100	100

Collect soiled towels and linen				
Practical nurses	7	43	29	57
Aides	14	93	50	43

Give out refreshments				
Practical nurses	4	100	0	25
Aides	3	100	33	100

Collect trash				
Practical nurses	13	85	85	77
Aides	27	93	85	78
Students	4	100	100	100

*Because the numbers of certain classes of personnel for some functions were very small, supplementary observations in addition to those given in Table 2 were made. The observations—which were always for complete days—have been included in this table. Doctors do not appear in this table because there was almost no overlap between their functions and those of the nursing personnel.

days (Table 2) both involved the same doctor—an assistant surgeon on a temporary assignment. His successor does not wear protective clothing.

As both of these tables show, the use of protective clothing is inversely related to occupational status level. The people of higher rank seem to have the privilege of taking the greater risks, particularly in the case of masks. The cap and gown are intended in part to prevent the spread of the disease to others; the mask is almost exclusively for the protection of the wearer.

It might be argued that the lower status employees should wear protective clothing relatively more often because they perform tasks which require more intimate contact with the patients and their effects. Thus, the aides and students do most of the work of collecting food trays and trash, making beds, washing furniture, picking up soiled towels. Certainly, this factor makes a difference, but it is not sufficient to account for the whole difference.

When we examine overlapping functions (those carried out by two or more levels of nursing personnel), differences, if any, are almost always in the direction of more frequent wearing of protective clothing by the lower-status employees. Table 3 gives the figures for the thirteen overlapping functions in which such differences occurred.

Why do persons with higher status wear protective clothing less often? For one thing, it is not considered necessary by people who know best. There is no good evidence that the systematic wearing of protective clothing makes any difference (even the person who planned and administered this program could cite no evidence showing its effectiveness) and people who know most about TB do not seem to consider it worth the trouble. Doctors, and to a lesser extent professional nurses, are, of course, most likely to recognize the probable futility of these procedures. The relative ignorance of the lower levels of ward employees makes it more likely that they will have doubts about whether it is safe to go without the protective clothing, especially on routine duties when they must enter patients' rooms repeatedly in a short interval. There are, of course, circumstances in which almost everyone would agree that the wearing of a mask and perhaps a gown was wise. It is the routine wearing of protective clothing for all contacts with patients that is generally rejected. Probably a more important factor is the likelihood that the employee can "get away with" a violation. A doctor need not worry about a "bawling out" for not protecting himself. A professional nurse might be criticized, but usually she is the highest authority on a ward. The chance of criticism increases down the scale. Students, who are new and unfamiliar with the situation (they put in four-week stints) and who worry about possible "demerits," wear protective clothing all the time in patients' rooms. Some ward employees, especially those of lower status, who are not "properly dressed" hurriedly don a mask and gown if they see the supervisor of the nursing education program on the floor.

Magic and the Tubercle Bacillus

Gauze or paper masks are rather difficult to breathe through. To make breathing easier patients and employees sometimes pull down the mask until their nostrils have a clear space. This, of course, destroys the point of wearing the mask and the mask then takes on the status of a charm necklace.

We can also find examples of institutional magic. In the state hospital patients are required to wear masks when they go to the first floor for a hair cut or for an x-ray and when they go to the eighth floor to see the social worker or the patient services director. They do not have to wear masks (and never do) when they go to the first floor for occupational therapy, to visit with their families, to attend socials or church services, or to see a movie, nor when they go to the eighth floor to the library and to play bingo. An examination of these two lists shows that patients must wear masks when they go somewhere on "business," but not when they go somewhere for "pleasure," even though they use the same parts of the building and come into contact with hospital personnel in both cases. The rules suggest that the tubercle bacillus works only during business hours.

The ward employee tends to wear protective clothing when carrying out her duties, but not when "socializing" with the patients. I kept a record over a short period of time on several practical nurses on the 3:00 to 11:00 P.M. shift. Table 4 shows the contrasts in their use of protective clothing. The nurses' contact with the patients was more prolonged and more intimate while socializing than while carrying out their duties. The average time spent in the room during this recorded period was less than half a minute for taking care of a duty and about three minutes for socializing. While giving out medicine or taking temperatures or bringing in food trays the nurses have very little close contact with the patients. While socializing, they often stand close to the patients, lean on their beds and other furniture, and handle their newspapers and other belongings. Logically, there is a greater need for the protective clothing—and especially the

TABLE 4.   Wearing of Protective Clothing by Practical Nurses When Carrying Out Duties and When "Socializing" with Patients

	Times Entered Room	Percentages Wearing		
		Cap	Gown	Mask
Carrying out duties	39	97	75	80
"Socializing"	23	91	17	9

mask, which was hardly used at all—while socializing than while carrying out the routine duties.

Apparently, these nurses believe they need protection only when working. They remark that the gown, and more especially the mask, is a barrier to friendly intercourse.

Man's Laws and Nature's Laws

Rationally considered, the controls and protections used to check the transmission of TB should depend on an estimate of the probability of such transmission occurring under given conditions and in given circumstances. The problem for persons responsible for controlling the transmission of TB is to set their controls and protections at a level where a "reasonable" risk is involved. Admittedly, this is not easy because of the uncertain knowledge about transmission and susceptibility and public anxieties about the disease. Even if one were able to establish general rules for a "reasonable" level of control on the basis of present knowledge about the disease, putting these rules into practice would still be a major problem. To deal with this problem realistically, the controlling agents need a good understanding of the social organization of the hospital, the disease concepts of the personnel, and the patterns of administrative thinking on the part of supervisory persons.

The practices surrounding contagion control in a TB hospital represent an effort to make man's laws approximate the laws of nature, and when nature's laws are not well understood, man's rules are likely to be more or less irrational and their observance vacillating and ritualistic.[3]

---

[3] Professor Everett C. Hughes pointed out to me the implications of the use of the same word "law" for both the regularities of nature and the rules of conduct made by man.

Medical Vocabulary Knowledge among Hospital Patients

Julian Samora, Lyle Saunders, Richard F. Larson

"When I use a word," Humpty Dumpty said, "it means just what I choose it to mean, neither more nor less."

Lewis Carroll

Some years ago, several nurses provided me with a list of expressions representing what patients either thought they heard staff say or conditions which they thought they themselves had. A selection from that list includes: "fireballs in the useless" (fibroids in the uterus), "smiling mighty Jesus" (spinal meningitis), "slipped-a-pippus" (slipped epiphysis), and a "strangulated unicorn" (?). Though in some ways humorous, these serve to illustrate misunderstanding between professionals and clients. The following very brief selection demonstrates how people speaking basically the same language may fail to communicate. While the patient appears to understand such words as *paraphernalia* and *catheterization,* her vocabularly is selective (as is everyone's). Communication fails. There is a tendency to emphasize communication problems between people who speak mutually unintelligible languages and to believe that such problems will disappear if people speak the same language. This naive view of communication does not take into consideration the variety of differences that can exist within cultures.

I'll tell you something, a good one on me. When my first child was born the doctor—like I told you I think it would be nice if they would reduce the language to where a person with hardly no education could understand these people; but me, I'm so frank myself that I tell them, "Look, let's knock this thing down and let's speak English to me because I don't know what the devil you're talking about." And they always have; the doctors

Reprinted by permission of the authors and the American Sociological Association from the *Journal of Health and Human Behavior,* Vol. 2, 1961, p. 83 (with abridgements). Copyright © 1961 by the Leo Potishman Foundation.

I've went to and those that seen my children have always been very nice about it. In other words, they knock it down to where it is just plain English to me. But this doctor kept coming in every day and asking, "Have you voided?" So I'd say, "No." So in comes the nurse with some paraphernalia that was scary. So I said, "What the devil are you going to do?" And she said, "I'm going to catheterize you, you haven't voided." Well of course I knew catheterization was. I said, "You are going to play hell. I've peed every day since I've been here." I said, "Is that what he said?" And she said, "Of course, Rusty, didn't you know?" And I said, "Well, of course why didn't he just ask me if I'd peed? I'd have told him."

Physicians' Views on the Level of Medical Information among Patients

Lois Pratt, Arthur Seligman, George Reader

In *Le Malade Imaginaire,* Molière satirizes the importance of the special relationship that exists between doctors and patients. That such a relationship can prove to be less than ideal is no great surprise. In the following article the authors provide a straightforward account of how (in the 1950s) professionals, in this case medical doctors, incorrectly estimated the level of medical information possessed by their patients. There is no reason to believe that the patients' level of information or their communication with practitioners has improved in recent years. For a current example of language ambiguities taken from the field of nursing, see Petrello (1976). Nevertheless, the medical professional is at home in the hospital environment, taking this environment for granted and often expecting patients to similarly recognize and abide by the implicit categories and rules that govern behavior in this setting. In contrast, the patient is in an alien environment, does not know the hospital culture, and therefore presents behavior that may not accord with the professional's expectations. As a result, patients may be labeled "good" or "bad" solely on the basis of how well socialized they are to hospital culture. The labels, in turn, may affect the level of care that the patients receive. For a description of hospital culture see Taylor (1970). Through an understanding of such cultural elements as religion, economics, social class, and ethnicity the medical professional may come to temper his expectations and avoid that categorization of clients which may impair the provision of quality health care.

In organizing medical services for ambulatory patients those planning them often forget the patient in the desire to offer all that is considered necessary for adequate scientific care. Likewise, they may overlook one of

Reprinted by permission of the authors and the American Public Health Association. From the *American Journal of Public Health,* Vol. 47, October 1957, pp. 1277–1283. Copyright 1957 by American Public Health Association, Inc.

the primary purposes of any medical care activity: to provide an optimal environment for the development and continuance of the doctor-patient relationship. Essentially this relationship resolves itself into a give-and-take between two human beings, the nature of the interchange being determined by a number of factors, such as the previous experience and knowledge of the participants, expectations of each toward the other, and ability to communicate. The effectiveness of the doctor-patient relationship should be one of the fundamental considerations in evaluating adequacy of medical care.

To shed some light on the adequacy of patient care in the medical clinic of a large metropolitan medical center a number of studies have been made. This paper will report findings that bear on the question of communication of information between physicians and clinic patients; more specifically, it will focus on the physicians' attitudes and beliefs about patient information. In addition, to provide a context within which physicians' views may be interpreted, a summary of findings on some related questions will be presented.

Methods

In the medical clinic 214 patients were queried about etiology, symptoms, and treatment of ten common diseases, namely tuberculosis, diabetes, syphilis, arthritis, menopause, asthma, cerebrovascular accident, stomach ulcer, leukemia, and coronary thrombosis. A 36-question multiple choice test was used. A sample question follows:

Tuberculosis of the lungs is due to:
1. Prolonged exposure to the cold
2. Infection with a germ
3. Anemia and vitamin deficiency
4. Don't know

These same questions were then made part of a questionnaire administered to 89 physicians in the same clinic which was aimed at determining how much information these doctors thought laymen should know and how much they thought patients in the clinic did know.

The third part of this study consisted of an intensive longitudinal analysis of 50 patient-physician relationships, the 50 patients being randomly selected from among those making new appointments in the medical clinic. Each patient visit to a physician in the clinic was observed and a record kept of the activity and conversation that took place; in addition, the patient was interviewed before making the first visit to the physician and after each visit with him. The observations of the patient-physician contacts provided data on the ways the patient's illness was discussed, while interviews with patients revealed their views of what they had been told.

Results

The multiple choice test of knowledge about ten common diseases revealed that, on the average, the clinic patients could correctly answer 55 percent of these rather routine questions. The range was from one-third correct answers for patients with less than an eighth grade education to two-thirds for those with a high school education. It was also found that knowledge varied considerably by disease; knowledge of coronary thrombosis, for example, was particularly low, with only two-fifths of the information answered correctly.[1]

In addition a random group of 50 new patients were questioned on their arrival at the clinic about the condition they suspected they had. Some of these patients had received care for this suspected illness from another clinic or physician, but the majority had not. Most patients were found to have focused concern on a particular disease possibility, and the findings pertain only to this group who suspected a particular disease. No patients were found to have a thorough understanding about all three aspects about which they were questioned—the etiology or nature of the illness, the usual treatment, and the prognosis. Four patients were classified as having thorough understanding of the etiology or nature of the illness; but none had a thorough understanding of the treatment or prognosis. The majority were classified as knowing almost nothing about the three aspects of the disease. The minority were classed as having some understanding of it. On the basis of the findings it may be concluded that the patients studied were rather poorly informed about several common diseases and about their own suspected condition.

The next question to be considered, then, is what difference does this make? How does the patient's knowledge of disease influence the way the patient interacts with the physician and the quality of care received from the physician? It was not possible to determine the effect of the patient's level of knowledge, because no patient in the sample was well enough informed about his disease.

What was observed, however, is that patients in our sample participated with the physician at an extremely low level. They seldom requested information from the physician (one-third of the patients never asked a single question on any visit), they seldom asked the physician to do anything, and seldom even made a statement to direct the physician's attention to

---

[1] [These findings are reported in more detail in Seligmann, McGrath, and Pratt (1957).]

something. While it is assumed that the physician should direct the conversation and activity, complete lack of initiative by the patient may be dysfunctional for the physician as well as the patient. While it has been impossible to test whether this low level of participation by the patients was related to their low level of information and understanding of illness, the simultaneous presence of these two conditions is consistent with the notion that they are related.[2]

What are patients' attitudes about receiving and demanding information from physicians? Before attempting to modify existing patterns of communication, it would be wise to know what information patients want to obtain from physicians; for if patients expect more information than they are now receiving one would proceed differently than if they expect and want little information. On the basis of our study data it has been concluded that for the clinic patients studied, there was no demand for detailed and fundamental information among the patients; but there is apparently a certain amount of latent interest in receiving more information than they now receive. The findings on this point are summarized: Patients seldom make direct demands for information to the physician, particularly of the sort that would give basic understanding of the disease; their abstract notions about what constitutes a good doctor seldom include information-giving as a requisite characteristic; by and large they evaluated their own clinic physicians as performing satisfactorily with regard to explanations and information-giving; but in contrast to the above findings, which suggest little concern with information, it was found that a majority of patients indicated to the interviewer in some direct or indirect fashion that certain specific pieces of information about the disease process, implications of the test results, and so on, were of some importance to them. In general there was very little conscious demand for a thorough explanation of the illness on the part of the patients; but there was an unformulated, latent need.[3]

At least as important as the patients' views on this problem of communication are those of physicians. The attitudes of physicians determine, in part, what patients are now told. Furthermore, it would be necessary to take their attitudes into consideration in any future plan to change communication practices. This would be especially true if it seems desirable to encourage physicians to devote more attention to this problem, for, according to one study, 19 percent of the internist's time is now devoted to patient education [Dowling and Shakow, 1952].

---

[2]An average of 1.4 requests for information per visit, 0.5 requests for action, and 2.7 statements to direct the physician's attention or to volunteer information.

[3]Our findings on this problem are discussed in more detail in a paper by George Reader, Lois Pratt, and Margaret Mudd [1957].

What, then, are the attitudes of physicians about having patients know about medical matters? The findings obtained on this question are based on a questionnaire administered to 89 physicians in the medical clinic. Each doctor was asked to indicate for each of 36 facts about disease whether or not he thought the fact should be part of the layman's fund of knowledge, from his own point of view as a doctor who has to deal with patients. For example, did he think laymen should know that tuberculosis is due to infection with a germ, or that treatment for stomach ulcer tries to cut down on acid stomach juices, and so on. These are the identical facts on which the clinic patients had been tested.

Here are the results. The doctors reported, on the average, that 82 percent of the facts included in the questionnaire should be known by laymen. Only 9 percent of the doctors thought patients needed to know no more than half the information; while 18 percent of the doctors thought patients should know it all. The types of information that doctors most commonly thought laymen should know tended to be facts involving a favorable prognosis for a disease. Thus, the physician is a little more anxious that laymen be given hopeful information than that they be given facts on the etiology, symptoms, and treatment of disease. Nonetheless the preponderant opinion was that laymen should know most of the information in our test.

These findings must not be interpreted as indicating that physicians feel it desirable to tell a patient the full extent of his illness. On the contrary, when the clinical teaching faculty of the same institution were asked how they would feel if a physician in their specialty were "always to tell patients the full extent of their illness," almost three-fourths said they would disapprove.[4] When these two sets of findings are considered together, it suggests that physicians hold it beneficial for laymen to have a rudimentary understanding of illness, but that in actual practice it is often unwise to give a sick patient all the facts.

Do patients now meet these standards of knowledge of the physician? It is clear from the foregoing figures that patients in general fall far short of physicians' standards of what laymen should know. The physicians thought 82 percent of the test information should be known by the ordinary layman, while patients knew only 55 percent of it, with even high school graduates knowing only two-thirds of the facts. This represents, then, one measure of the gap between physicians' standards of what patients ought to know, and the actual level of patients' knowledge. The fact that patients fall far short of physicians' standards underlines the suspicion (reported earlier), that the

---

[4]From a study now [1957] in progress at the Bureau of Applied Social Research of Columbia University, by David Caplowitz.

patients may not be sufficiently informed to communicate with physicians with the highest degree of effectiveness.

The next question considered is: How do physicians perceive patients' level of knowledge about disease? Are they accurate in their evaluations, and do they overestimate or underestimate patients' knowledge? This question is thought to be significant in an investigation of communication problems, because physicians' judgments of patients' current knowledge undoubtedly influence what they discuss with patients and how they discuss it. Concerning the importance and direction of this influence, some limited findings will be presented later.

A first attempt to measure physicians' judgments about patients' level of knowledge was made by asking 89 clinic physicians to estimate the proportion of the clinic patient population who knew each of the 36 facts about disease. The estimates were then compared with the actual results on the knowledge test for the patient population. This is admittedly a gross measure of physicians' judgments because they were asked to evaluate an entire group rather than specific patients. Nonetheless, it provides an indication of how they perceive the clinic patients. It was found that well over half the estimates made by doctors were in error by at least 20 percent, the median error for doctors being 23 percent. Eighty-one percent of all doctors had an over-all tendency to underestimate patients' knowledge. This tendency to underestimate occurs in spite of the fact that patients' actual level of information is quite low.

What effect do these perceptions by physicians of the patients' knowledge have on their discussions with patients about illness? The data available on this problem consist of a measure of the physician's tendency to underestimate, overestimate or accurately judge the knowledge of the patient population, and a rating of the amount of explanation given by the physician to one or two patients.[5] It was found that those physicians who seriously underestimated the knowledge of the patient population tended to have more limited discussions with the patient about his problem than did the physicians who more accurately evaluated patients' knowledge or overestimated it.[6]

In addition to this statistical relationship, the intensive observation of 50 patient-physician relationships provided countless clues that the dynamics of the situation were somewhat like this: when a doctor perceives the patient as rather poorly informed, he considers the tremendous difficulties of translating his knowledge into language the patient can understand, along with the dangers of frightening the patient. Therefore he avoids involving

---

[5] The first measure is based on the questionnaire study of 89 physicians, and the second on observation of 50 patient-physician relationships.

[6] Too few physicians overestimated patients' knowledge to analyze this group separately.

himself in an elaborate discussion with the patient; the patient, in turn, reacts dully to this limited information, either asking uninspired questions or refraining from questioning the doctor at all, thus reinforcing the doctor's view that the patient is ill-equipped to comprehend his problem. This further reinforces the doctor's tendency to skirt discussions of the problem. Lacking guidance by the doctor, the patient performs at low level; hence the doctor rates his capacities as even lower than they are.

What are the actual practices of physicians in giving explanations to patients about their illness? Our findings on this question are based on observations of 50 patient-physician relationships during the entire course of these relationships.[7] On the basis of examining all the conversation between patient and physician, an attempt was made to code the amount and type of information given by the physician to the patient as objectively as possible. Five types of information about the patient's illness were considered: (1) reasons for test; (2) test results; (3) etiology of illness or what the illness consists of; (4) what the treatment is supposed to do; and (5) prognosis, possible complications, or other statements of what can be expected in the future.

It will not be possible at this time to report on the ways each of these areas were handled by physicians. The findings will be illustrated by discussing just one area—the reasons for tests: one-third of the patients were told nothing beyond the fact that tests x, y, and z were to be done (that is, they were given no explanation of the tests on any level); one-half of the patients were told, with regard to at least one test, what organ or possible disease was being investigated by the test (for example, they might have been told they were to have an x-ray of their chest); the remaining 14 percent of the patients received an explanation, with regard to at least one test, of the type of evidence the tests would provide, or what the test means in terms of a possible disease.

The findings for the physicians' handling of the other information areas were similar. Physicians were significantly more likely to give some explanation rather than none at all. A small minority received what could be called a rounded explanation, while the majority received a limited number of isolated facts. It was further found that physicians were more likely to avoid completely discussion of the prognosis and etiology than they were to bypass the more immediately practical issues of tests and treatment. It is strongly suspected that the limited explanations given by physicians in this sample is bound up with the low level of knowledge of the patients and the lack of overt interest shown by the patients in receiving information.

---

[7]Both junior physicians and attending physicians were observed. While certain differences were found in the explanations given by these two groups of physicians, the patterns to be reported below apply to both groups.

How much do patients learn about their illness from physicians? If a physician explains the problem carefully, does the patient always learn more than when the physician does not give a careful explanation? Are other factors—such as the patient's anxiety, interest, or education—such crucial determinants of what the patient learns from the physician, that undue emphasis should not be placed on the physician's giving elaborate explanations to all patients? The limited investigation made of this problem consisted of classifying patients in terms of how thorough an explanation their physicians gave them and then cross-classifying patients in terms of whether they improved in their understanding of their condition after interacting with the physician. It was found that the patients who received some explanation were more likely to increase their understanding of their problem than were those who did not receive explanations, but there was by no means a perfect relationship. While the measures are crude, it appears safe to conclude that what the doctor tells the patient is certainly not the only factor determining how much the patient learns about his condition. Because of the small number of cases in the sample, it is not possible to trace what the most significant other factors are which intervene between what the doctor says and what the patient actually learns. Furthermore, it was not possible to ascertain definitively what patients can learn when they receive well rounded explanations, for so few received systematic explanations.

The final consideration is: what difference does it make if a doctor gives or does not give a thorough explanation to the patient about his illness? That is, does it affect the patient's health? It is not feasible at this stage of the research to attempt to determine whether patients who are informed by their physicians actually make better recovery from their illness than those who are not informed. It was thought more practical to attempt to specify some of the more direct and specific effects that the doctor's explanations might have. First, were patients who received thorough explanations able to participate more effectively in the conversation and planning with the physician? It had been strongly suspected from the observations that the patients who were most confused about their condition and about what the doctor was doing or thinking, were the ones who participated least actively in discussions with the physician. Therefore, the number of requests for information made by the patient was used as a crude index of the extent of the patient's participation. It was found that the patients who received some explanation from the physician tended to ask slightly more questions than did those who were given almost no explanation. This finding is far from conclusive, but is consistent with the notion that the patient is able to interact more productively when the physician provides at least a minimum framework of information within which the patient can arrange his thoughts and formulate his questions.

Another possible effect of the physician's explanations might be the extent to which patients accept the physician's diagnosis and plans for treatment. It was found that the patients who received some explanation of the problem from their physicians were slightly more likely to agree fully with the diagnosis and plans of the physician, than were those patients who received negligible information about their condition. The relationship is far from perfect, partly, perhaps, because refined measures have not yet been developed. However, the relationship found does suggest that the patient who receives regular explanations from the physician about what he is doing and what he is finding, may accept more fully the physician's plans and goals, and hence this patient may be better cared for. As reported in another paper, agreement with the physician's diagnosis and plans is apparently a crucial factor; for the patients who agreed with the physician's diagnosis and plans were found to complete their care in every case, while a significant number of those not agreeing completely with the doctor's formulation, left the physician [Pratt and Mudd, 1956].

Summary and Conclusions

This paper has reported on findings from studies of problems of communication between patients and physicians in a medical outpatient clinic. It was found that:

Patients were quite poorly informed about their own condition when they came to the clinic and about ten common diseases. It was suggested that this might be partly responsible for the almost complete lack of initiative shown by the patients with the physicians.

The patients gave little evidence of conscious, aggressive demand for information about their condition from the physician; but there appeared to be an unformulated, latent desire for more information among the majority.

Physicians working in the clinic thought that basic facts on the symptoms, etiology, and treatment of common diseases should be known by laymen. The fund of information that physicians indicated should be known by laymen was considerably more extensive than patients were actually found to have.

Physicians apparently cannot judge very accurately the level of medical knowledge in a patient population. The direction of their error was rather consistently to underestimate patients' knowledge, despite the low level of knowledge among patients. Physicians who seriously underestimated patients' knowledge were less likely to discuss the illness at any length with the patient, than were the physicians who did not seriously underestimate patients' knowledge.

A majority of patients were found to have been told a limited number of isolated facts about their condition; few were given a systematic explanation of either the etiology, prognosis, purpose of the tests, test results, or treatment.

Finally, patients who were given more thorough explanations were found to participate somewhat more effectively with the physician and were more likely to accept completely the doctor's formulation, than were patients who received very little explanation.

The Two Languages of Nursing and Medicine

Joan E. Lynaugh, Barbara Bates

"The nurse must communicate her recommendations without appearing to be making a recommendation statement. The physician, in requesting a recommendation from a nurse, must do so without appearing to be asking for it." In this way Leonard Stein (1968) begins discussing the rules of "the doctor-nurse game." In looking at the language used by nurses and doctors, Lynaugh and Bates discuss the social structure of the medical system. They encourage our examination of what Merton has termed "zones of ambiguity"—areas of overlap in role performance between professionals with different training and orientations. This ambiguity can be a source of tension for individuals within and between disciplines. Such tensions may affect optimum provision of services to clients. There is a significant amount of literature on this subject. Among the available books and articles are those by Duff and Hollingshead (1968), especially Chapters 5 and 11; Bullough and Bullough (1971); Jaco (1958), especially Section VII; and the classic article by Stein, mentioned above. Various authors, among them King (1962) and Simmons and Wolff (1954), provide further interesting insights on the subject.

C.P. Snow has crystalized one of the critical problems of the 20th century: the failure of two cultures to communicate with each other. The two cultures he described comprised scientists and intellectuals; the gulf between them was created chiefly by excellent, but separate, highly specialized, educational systems. He has summarized:

Persons educated with the greatest intensity we know can no longer communicate with each other on the plane of their major intellectual concern. This is serious for our creative, intellectual and, above all, our normal life. It is leading us to interpret the past wrongly, to misjudge the present, and to deny our hopes of the future. It is making it difficult or impossible for us to take good action [Snow 1964:60].

In the course of working together to develop a nurse practitioner program, we have become aware of a similar failure in communication between nursing and medicine. Its cause may be comparable—separate, highly specialized educational systems. Its risks are the same—impaired ability to cooperate effectively, mutual misunderstanding and antagonism, and poor performance.

Our two subcultures, nursing and medicine, and the gap between them show up in the different ways in which our professions use words. At times we use different words for the same thing. This gap in communications can be bridged by simple translation of terms. At other times we not only use different words, we also have different perceptions of the same process. Here a simple translation is sufficient, and we unwittingly confuse, alienate, or antagonize each other.

A dictionary of words and the uses of words, as nurses and physicians commonly speak and write them, might sensitize readers to the potential problems of communicating across professional lines. Possibly it could help to improve communication and to increase the two professions' understanding of their own and a somewhat foreign subculture. Readers are invited to join in what we have found to be an enjoyable game—finding new words for a nursing-medicine dictionary.

The Dictionary

Rather than alphabetizing, we have chosen to classify words and phrases into somewhat arbitrary but useful categories: neutral phrases, phrases that indicate the theoretically different orientations of the two professions, phrases that reflect professional territoriality, and phrases that reflect habits and attitudes that affect collaboration.

Neutral Phrases. Neutral phrases are relatively few, but intriguing and inexplicable (see Table 1). Although we use different words to describe our actions, these are quite easily interpreted and cause no problems in communication.

Phrases Indicating Different Professional Orientations. A number of studies have suggested that nurses and physicians look at patients and at patient care from different vantage points and have correspondingly different perceptions of the problems involved [Bates, 1970]. While the physician focuses primarily on diagnosis and treatment, the nurse is more psychosocially and sometimes more personally oriented. The physician tends to emphasize structure, whether normal or diseased; the nurse concerns

TABLE 1. Neutral Phrases

	Nursing	Medicine
Visit to a patient at home	Home visit	House call
Methods of effecting patient care	Nursing care plan	Medical regimen
	Intervention	Treatment
	Comfort measures	Symptomatic therapy

herself[1] more with function. The central questions to which each profession addresses itself are basically different. (See Table 2.)

As the orientation of nursing separates further from medicine, the differences have crept also into the chapter headings of textbooks. For instance, a nursing text has a chapter heading, "Patients with a problem in transporting material to and from cells" [Beland, 1970]. A comparable chapter in a medical text is headed, "Diseases of the cardiovascular system [Beeson, et al., 1971]. Another nursing text [Smith and Gips, 1963] has a heading, "The patient with turculosis"; the medical text [Beeson, et al., 1971], has "Diseases due to mycobacteria."

The disease orientation of m medicine is caricatured in medical center dialect, in which patients become "clinical material" and "teaching material." Patients having special value are "fascinating patients," "good clinical material," or "great cases." Nurses do not use these words, they neither seek nor receive the intellectual rewards that these phrases imply. The gap between the subcultures is overt.

The person orientation of nursing is exemplified by phrases like "good patient," "patients who really need help," or "making people comfortable." The "action" is in the interaction with patients who look to the

---

[1]The authors concede a certain restlessness with their inability to cope more successfully with an obvious problem of word usage: i.e., physician equals he; nurse equals she. They add, "Conventional identification of gender won out over clumsy circumlocutions. Our apologies."

TABLE 2.   Phrases that Indicate Different Professional Orientations

	Nursing	*Medicine*
Central questions of the profession	What are the patient's problems, how is he coping with them and what help does he need?	What is the patient's diagnosis and what treatment does he need?
Phenomena dealt with	Discomfort	Symptom
	Patient concern	Disease
	Vision	Eyes
	Hearing	Ears
	Mobility	Musculoskeletal and neurological systems
	Elimination	Diseases of the colon and rectum
	The patient with tuberculosis	Diseases due to mycobacteria
	The patient with disease of bones and joints	Diseases of joints
Professional specialty areas	Maternal and Child Health	Obstetrics and Pediatrics
Process of improving the patient's future health	Promotion of health and well-being, health care supervision	Preventive medicine
Expressing esteem for the physician	He really knows his patients	He really knows his medicine
People served	Patients	Clinical material, teaching material, cases*
People served who are especially valued	Good patients, nice patients, cooperative patients, patients who really need help	Fascinating patients, good clinical material, great cases

*medical center dialect

TABLE 3. Phrases which Reflect Professional Territoriality

	Nursing	*Medicine*
Evaluative process in patient care	Gather or collect information, take a nursing history	Take a history
	Assess	Diagnose
	Physical assessment	Physical diagnosis
	A problem	A diagnosis
	Problem solving	Diagnostic process
	Appears, seems ("The patient appears to have stopped breathing.")	Is ("The patient is dead.")

nurse for help in sorting out their health problems, achieving comfort, answering their questions, or simply providing human contact. Nursing tries to implement this person orientation using scientifically based approaches to patient needs. Rewards in nursing grow out of accurate recognition of, and successful intervention in, health and illness problems.

Phrases Reflecting Professional Territoriality. As we have noted, diagnosis is central to the profession of medicine. It is also an area that physicians sometimes guard with fierce territoriality. Nurses respond by declaring diagnosis as off limits, taboo. The nurse is reluctant to move onto diagnostic grounds, and when she does so, she refuses to call it that. She has developed a series of alternate phrases to describe the process of patient evaluation; some are listed in Table 3.

Phrases Affecting Collaboration. A final group of phrases, shown in Table 4, reflect attitudes and habits that affect collaboration between nurse and physician. Most of them reflect the physician's traditional view of himself as the central figure in health care, issuing directives to others and

TABLE 4.   Phrases that Affect Collaboration

	Nursing	*Medicine*
Method of sharing information	Communication (physician to nurse and nurse to physician)	Orders (physician to nurse)
Method of asking the other to do something	Suggest	Request, order
Method of sharing work	Collaboration	Delegation
Optimal nursing response to physician's orders	Integrates orders into the patient care plan	Follows orders to the letter
Perception of the nurse in relationship to the physician	Colleague Nurse, nurse practicioner	Assistant Physician's assistant, paraphysician, paramedic, nonphysician
	Nurses	Girls*
Method of expressing esteem for the nurse	She really is a good nurse	She really ought to go to medical school
View of the whole process	Health care	Medical care

*dialect of the practicing physician

defining others chiefly in terms of himself. Collaboration among equals does not come naturally to him, and the concept may actually arouse considerable hostility. He frequently prefers to define nurses working with him in terms of his own profession, not theirs: physician's assistants, paraphysicians, paramedics, and, that most anonymous of terms, nonphysicians. He has little awareness that these terms may diminish the indentity of others. Even his most sincere and highest compliment goes awry because of this bias: "She really ought to go to medical school."

Physicians' orders are, of course, important, especially when rapid decisions are required. A communication system thus limited and restricted to a purely medical orientation, however, interferes with the full development of a comprehensive patient care plan.

On Becoming Bilingual

When separate cultures are forced by circumstance into close proximity, the dominant group seeks to control the others and to impose its own mores and values. Such a forced homogeneity is achieved only through the loss of variety and the intrinsic values of the less dominant system. It is our belief that modern patient care requires the full contribution of many disciplines, most frequently those of medicine and nursing. To maximize these contributions rather than block them, nurses and physicians may need to become bilingual, both in the use of words and in the understanding of each other's subcultures.

Words are currency for intellectual exchange. In our professional dialects, they reflect the changing influence of knowledge, social pressures, and fashion. Although nursing and medicine speak different dialects, they are intrinsically compatible and interdependent professions. Mutual comprehension of nursing dialect and medical dialect paves the way to our common interest, patient care.

Complex patient care problems require collaborative effort and discussion of problems with a minimum of "game playing" [Levin and Berne, 1972; Stein, 1968]. The physician who knows the meaning of "health-care process" in nursing dialect and the nurse who really comprehends "diagnostic process" in medicine are well on their way to genuine sharing of patient care responsibilities. If the nurse and physician need an interpreter, whether animate (the patient) or inanimate (the order book), they run the risk of bias, misunderstanding, and error. They also miss the satisfaction of sharing each other's skills in solving patient-care problems.

New working relationships between nurses and physicians are an inevitable result of demands for more and better health care. The nurse and physician cannot avoid one another, nor will rigid standing orders or protocols for care take the place of personal exchanges of information and plans. Quick exchanges require that words and phrases have the same meaning.

The flood of information about wellness and illness has swamped health workers. The opportunity to divide the responsibility for acquiring new information may be an additional pressing reason for bilinguality for both health professions.

Improving Communication

Interdisciplinary learning in formal settings may or may not improve comprehension between professions, but our experience has shown that face-to-face discussions about practice, the meaning of words and titles, and professional territories yield some immediate results in improved mutual comprehension. Members of both the nursing and medical professions need to be self-conscious about understanding the other [Leininger, 1971; Howard and Byl, 1971].

Basic to common comprehension of our subcultures is individual commitment to a broad perception of human needs. If the nurse and physician believe that patients require education, counseling, advocacy, comfort, and support in conjunction with diagnosis and therapy, then the effort to understand one another is worthwhile. Similarly, each needs not only to accept responsibility for his own professional sphere, but also to understand and accept the goals of his colleagues. If the comprehensive view of patient care is not a strongly held value, then real communication about patients probably will not occur.

Becoming bilingual is another route to better utilization of health workers. Nurses and physicians involved together in role change come to recognize this phenomenon. The nurse in the coronary care unit speaks and understands the specialized dialect of coronary care perfectly. The cardiologist unconsciously responds with pleasure and trust, valuing the person who has taken the trouble to learn his language. Physicians who seek to provide comprehensive care learn to speak some "nursing" and probably some "social work." Here too, the nurse—or social worker—responds favorably, sensing that she and her contribution are understood. Her own subculture and value system need not be submerged in the dominant medical system.

The advent of problem-oriented record keeping may enhance the development of bilingual tendencies in systems where such records are used by more than one discipline [Weed, 1970]. Use of the progress record by nursing and medicine is becoming common in hospitals. Using the same record may enhance both mutual understanding and sharing of patient care plans.

Risks in Being Bilingual

The nurse who chooses to become bilingual runs the risk of being misunderstood by nurses and physicians who remain unilingual. Nursing, in spite of its numbers, is still a developing profession, with all the self-consciousness of youth. In this sense, nurses are intolerant of members of their profession who deviate from "real nursing." To the degree that "real nursing" is seen as being diluted by the acceptance of additional medical tasks, the bilingual nurse may be seen as a deserter or traitor to the profession. The nurse who assumes a role as physician's assistant does in fact run the risk of becoming an emigrant to the slums of medicine as a "junior doctor.'' If this happens, she not only loses her capacity to speak nursing, but also her credibility as a nurse.

There are comparable risks for the physician who chooses to learn and use the language of nursing and to recognize the nurse's value system. His competence in diagnosis and treatment—the hard science of medicine—has been won at considerable cost. He values it highly and it forms an important part of his professional self-image. He may be reluctant to dilute it with a different kind of orientation and value system, especially if that orientation appears to him softer, less scientifically rigorous, and perhaps more feminine. And, like the nurse, he worries about what his colleagues may think, even when he is comfortable with the two languages.

But improved understanding between nursing and medicine is essential if each is to realize its full potential. In making the effort, we are not so much embarking on a new task as reaffirming an old purpose common to us both: ''To cure sometimes, to relieve often, to comfort always'' [Anonymous, 1968:410].

An Interview with Thomas Szasz

Richard Ballad

Thomas Szasz raises some strongly significant issues with regard to the nature and definition of mental illness. In discussing the complex ethical aspects of psychiatric interventions and the sometimes arbitrary labeling of a condition as a condition, Szasz touches on a fundamental product of cross-cultural research: that behaviors or physical characteristics which are labeled as symptoms and/or conditions in one culture do not necessarily warrant such a label in others. Some well-known examples of problems in disease definition include: dyschromic spirochetosis (Mechanic, 1968:16; Zola, 1966:618; Dubos, 1965:251), schistosomiasis hemotobia (Warren, 1974:52), and worm infestations (Saunders, 1972:509). While such differences in definition may be quite pronounced at the cross-cultural level, one tends to lose sight of the relative and sometimes arbitrary aspect of diagnoses within our own culture. Various conditions thought to be normal for the elderly are considered illnesses of a serious nature if seen in youths. Behaviors, as in the case of homosexuality, are apparently placed on and taken off lists of disorders by fiat, as in an action by the American Psychiatric Association (Los Angeles Times, 1974). Szasz provides a good basis for discussion of such issues and readers wishing to pursue these topics are directed to his many works (1960, 1961, 1970, 1973 for example). In *The Death of Psychiatry,* E. Fuller Torrey (1974) also presents a broad perspective (with a good deal of bibliography) on the shortcomings of the field. It should be noted that Szasz's views are often controversial and he has his critics; however, his position becomes particularly relevant in the discussion of mental illness in a multicultural society (see, for example, "A Case of a 'Psychotic' Navaho Male" and "That Nigger's Crazy," in this collection).

Dr. Thomas Szasz sent shock and rage through the psychiatric fraternity in 1961 with his book *The Myth of Mental Illness.* He has remained the most stinging gadfly of his profession. He acknowledges brain disease, brain damage, brain defects, but not *mental* illness. "Disease," he says, "cannot be cured by conversation." What so many doctors call mental disease, Szasz calls human conflict expressed in ways society can't live with. He has become this country's leading spokesman for the newest trend in behavioral science—the belief that science belongs on the side of the people it studies, rather than aligning itself with a society that wants to control differentness. Szasz is opposed to all involuntary hospitalization, and he has wakened America's conscious to many "crimes" committed in the name of "mental health," from abuses in private practice to our system of criminal justice.

Within a year after *The Myth of Mental Illness* appeared, the New York State Commissioner of Mental Hygiene called for Szasz's resignation as a professor at the state university's Upstate Medical Center at Syracuse, a position Szasz has held since 1956. After great turmoil, including the resignation of the chairman of the department of psychiatry, the rebellious Szasz emerged secure in his job. He is still there.

Yesterday's shock artist is today's authority. Many of Szasz's aphorisms have become slogans for Young Turks in medicine who stand with the patient rather than the hospitals and the jails. The following are excerpts from his book *The Second Sin,* published in 1973:

- "If a man says he is talking to God we say he is praying. If he says God is talking to him we say he is a schizophrenic."
- "Treating addiction to heroin with methadone is like treating addiction to Scotch with bourbon."
- "Mental hospitals are the POW camps of our undeclared and unarticulated civil wars."

Szasz pours them out, and they inspire retaliation. The late Dr. Manfred Guttmacher, a distinguished forensic psychiatrist, wrote: "A bird that fouls its nest courts criticism. Dr. Szasz doubtless enjoys the contentions he is creating."

Dr. Guttmacher was right; Szasz gets a huge kick out of twisting tails. He criticized Dr. Bernard Diamond, chief psychiatrist for Sirhan B. Sirhan, who assassinated Robert F. Kennedy. He ridiculed the idea of Sirhan's being portrayed as unaware of what he'd done because he was presumably insane at the time. Dr. Diamond, in turn, called some of Szasz's ideas on psychiatry and the law "irresponsible, reprehensible, and dangerous."

But now Szasz has many defenders. Some have joined the American Association for the Abolition of Involuntary Mental Hospitalization, of which Szasz is co-founder and chairman of the board. The American Humanist Association named him the 1973 Humanist of the Year. Far-out admirers have talked of forming "The Insane Liberation Front" in his honor.

Dr. Thomas Szasz, at 53 [in 1973], is a bright-eyed, wiry man of medium height. He favors conservative gray suits and lives in a modest, split-level home. In 1970 he was divorced quietly from his wife of 19 years. Their two daughters, Margot, 20, and Suzy, 18, live with him.

Szasz was born in Hungary in an upper-middle-class Jewish family. His father had a law degree and was overseer of several estates. In 1938, young Szasz came to the U.S. to avoid the impending Nazi take-over. He was an honors graduate of the University of Cincinnati in 1941, with a major in physics, and three years later he was graduated at the top of his class from that university's medical school. He interned at Boston City Hospital, took his residence in psychiatry at the University of Chicago Clinics, and his analytic training at the Chicago Institute for Psychoanalysis. He has maintained a private psychiatric practice since that time.

Dr. Szasz has written more than two hundred articles and eight books and has recently edited an anthology called *The Age of Madness* (1973).

Some of his better-known works are *Psychiatric Justice* (1965), *The Ethics of Psychoanalysis* (1965), *The Manufacture of Madness* (1970), and *Ideology and Insanity* (1970).

This interview was conducted by *Penthouse's* Richard Ballad.

Penthouse: What do psychiatrists do when they are said to be treating mental illness?

Szasz: In my view, when psychiatrists "treat" so-called mental illness, they actually intervene, in one way or another, in a conflict. Now, in the face of a conflict, there are three alternatives: you side with one party, side with the other, or try to remain neutral and act as an arbitrator or judge. Psychiatric interventions—which is the term I prefer to "psychiatric treatments"—are actually a confused and confusing mixture of these three kinds of social actions.

Penthouse: Give us some examples.

Szasz: Let's first take the case of a person who goes of his own accord to a private psychiatrist—say, someone like Dr. Daniel Ellsberg. Such a person hires the psychiatrist to help him with whatever he, the so-called patient, considers to be his problem, and to help him deal with it the way he, the client, wants to deal with it. Such a person is likely to have secrets—from his wife, his employer, the government—which he may share with his psychiatrist, but which the psychiatrist is expected to keep confidential. In Ellsberg's case, for example, the psychiatrist may have come into the possession of information which the U.S. government wanted to have. In short, in the conflict between Ellsberg and the American government, Ellsberg's psychiatrist acted as an agent of his client—protecting his client's interests, even where these might have been in conflict with the interests of the government.

Penthouse: But, isn't this an exceptional case?

Szasz: Only insofar as government agents burglarized the psychiatrist's office—which, I assume, is not yet common practice. For the principle it illustrates, however, it is not unusual at all; it is typical. In the less sensational cases, the patient may confide secrets to the therapist that have to do with his conflicts with his wife, or a wife may confide her conflicts with her husband; the therapist will then be acting for the interests of one marital partner and against those of the other.

Penthouse: Give us some examples of other things psychiatrists do.

Szasz: In my first example, the psychiatrist did something *for* the patient. In the case of the husband and wife—which is economically and statistically more important than the first—the psychiatrist does something *to* the patient: for example, a husband contacts a psychiatrist, tells him that his wife has delusions or is depressed, and the psychiatrist then commits the wife to a mental hospital. The wife, the ostensible patient, does not want to be in the hospital; she wants to be left alone. Here then, the psychiatrist acts not as the patient's agent, but as his or her adversary. Finally, when a psychiatrist is hired and paid to "evaluate" individuals—for example, for a court, a draft board, the Peace Corps, an insurance company, and so forth—he acts as an arbitrator or judge. He is, in principle, neither the patient's agent nor his adversary; he is the agent of whoever hires him and pays him—assuming that he does his job honestly.

Penthouse: How can people tell what sort of a thing a psychiatrist will do; whether he will act for or against what you call the patient's "self-defined interests?"

Szasz: They often can't. That's why I have gone to such great pains, in several books, to try to show that there are a minimum of two very different kinds of psychiatry—voluntary and involuntary; and that the difference is at least as important as the difference between, say psychotherapy and organic therapy.

Penthouse: Are you opposed to involuntary psychiatry?

Szasz: Indeed I am.

Penthouse: Why?

Szasz: Because I consider all involuntary psychiatric interventions to be punishments. Because I believe that physicians should be healers, not jailers. And because I believe that no one should be punished who did not break the law and who was not duly tried and convicted in court for it.

Penthouse: Not many psychiatrists share your idea that involuntary psychiatry is punishment.

Szasz: Not many psychiatrists. But many writers do. James Thurber described this in *The Unicorn in the Garden.* Of course, the victims of involuntary psychiatry think it's punishment, but their opinion doesn't count; they are considered "crazy." I suspect it's the main reason people are afraid of psychiatrists. After all, dermatologists and gynecologists are not in the business of locking people up, but psychiatrists are. And people know this. So what I am saying is at once shockingly novel, because it is the exact opposite of what medical and psychiatric orthodoxy says; and yet it is terribly obvious, because no one wants to be locked up in an insane asylum. That's why we have commitment laws and closed wards in mental hospitals.

Penthouse: You often complain that psychiatrists do not keep their patients' confidences. You mention, for example, the psychiatrist who released reports on a man who shot and killed several people from a tower at the University of Texas. Why do psychiatrists do that?

Szasz: Because they are no more honest than politicians. They often comply with popular expectations and pressures. There are countless such cases. For example, there was Lee Harvey Oswald, the man who supposedly killed President Kennedy. A psychiatrist saw him when he was in his teens. After Oswald was apprehended and killed—perhaps even before he was killed, I don't remember the exact timing—this psychiatrist gave out the whole story of Oswald; that is, when he saw him, and what he thought was wrong with him, and Oswald's mother, and so forth. An utter breach of confidence, in my opinion.

Penthouse: What about President Nixon's psychiatric record? Didn't he see a psychiatrist in the 1950's?

Szasz: He saw a physician who at the time was said to have specialized in psychosomatic medicine. He subsequently became a psychotherapist. The doctor also talked—perhaps blabbered would be a better term. The very fact that he acknowledged that Mr. Nixon had been his patient was in my opinion a breach of confidence. But that wasn't all: he also published a story in one of the mass magazines in which he went on at length about how mentally healthy Mr. Nixon was. This too was improper. He shouldn't have said anything.

Penthouse: Doesn't the ethics committee of the American Psychiatric Association to anything about this?

Szasz: You must be joking! Ethics committee! You know what such committees are for? To protect the *profession*—not the patient or the public. This is the whole problem with professions, especially when they manage to instill awe and fear in the public. George Bernard Shaw said that "every profession is a conspiracy against the public." Nowhere is this now more true than with respect to psychiatry.

Penthouse: In your writings, you cite the names of many public figures who have been "psychiatrized against their will." Can you mention some of them and just what happened?

Szasz: The list is a mile long. Ernest Hemingway was involuntarily hospitalized and given electric shock treatment. Secretary of Defense James V. Forrestal was apprehended, supposedly because he was suicidal. He was taken to the Bethesda Naval Hospital and was placed in a room on the top floor—the eleventh, I believe. A few weeks later he was found dead on the pavement in front of his window. Earl Long, the former governor of Louisiana, was incarcerated in a psychiatric hospital in Texas. When he was returned to a Louisiana mental hospital, he freed himself by firing the head psychiatrist of the Louisiana state mental health system. Long was a smart man. He understood psychiatric gangsterism better than most politicians do.

Finally, I want to mention the Goldwater case. During the 1964 presidential race, Senator Goldwater was, as you may recall, called crazy by about one thousand psychiatrists. Now, the interesting thing—and to me the terrible thing—about the aftermath of that affair was that Senator Goldwater sued Ralph Ginzburg, the publisher of *Fact* magazine, where this psychiatric defamation was published. Ginzburg was found guilty of libel and had to pay a substantial sum to Goldwater for damages. But, interestingly, Goldwater didn't sue any of the psychiatrists, even though they were the ones who produced and supplied the libelous material to Ginzburg. This shows, I think, how afraid politicans are of psychiatrists, of the psychiatric profession as a whole and that they consider psychiatrists more sacrosanct than Presidents or White House candidates. It's a dangerous situation.

Penthouse: You have criticized the symbiotic relationship between medicine—especially psychiatry—and the state. How did this symbiosis develop?

Szasz: This is a complicated matter, but in a nutshell, as the prestige and popularity of organized religion diminished, following the Enlightenment, medicine took over many of the functions formerly performed by the churches. Physicians became the new priesthood and it has been the psychiatrists especially who have played the roles of priests. They are our secular and "scientific" priests.

In a theocratic society the religious values, as interpreted by the priest, are enforced by the government; for example, you must close your shop on Sunday, or Saturday. In a therapeutic society, the medical values, as interpreted by the physician, are enforced by the government; for example, you must be vaccinated against smallpox and you cannot buy a hypodermic syringe.

Penthouse: If you are so critical of psychiatry, why do you teach and practice it?

Szasz: I am not critical of *all* of psychiatry. I am no more against psychiatry than a 16th-century priest who opposed the Inquisition was against

Catholicism. Of course, many orthodox Catholics in the 16th century would have said such a priest was against Catholicism, and many orthodox psychiatrists would now say that I am against psychiatry. This proves only that there is a conflict between me and orthodox psychiatrists, which is obvious. It does not prove that I am "against" psychiatry and that they are "for" it. The situation is a lot more complicated than that.

I object to only two things. First, I object to any and all *involuntary* psychiatry; to any kind of psychiatric measure that's imposed on a person against his will. Second, I object to the widespread mislabeling in psychiatry; that is, calling personal problems "diseases," calling prisons "hospitals," calling conversation "treatment," and so forth.

Penthouse: What do you approve of?

Szasz: I approve of any kind of psychiatry that's voluntary and to which the so-called patient consents, and which is correctly labeled—or at least approximately so. If people want to do it, they should have the right to use all the existing psychiatric measures and any others that anyone wants to add—you name them: psychoanalysis, psychotherapy, group therapy, drugs, hospitalization, electroshock. They are all okay for those who *want* them. If someone like Senator Eagleton wants to go to a hospital and hire a doctor to give him electrically induced convulsions, why shouldn't he? I think he is making a bad mistake in doing so, but that's only my opinion. He is entitled to have his opinion and to act upon it.

Penthouse: You are personally opposed to electroshock. Why?

Szasz: It's a barbarity. I have never used it and never would. I wouldn't dream of recommending it. If someone asked me about it, I would point out that neurologists go to great lengths trying to prevent seizures in persons who have epilepsy, because every time a person has a grand mal seizure, his brain gets damaged. Nevertheless, psychiatrists claim that giving someone a seizure is a form of treatment. But then the history of medicine is full of instances of so-called cures that were actually harmful. You know the old saying, "The cure is worse than the disease." It applies to a lot of things psychiatrists do—electroshock, lobotomy, often the use of drugs, and sometimes even psychotherapy or psychoanalysis.

Penthouse: Despite this you would not want to see these things abolished?

Szasz: Certainly not! In my view of life, the foremost value is individual freedom and responsibility. People should have a chance to make their own choices. I am willing to state my views—for example, I think that anyone who has electroshock is an idiot, but I would not want to impose my views on anyone. For one thing, I *could* be wrong. But even being right should not give one the right to impose his views or will on others. I view all this on the model of religion and religious freedom. It isn't only electroshock and lobotomy that I don't think much of. I don't think much of being a Jehovah's

Witness or a Christian Scientist; but I certainly think people should have a right to these religious beliefs and the practices they entail. And I think the same way about medical beliefs and practics.

Penthouse: Then you are not an antipsychiatrist, as so many seem to think?

Szasz: Of course not. I am against psychiatric coercion and deception, but I'm not antipsychiatry! There is now a whole literature on what is called "antipsychiatry," and I am supposed to be one of the originators of this whole movement. Words are very important, especially in psychiatry. So I reject the term "antipsychiatry." It's a bad term. It's misleading. It fails to make the distinction between voluntary and involuntary psychiatry. If one values individual freedom and dignity, then one must, of course, oppose involuntary psychiatry; at the same time, one must *not* oppose voluntary psychiatry, not try to prevent people from choosing psychiatric interventions that one personally dislikes or disapproves of.

Penthouse: You often refer to religion. Are you religious?

Szasz: Not in any formal sense. In the sense that I hold some values dear, yes. In a sense, everyone is religious. Man is fundamentally a religious being.

Penthouse: What do you think about death? What happens when we die? As a scientist, aren't you curious about it?

Szasz: Not really. This may sound foolish, but I think I know what happens when we die.

Penthouse: What?

Szasz: We are dead. That's it.

Penthouse: But do you accept the *possibility* that you might not know *everything* that happens when we die?

Szasz: Well, of course. All I am saying is that I don't believe in a life after death—whatever that phrase means. I have just never had the usual hang-ups about death. Life is very precious. But when one dies, one dies. That's the way it is, I think.

Penthouse: You often refer to John Stuart Mill and Ralph Waldo Emerson. What other men do you admire? Who influenced you?

Szasz: The great writers and playwrights—Shakespeare, Molière, Dostoevski, Camus, and countless others. Among contemporaries, people like Wittgenstein, Bertrand Russell, Karl Popper.

Penthouse: How about psychoanalysts?

Szasz: I admire all three of the great founders of psychoanalysis; not uncritically, though. Freud, Jung, and Adler were, all three of them, immensely gifted and creative and important people. It's too bad people no longer read them very much—read their original works. They are better than 99 percent of the current stuff.

Penthouse: What do you admire about these men or their work?

Szasz: I admire Freud's brilliance and his systematic style of work;

Jung's humaneness and sensitivity to man's moral and religious nature; and Adler's common sense and directness. It seems to me, too, that Jung and Adler must have been superb psychotherapists, which Freud clearly was not.

Penthouse: In your new book, *The Second Sin,* you say that, "The narcotics laws are our dietary laws." Why don't you consider the addict a sick person?

Szasz: Because a bad habit is not a disease. In fact, I maintain that not only is the addict not sick, but there is no such thing as "addiction" and no such person as an "addict." There are, to be sure, people who take some drugs which some other people do not want them to take; and if the latter have more power than the former, then they can and sometimes do call the former "addicts."

Penthouse: Do you say this for effect or do you really believe it?

Szasz: Both. But look at the similarities between this drug situation and the situation as it was not so long ago with religion. A few hundred years ago, if a person was not a Christian, or was not a Christian in just the right way, he was considered a heretic. Today we know there are no heretics. Heretics were simply people whose religious habits offended those who defined the true faith. I hold that, in the same way, addiction is a sort of pharmacological heresy.

Penthouse: I presume you don't think much of methadone?

Szasz: It's as good a narcotic as another. It's much like heroin—just as Orthodox Judaism is much like fundamentalist Christianity, which is why they make such perfect antagonists.

Penthouse: Isn't methadone a treatment?

Szasz: Of course it's a "treatment." It must be. The United States government says so. The American Medical Association says so. The American Psychiatric Association says so. So most people are likely to go along and believe this. I don't. But I don't expect most people to agree with me on a thing like this, which is almost entirely a matter of fashion, of fast-changing definition.

Penthouse: At one time heroin was used as a treatment for morphine addiction. You think the same thing may happen to methadone?

Szasz: Yes, I think there is an excellent chance for that. As methadone is used more widely and over a longer period, more and more people will be "abusing" it, and then the medical profession and the government will decide one nice day that it's no longer a "treatment" but a disease!

Penthouse: You are opposed to prescriptions. Wouldn't a lot of people hurt themselves and perhaps hurt others if anyone could buy any drug he wanted?

Szasz: If people buy drugs and hurt themselves, that's their problem. If they hurt somebody else, they should be punished especially hard instead of it being an extenuating circumstance calling for mercy. Under Roman law, a person who committed a crime while intoxicated was punished especially hard. That was two thousand years ago. What we need is a little catching up. But you don't penalize people by stopping them from buying and taking drugs. That is not a crime.

Penthouse: Give us some other examples of this alliance between medicine and the state.

Szasz: There are so many, and we are so embedded in them, that we are unaware of them, as people are unaware of the air they breathe—until they get asthma. A few years ago, abortion was a crime. Now it's a treatment—and Blue Cross pays for it! Pimping is a crime, but when a so-called sex therapist like Dr. Masters gets you a prostitute and calls her a "surrogate wife," then pimping becomes a form of treatment, which you can take off your income tax. Sending your son or daughter through college is not tax-deductible, but "sex-therapy" is. If that doesn't drive home the truth about the alliance between medicine and state, the politicalization of illness and treatment, I certainly don't know what would.

Penthouse: You don't believe there is such a thing as "mental illness." Well, how does schizophrenia develop, and other behavior conventionally called "mental illness"?

Szasz: I don't want to be difficult, but I must insist that schizophrenia doesn't develop. A certain kind of behavior develops, and that may be called "schizophrenia." Assuming that, and assuming we have the same sort of behavior in mind, this would be my answer. There are two basic ways of being badly screwed up in childhood: by being neglected too much or by being interfered with too much. Being left alone, being left unoccupied, unstimulated—or, on the other hand, being overprotected, intruded upon, overstimulated—both are pretty nearly intolerable for children—as well as for adults. To develop what we in our culture call "properly," we must be able to grow up and live in some middle range between too much aloneness and too much togetherness.

Penthouse: Some researchers claim that diet—and especially some vitamins—can affect schizophrenia and may be used to treat it. Could you comment on this?

Szasz: I can't comment on the biology of this matter, because I don't know what dietary influences or vitamins do for whatever may be physiologically the matter with some "schizophrenics"—if anything. But I do want to emphasize that if schizophrenia is a disease, like diabetes, to which medically oriented pyschiatrists often compare it, then the "schizophrenic" patient should have the same rights as those of the diabetic patient. Foremost among these are the right to reject treatment, the right to reject being diagnosed—indeed, the right to reject being a "patient" at all, in the sense of having the right to refuse to submit to medical ministrations. At the same time, as I said before, people should have the right to whatever treatment they want—vitamins, electroshock, even lobotomy; but *only* if they want it.

Penthouse: Why do you emphasize the right to reject treatment?

Szasz: Because psychiatrists and medically oriented psychiatric researchers make constant claims about this or that being physiologically wrong with "mental patients"—as if establishing the presence of an objectively identifiable disease would legitimize treating such patients. It wouldn't. Syphilis is an objectively identifiable disease. But there is no law, in New York State, authorizing a physician to treat a person for syphilis who does not want to be treated. In other words, what makes treatment legitimate in medicine is that the patient wants it; whereas what makes it legitimate in psychiatry is that the physician *claims* that the "patient" is "sick." I insist on distinguishing between illness as a biological condition and the act of treating a person—with or without his consent—which is a political event.

Penthouse: Your objection to involuntary mental hospitalization and treatment leaves open the problem of what to do with people who are dangerous, those who commit crimes.

Szasz: Here I must refer you to my two books, *Law, Liberty and Psychiatry* and *Psychiatric Justice,* where I discuss this subject in detail. Briefly, my position is that in a free society, no one should be deprived of liberty without due process of law. And to me, due process implies that the only justification for loss of liberty is the commission of an illegal act. Mental illness can never justify it, just as heresy can't—just as being too fat or too thin can't. In other words, if someone is suspected of breaking the law, he should be accused, tried, and if convicted, sentenced. If the sentence calls for loss of liberty, then the offender should be confined in an institution that's penal, not medical, in character. Of course, in many cases where such sentences are imposed, they really should *not* be imposed if we are to be truly concerned with the protection of public safety and the maintenance of human dignity. In any event, I don't want doctors to be jailers or torturers. We have already forgotten what doctors did in Nazi Germany, and we don't *want* to know what they do in Communist Russia.

Penthouse: All right, so we send criminals to jail without considering insanity as an extenuating circumstance. But our jails are very bad. Very few people come out of them fit for society. What good does it do to send them there unless you hold everybody for life terms?

Szasz: Of course our prisons are bad. I didn't say they were good. Nor did I promise to solve all social problems. I am only trying to clarify what psychiatrists do and to identify what I think is good or bad among the things they do, and why. If prisons are bad, and if we want to do something about this, the remedies are obvious enough. We should send fewer people to prison and we should make the prisons better. Placing lawbreakers or suspected lawbreakers—and indeed, innocent persons suspected of being "dangerous," whatever that term might mean—in mental hospitals, which are themselves horrible prisons, is not my idea of prison reform.

Penthouse: You say that committing suicide should be a human right. But suppose I tried to jump out of a window? Wouldn't your impulse be to restrain me?

Szasz: Yes, of course. I would try to stop you, partly because I would assume that that's what you would want me to do; otherwise you wouldn't be trying to kill yourself right in front of me. But the point is that I would *not* call police; I would *not* commit you to a mental hospital; I would *not* even try to persuade you to see a psychiatrist. What I might say is, "Look, you are insulting me. You call me on the telephone. You say you want to talk to me, to do an interview. You come and we talk. And then you want to jump out of *my* window. How can you do this to me? Why did you deceive me?"

Penthouse: Suppose I then told you: "All right, I'm going to get a room of my own, check in, and jump out of *my* window." Then what?

Szasz: I would offer to talk about it with you. That's all. The rest would be up to you. Perhaps I would also ask you why you tell me that you are going to kill yourself. Why don't you keep it to yourself?

Penthouse: You seem reluctant to say much about the possibilities of altering behavior chemically. Why is that?

Szasz: Because I do not consider myself particularly knowledgeable about biochemistry or pharmacology. Of course, I recognize that it is possible to alter behavior chemically. But I try to focus on the ethical and political aspects of how such alteration is brought about rather than on the alteration itself.

Penthouse: I'm sorry. You'll have to clarify that.

Szasz: I know that chemical substances alter behavior. That's not in dispute. Right now, we are drinking vodka tonics. If we drink enough of the stuff, we shall produce an alteration in our behavior due to alcohol. That's the model. The idea is simple enough: alcohol, nicotine, opium, methadone, barbiturates, amphetamines—it's a long list. All these drugs alter behavior. So I am not denying any of this or that drugs may be useful for what is now called psychiatric treatment.

Penthouse: But shouldn't medical men, chemists, biologists, be working full speed on this? Aren't you excited about the possibilities?

Szasz: I am not particularly excited about this area simply because I happen to believe—and, of course, I could be wrong about this—that most of the things we call "mental diseases" are personal problems, human problems; and there isn't much you can do about human problems by drugging the person who has them. Second, I am not too excited about this area because it seems to me that, by and large, drugs affect mood and behavior in one of two ways: they stimulate or they depress—that is, they make you feel more energetic and awake (at least for a while) or they make you feel less energetic and more sleepy. Now, each of these effects may be useful. In fact, I happen to believe that we have too many restrictions on drugs that have these effects. They should be freely available. And this carries me to my third point, which is the moral and political one. Who now controls, and who will control in the future, the use of these drugs? The government? The medical profession? The free citizen of a free society? It may be foolish to plunge ahead and develop more and more psychopharmacological agents when we can't seem to decide how to use the agents we now have. After all, opium has been around for thousands of years; and we now consider it "progress" to prohibit its use and to replace it with synthetic drugs. And last but not least, I think we should grapple—and I mean politicians, lawyers, civil libertarians and people in general—with the basic question of whether such drugs should ever be used involuntarily, and if so, when, how, by whom, on whom, and what sort of protections will the citizen have against being drug-controlled by physicians and politicians? It's not enough to write science fiction about this. It's necessary to confront it as the political—not medical—problem that it is.

Penthouse: One last question: In many of your books you are concerned with the dangers of medical oppression, or a kind of therapeutic tyranny. You have coined the term "therapeutic state." Could you clarify what you mean?

Szasz: For nearly twenty years now I have been writing about the fundamental similarities between the persecution of heretics and witches in former days and the persecution of madmen and mental patients in ours. Briefly, my view is that just as a theological state is characterized by the preoccupation of the people with religion and religious matters, and especially with the religious deviance called heresy, so a therapeutic state is characterized by the preoccupation of the people with medicine and medical matters, and especially with the medical deviance called illness. The aim of a therapeutic state is not to provide favorable conditions for the pursuit of life, liberty, and happiness, but to repair the defective mental health of the subject-patients. The officials of such a state parody the roles of physician and psychotherapist. This arrangement gives meaning to the lives of countless bureaucrats, physicians, and mental health workers by robbing the so-called patients of the meaning of *their* lives. We thus persecute millions—as drug addicts, homosexuals, suicide risks and so forth—all the while congratulating ourselves that we are great healers curing them of mental illness. We have, in short, managed to repackage the Inquisition and are selling it as a new scientific cure-all.

IV

HEALTH CARE IN
A PLURALISTIC SOCIETY

The world is getting smaller. Colonel Sanders is everywhere. Few places on earth remain unreached by television and radio. All places display reminders of how profound are the effects of intercultural contact. But this uniformity is only an illusion. It is true that we can travel more rapidly than before and can recognize things familiar to us wherever we go. The people we encounter, however, will often possess knowledge and profess beliefs totally foreign to almost all of us. In a sense, then, the world has gotten larger: with rapid travel we may meet greater diversity—if we care to recognize it. That cultural diversity exists is axiomatic. The difficult task lies in determining what are the differences and similarities and what their possible implications are.

Corollary to the belief in a shrinking world is the conviction that the United States is a melting pot. It is obvious that the population is composed of people from many backgrounds. This complexion, in turn, has yielded what might be termed "American culture." As a general concept, "American culture" conveys a particular meaning, but when used to describe the specific beliefs of different groups and individuals it may confuse. Lulled into believing that the United States is truly a melting pot, practitioners often believe that there are no significant differences in the beliefs and attitudes held by different peoples. Such an attitude can give rise to various difficulties in the delivery of health care. Increased cultural awareness on the part of practitioners would seem to provide a partial solution to some of these problems. Such an approach has great value but it demands caution. Perhaps something special has happened in our thinking as a result of the emphasis on cultural awareness. A negative side effect of attempts at increased cultural awareness has been to identify all members of an ethnic group as carriers of an idealized culture. Using such generalized knowledge about a particular ethnic group as a blueprint for providing health care ignores individual differences and most certainly will result in stereotyping. This is not to deny that some routine in medicine is essential.

In a pluralistic society beliefs are not patterned solely by ethnicity. Individuals begin to be seen as members of various "subcultures." In addition to being ethnically identified, an individual may also be identified according to social class, economic status, politics, religion, sex, age, occupation (the list is hardly exhausted). Each category cross-cuts the others and together they form what has been termed the "subcultural matrix." Each category has, furthermore, been correlated with different health attitudes. The consequent picture is indeed a complicated one, and the task of designing programs and promoting professional attitudes that emphasize flexibility becomes a major challenge.

In *The Mind Game* (1972), E. Fuller Torrey contends that the effectiveness of psychotherapists in all cultures is governed by how well they adapt and satisfy what has been identified as the four components of psychotherapy. To a great extent these are also components of medicine in general. They are: a shared world-view, the personal qualities of the therapist, the patient's expectations, and the techniques of therapy. A *shared world-view* involves the therapist's ability to assign an acceptable name to what is wrong with the patient; the patient will believe he or she is in good hands since the practitioner "understands" (names) the problem. The *personal qualities of the therapist* are of prime importance in the patient-practitioner relationship. Each player has specific *expectations* of the other and the extent to which these expectations are met will influence treatment. The self-fulfilling prophecy is at work with respect to patient expectations. Patients are impressed, for example, with the trappings of medicine. Those things that identify a person as a healer or a building as a place to get cured serve to reinforce the patient's faith in the system and improve chances for success in treatment. *Therapeutic techniques* in all cultures meet with varying degrees of success. Deviation from proven methods may bring skepticism or rejection. The form that these four somewhat overlapping components take will necessarily differ with culture. Compliance with cultural expectations will help to determine the effectiveness of treatment.

The articles in this section provide a variety of perspectives on a broad range of issues related to cultural variability and health care. Donald Jewell illustrates how a lack of information about a person's culture can proceed from misjudging behavior to misdiagnosing that behavior, which was not understood in the first place.

André M. Tao-Kim-Hai, conditioned by his previous medical experience as a youth, interprets from his own perspective what transpires during his hospitalization. Communication problems abound. The staff's lack of knowledge of the patient's culture, coupled with his failure to accept "normal" procedures, creates havoc.

Loudell Snow suggests that something goes consistently wrong in the interaction and communication between the patients in her special sample and the physicians whom they contact. The result of the exchange is that patients are "encouraged" to seek treatment elsewhere.

Luisah Teish argues that diagnosing is often accomplished in accord with stereotypes of the people to be treated. This has been the case in the past and still persists.

Cervando Martinez and Harry Martin outline the medical belief system of many Mexican-Americans. The authors also introduce and discuss peoples' ability to use dual medical systems.

Gwen Anderson and Bridget Tighe stress the importance of understanding culturally valued behavior and acceding (if at all possible) to the culturally influenced needs of the patient. Their discussion of Gypsy health behavior provides an opportunity to examine the central role and importance of family in providing care.

William Nolen acknowledges the different attitudes of many doctors toward men and women with regard to the nature of treatment and information provided. The article focuses on sex-stereotyping and the doctor-patient relationship.

Though not restricted to the subject of ethnicity, the selections in this section emphasize the importance of recognizing and understanding cultural differences regarding health-care beliefs. The idea of the subcultural matrix and the views of E. Fuller Torrey serve as a backdrop for considering the subject of cultural variability in a pluralistic society.

A Case of a "Psychotic" Navaho Indian Male

Donald P. Jewell

"One flew east, one flew west, one flew over the cuckoo's nest." So begins Kesey's well-known book, *One Flew Over the Cuckoo's Nest* (1962), and the reader soon begins to question where it is that illness actually lies. In the following article the reader is provided with an opportunity to examine a number of problems relating to a cross-cultural view of mental illness. The subject's condition is misdiagnosed because of the authorities' lack of understanding and early inability to identify his culture. What appears to be ill behavior turns out to represent a normal reaction to circumstances for an individual with Bill's cultural background. There is also an interesting reference to the role of the institution as a conditioning force. We are given the opportunity to view the hospital as an enculturating agent. This, of course, can be seen in both a positive and negative light. Some readers might wish to extend the discussion of misdiagnosing to include the views of such authors as Thomas Szasz. Most notable would be his thoughts in *The Myth of Mental Illness* (1960, 1961). Also, Rosenhan's (1973) "Being Sane in Insane Places" provides some insight into the complexity in diagnosing and labeling illnesses. Readers specifically interested in the Navaho and health should begin with Adair and Deuschle (1970); Lynch (1969), part II, six articles; Primeaux (1977); and Kniep-Hardy and Burkhardt (1977).

Increased psychological and ethnological rapprochement has resulted in a greater understanding of American subgroups and the processes of acculturation. Examples of this integrated approach are to be seen in Barnouw's

Reproduced by permission of the Society for Applied Anthropology from *Human Organization,* Vol. 11, No. 1, 1952. Copyright 1951 by the Society for Applied Anthropology.

☐This study was undertaken during the writer's internship in Clinical Psychology at Patton State Hospital, Patton, California. This writer wishes to gratefully acknowledge the supervision of this study by Mr. William Walcott, Clinical Psychologist and Supervisor of Interns. This study was made possible by the interest and cooperation of Dr. Otto L. Gericke, Superintendent of the hospital.

[1950] study of Chippewa Indian acculturation and, on the individual level, Devereux's [1950] psychotherapy of an alcoholic Sioux.

Sometimes identified as the "culture-personality" orientation, this approach has reached a degree of clarification which justifies consistent designation. It is suggested here that it be defined as ethnopsychological. It is an approach which, as Kluckhohn [1947] has shown, has about a century of development. Ethnopsychology has generally concerned itself with the definition of general normal personality characteristics of other cultures, only occasionally with the neurotic individual, and rarely with the psychotic.

Purpose of This Study

The writer had the opportunity recently to make a rather extensive observation of a Navaho Indian institutionalized as a psychotic in a California state mental hospital. By drawing from the literature of Navaho ethnopsychology and the writer's own experience among the Navaho people, it was hoped that the dynamics of the patient's maladjustment would be revealed. It was also anticipated that some sort of psychotherapy would evolve.

This report is a summary of those endeavors to understand and assist the Navaho patient. Cultural and linguistic obstacles prohibited an ideal approach, but enough was accomplished to permit considerable insight into the patient's behavior. There were features about the patient's personality which would not fit harmoniously with concepts of psychiatric symptomatology derived from European culture, those concepts dealing particularly with the dynamics of the patient's diagnosis of catatonic schizophrenia. The unique characteristics of this individual's personality lead, in fact, to the question as to what extent he should be considered psychotic, and whether that consideration should be viewed from Navaho or Anglo perspective.

During his many interviews with the patient, some of them with the aid of a Navaho interpreter, the writer developed an increasing awareness that to call the patient psychotic was an arbitrary matter. When this Navaho is referred to as psychotic, then, it is merely because he carried such a diagnosis during his 18 months of hospitalization as a mental patient.

Orientation

Considerable literary attention has been given to the general psychological characteristics of Navaho Indians [Henry, 1947; Kluckhohn and Leighton, 1948]. These have related psychological findings to ethnological contexts, and so offer a background against which the atypical Navaho individual may be examined.

On the behavioral level, the Navahos are in many ways unique, not only with respect to white people, but other Indian tribes as well. One of their most characteristic traits may be seen in crisis situations. Kluckhohn and Leighton describe it as a passive resistance, the individual masking his fear by quiet unmovingness, an appearance of stoicism. If forced into action, the response is a mechanical, apparently uncomprehending behavior [Kluckhohn and Leighton, 1948:108].

Another form of withdrawal is often expressed in periods of depression, apparently a morbid preoccupation with health [Kluckhohn and Leighton, 1948:110].

These being salient aspects of the typical Navaho personality, the question now arises as to how those traits would be characterized on the psychotic level. Under prolonged psychological stress, what would develop from the stoicism and moods of morbid preoccupation?

In an endeavor to answer this question a survey was made of those mental hospitals which would most likely be caring for Navaho patients. The Bureau of Indian Affairs' policy is not to concentrate Indian patients, but to subsidize their care in whatever hospital they may have been committed. It is thus possible that a few Navahos may be hospitalized some distance from their reservation area of New Mexico, Utah, and Arizona, and have not been located in this survey. It is felt, however, that a survey of those mental hospitals in the Southwest only would be adequate to show general trends. The findings are summarized in the following table.

Diagnosis	Number	Sex and Age
Psychosis with syphilis of the C.N.C.	2	1f: 47; 1m:31
Psychosis with cerebral arteriosclerosis	1	1f:62
Psychosis due to trauma (organic)	1	1m: 47
Epilepsy	8	6m; 20, 24, 29, 33, 37, 39; 2f: 20,32
Schizophrenia, Simple Type	1	1m: 25
", Mixed Type	1	1f: 26
", Hebephrenic Type	1	1f: 30
", Catatonic Type	7	4m: 26, 28, 28, 36, 3f: 20, 30, 38
Depressed State	1	1f: 37
Manic Depressive Psychosis, Manic Type	1	1m: 42

Legend: f: female; m: male

Summary of survey of Navaho Indian mental patients hospitalized in southwestern United States, excluding mental defectives. (Acknowledgement of the hospitals cooperating in this survey must be regretfully omitted due to the need to protect the identity of the patients.)

Elimination of the organic psychoses leaves one manic, one depressive, and 10 schizophrenics. Of the schizophrenics, seven are catatonic. This is an unusually high incidence of catatonic schizophrenia, and seems to indicate that Navahos are predisposed toward that particular psychosis. This immediately suggests that the above described stoicism has been carried to pathological extremes, and possibly that the stoicism is actually a transient form of catatonia. It was with this problem in mind that the Navaho patient discussed in this report was studied.

The Patient

The patient was a 26-year-old Navaho male. For purposes of anonymity he will be referred to as Bill. He came to the writer's attention through a survey of Indian patients at the hospital. He was the only Navaho of 13 Indian patients scattered throughout the various wards and cottages, and of the 4,000 general patient population.

The outlook for examination and therapy seemed at first quite discouraging. The patient was in a cottage ordinarily reserved for the most regressed patients. Unlike most of the others in this cottage, however, he was not there because of repeated failure of such routine therapies as shock treatment, occupational therapy, etc. It was unusual for a patient in his condition, who had been at the hospital for eight months, not to have received at least electric shock treatment.

A preliminary period was spent at the cottage, observing Bill's behavior. He was very withdrawn. Most of his day was spent in inactive sitting or sleeping. He would rouse himself only for eating or attending to other personal needs. He would assist with floor waxing, dish washing, or other activities the attendants might require of him, but in a perfunctory and apathetic manner. His behavior was not patently catatonic, but certainly suggestive of it.

Most of the attendants reported never having heard Bill speak. A few, however, indicated that Bill would occasionally approach them and, in almost unintelligible English, ask if he could go home.

Shortly thereafter Bill was brought to the writer's office where he was greeted in Navaho. Bill responded in that language, glancing briefly at the writer before returning his gaze to the floor.

This closer inspection of Bill revealed occipital flattening, resulting from the cradle board as a child, and the pierced ear lobes of a conservative Navaho. During this first interview he complained about the close hair cuts he received at the hospital, further evidence that he belonged to the old fashioned, "long hair" conservatives of the reservation.

The interview proceeded very slowly, but gradually a system of communication began to evolve. By utilizing mutually understood Navaho and English words, by means of pantomime, and with the aid of penciled sketches, the system became increasingly refined during the following interviews.

Bill was seen three hours a week for three months. The writer then took an eight months leave of absence from the hospital, during which time he spent several months in Bill's home area near Shiprock, New Mexico.

While in the Shiprock area, the writer endeavored to locate Bill's family to advise them of the patient's circumstances. Bill had previously drawn a map indicating the approximate location of his family's *hogans* (dwellings), but it proved impossible to find them. The *hogans* were located about five miles from the nearest road, and even if a horse and interpreter had been available the chances of locating the specific *hogans* were slight. The situation was complicated by the fact that the family did not have American names and the writer did not know their Navaho names. Missionaries and Bureau of Indian Affairs personnel were consequently given the problem of finding the family but several months elapsed before they were equipped with sufficient information to do so.

Although he could not communicate with Bill's family, the writer succeeded in talking with several Navahos who had known Bill, and in obtaining ecological and further case history material.

Shortly after the writer's return to the hospital a Navaho interpreter was brought in from the Sherman Institute, a large Indian school not far from the hospital. Interviews with the patient through the interpreter corroborated the case history material obtained, and further satisfied the writer in his clinical evaluation of the patient. Both of these areas are separately discussed in the following text.

Case History

The gathering of Bill's history extended over a period of 11 months, and was obtained piecemeal from a variety of sources. In summarizing, however, this material will be integrated for greater coherency.

Bill was born in a part of the reservation noted for being both very conservative and poverty-stricken. Only 50 miles away is the markedly contrasting community of Shiprock, considered to be one of the most acculturated Navaho communities. It is also prospering from recently developed uranium operations in the region.

During his early years Bill saw very little of Shiprock, and was reared in the traditional Navaho way. He was born during an eclipse (it is not known whether of the sun or moon), and was thus destined to take part in a periodic ceremony identified to the writer as the "Breath of Life" sing. The first of this series of ceremonies was held while he was still an infant, the second about six years ago. During the ceremony he inhales the breath of a great deity, and is thus assured of continued good health in the respiratory and vocal organs.

Bill lived with his immediate family until he was six years of age. He had only one younger sister at that time, although the family was later to include seven living siblings. He did not become well acquainted with his family, however, as he was given to his grandfather when he was six years old. The grandfather, a widower, lived several miles deeper into the reservation and required Bill's assistance as a sheep herder.

Bill worked for his grandfather as a sheep herder until he was 17, except for one interruption when, at the age of 15, he spent 50 days in the Shiprock hospital with a back ailment. Bill reports that the old man never talked to him.

At his grandfather's death Bill went to work for the railroad in Colorado. This was cut short by an illness which confined him to the Navaho Medical Center in Fort Defiance, Arizona. The illness was diagnosed as tuberculosis, pulmonary, moderately advanced. He was in the hospital for eight months and was discharged in the summer of 1944.

Bill returned to railroad employment, and worked in Utah, Oregon, and Nebraska. He was always part of Navaho crews and thus never exposed to acculturative influences. His father and a younger brother were also part of these crews.

Bill returned home for a brief visit in 1949, accompanied by his brother and father. He had saved $1,022. Subsequently, he went to Phoenix, Arizona to pick cotton, a job that had been found for him by the employment agency at Shiprock. This was his first trip from home without a family member.

The employment at Phoenix did not last long and in December, 1949, on the advice of an Indian friend he went to Barstow, California seeking railroad employment. At the section camp there his attempt to find work was unsuccessful, and after three days he started by bus back to Phoenix.

On this return trip he stopped for dinner at Colton. A white man he met there promised to obtain railroad employment for him. The stranger said that he required funds for his effort and in some way relieved Bill of his savings which had now dwindled to $725.

Bill returned home penniless, pawned some jewelry, borrowed some money, and returned to Colton to try to find the man who had taken his savings. He also looked for Navahos who might have information about employment. The many hours of waiting around the bus station searching for his man apparently caused suspicion, for he was arrested for vagrancy.

In jail he met some Navahos with whom he went to Barstow after his release. But in Barstow he was still unable to find employment and after six days he was completely out of funds. He started walking toward Phoenix, and was picked up by a man driving a truck. This man gave Bill one day's employment which allowed funds for a return to Barstow and another attempt to find work.

He managed to raise a little money doing odd jobs about the section camp near Barstow, and then returned to San Bernardino on the first lap of his return to Phoenix and home. It occurred to him that if he could get to a hospital, the officials there would send him to a reservation hospital, from whence he would be sent home. This was logical thinking: on the reservations, the hospitals, schools, and trading posts are the major source of assistance in all sorts of troubles.

As this idea occurred to Bill, he noticed a woman dressed in white whom he took to be a nurse. He approached her and endeavored to explain that he was sick, but his endeavors were misinterpreted and he was taken to jail.

At the county jail Bill was apparently mistaken for a Mexican since a Mexican interpreter had tried to interview him. When the interview failed he was transferred to the psychopathic ward. Interviewed by the medical examiner there, he reportedly demonstrated an anguished appearance and repeated, "Me sick." He was diagnosed as Schizophrenia, Catatonic Type, and delivered to the state mental hospital.

Upon admission to the hospital, Bill was first taken to be a Filipino. The psychiatric admission note indicated that he was, ". . . confused, dull, and preoccupied. He has a look of anguish and appears to be hallucinating . . . He repeats, 'I don't know.' " He was diagnosed as Dementia Praecox, which was later specified as Hebephrenic Type.

Several months later the psychiatrist on Bill's cottage tested him for *cerea flexibilitas* (waxy flexibility) and, finding it to be present, altered the diagnosis to Catatonic Type.

Eight months after his admittance he was discovered by the writer.

Psychological Aspects

Concomitant with gathering the case history material presented above, endeavors were made to evaluate the patient's intelligence and personality. The lack of culturally unbiased examining techniques made this extremely difficult.

Bill's performance on the various tests that were administered led to a conclusion that his probable I.Q. was in the vicinity of 80. This had to take into consideration the patient's slowness. At best, a Navaho refuses to be put under pressure of time, and to what extent Bill's slowness was cultural rather than psychotically pathological was a question of primary concern.

Bill's apathetic and withdrawn behavior has already been described. For diagnostic purposes, however, this syndrome is confused by cultural factors. It is common for Navahos, with their morbid fear of hospitals, to demonstrate just such a withdrawal patterning [Kluckhohn and Leighton, 1948:108–109]. It is not known whether or not this would reach a stage of *cerea flexibilitas* or how long this behavior will persist. Accordingly it was concluded that Bill's apparent catatonia should not be accepted as a symptom of schizophrenia until underlying signs of schizophrenic processes could be detected.

During the first interview Bill was given the Draw A Person Test. The figure he drew was indistinct and without facial features and clearly reflected his withdrawal.

On the seventh interview the test was again given. Compared with the earlier attempt, the second drawing clearly reflected an improvement. It probably indicated the therapeutic benefits derived from the extensive individual treatment the patient was receiving.

The second drawing filled the paper, the facial features were portrayed, the arms were extended, and the drawing generally implied those signs which are held to indicate good contact with reality.

Although Bill's second drawing seems to infer considerable personality change, no changes could be observed in his behavior. He continued to appear apathetic and withdrawn. On several occasions he indicated his reluctance to talk because, "me no good this place," pointing to his chest. This suggested the characteristic organ cathexes of schizophrenia. However, the patient's thinking behind this statement was made clear during the later interviews through an interpreter.

Bill was concerned about the fact that he had not completed the second series of the "Breath of Life" ceremony. This matter had gone too long unattended, and he assumed that he must conserve his vocal energies until they could be supplemented by the breath of the deity. He expressed a great need to return home to pursue the ceremony.

In continued endeavor to detect schizophrenic underlay of his apparent catatonia, Bill was given a series of tests, none of which revealed responses normally associated with schizophrenia.

During the early course of the interviews with Bill, although not satisfied that the patient was not psychotic, the writer recommended that the best therapeutic environment for him would be his own home. This recommendation was not acted upon, partly because no one knew where his home was, or how he could be supervised there, but chiefly because he continued to appear catatonic.

Later, as the writer became convinced that the catatonia—if such it could be termed—was not symptomatic of underlying schizophrenia, efforts were renewed to release the patient. The outcome of these endeavors are summarized on the following section.

Outcome

As mentioned earlier, the final interviews with Bill were carried on with the aid of a Navaho interpreter. Bill conversed quite freely with the other

Navahos and expressed gratitude at being able to talk to someone in his own language. The conversations did not add much to the history and understanding previously gained, but did offer an opportunity to inquire for the presence of hallucinations, delusions, and more subtle clues of schizophrenic thinking. Unless Bill's anxiety regarding the uncompleted "Breath of Life" ceremony could be considered bizarre, nothing of significance was elicited.

The interpreter's reaction to the interviews represented their most significant outcome. He was a professional interpreter, with vast experience in interviewing Navaho youths in strange environments. He expressed a strong conviction that Bill's behavior and attitudes were not unusual under the circumstances.

The interpreter communicated his feelings to the superintendent of the Sherman Institute who took an immediate and active interest in the case. After several interviews with Bill, satisfied that he could observe nothing about Bill's behavior which could be considered atypical under the circumstances, the superintendent offered to accept him into the flexible program of the Sherman Institute.

Bill was accordingly released under custody of the superintendent and careful plans were made to assure his adjustment at the school. At first, he was quartered in the school hospital, but allowed to participate in the school's social and recreational activities. He was employed with the animal husbandry and gardening program.

The writer's last visit to the Sherman Institute disclosed that Bill's adjustment had been quite rapid. He had put on weight and after about two weeks announced that he "felt right a home, now."

It had been difficult at first, because in spite of all precautions the students had learned something of Bill's past hospitalization. To the Navahos the hospital symbolizes death, and death is particularly abhorrent to them as they have no clearly structured concepts of an after-life. The students consequently shied away from Bill a little when he arrived, but he has since found acceptance.

He will go back to the reservation in the spring, at the close of the school year, and attend to the unfinished business of the "Breath of Life" ceremony.

Concluding Discussion

In the course of this Navaho's commitment and 18 months of hospitalization, he was routinely examined by several psychiatrists, all of whom concurred with the diagnosis of schizophrenia. Without verbal communication with the patient, diagnosis was necessarily derived from observation of his overt behavior. Diagnosis was apparently confident as the patient was not referred to staff clinic or for psychological testing, the normal procedure with questionable cases.

Most of the psychiatrists' diagnostic observations were based on information received from the attendants of Bill's cottage, who reported the patient's withdrawn and apathetic behavior. Upon closer examination the patient would demonstrate *cerea flexibilitas*. Because of these factors the patient was assumed to be catatonic and hence schizophrenic.

Actually, many of the classic symptoms of catatonia were not present in this patient. He was not markedly stuporous or mute; he was clean in his personal habits and would eat willingly; he tended to doze as he sat rather than stare fixedly into space as does the typical catatonic. The writer, too, examined Bill for *cerea flexibilitas,* but learned later that the patient held grotesque positions because he thought it was expected of him.

With the assumption, however, that the patient's overt behavior could be interpreted as symptomatic of catatonic schizophrenia, it remains to be explained why testing and closer observation did not reveal the underlying ego disintegration which should be expected.

General personality traits of the Navaho people, as briefly reviewed earlier in this paper, could possibly infer a potential for schizophrenic disintegration. Navahos do not have the imaginative activity and the inner control which is so important to adjustment in the Anglo world. The scales are balanced, however, by a defense of rigidity and constriction. In a threatening situation they strive to maintain ego structure by psychic withdrawal.

The few tests that were applicable in examining Bill did not permit a very intensive examination of the dynamics of his withdrawal, but all indications were that he continued to maintain ego strength. He could account for his acts rationally, he performed very well with conceptualization, he maintained orientation for time and place, and could hold in mind simultaneously various aspects of situations or problems. His visuo-motor performance exhibited no signs of distorted perspective. Many of his expressions could be considered naive, but hardly bizarre.

The apparent incongruity between the patient's overt behavior and underlying personality dynamics, although not fully understood psychologically, should not be considered as psychotic manifestation. Culturally derived, it can probably be explained as a defense mechanism characterized by an extreme and sustained withdrawal.

To what extent Bill's case may be typical of other Navaho patients diagnosed as catatonic schizophrenia cannot, of course, be proposed. It would be necessary to know if those patients were similarly diagnosed on the basis of overt behavior alone.

It is also unknown to what degree Bill may personify on-reservation Navaho youth. Superficially at least, his history appears quite typical. His lack of school, his years as a sheep herder for his grandfather, his attack of tuberculosis, and his railroad employment, are circumstances and events common to many Navahos. His grandfather's apparent lack of affection implies an almost feral existence for the growing boy, but even this situation is not unusual. It is, in fact, difficult to discern some way in which this patient could be atypical as evaluated against his cultural background. Except for his possible low intelligence, he appears to represent a typical Navaho youth, a fact heavy with implication when his 18 months of hospitalization as a mental patient is considered.

The previously cited survey of hospitalized Navaho mental patients shows an amazingly small percentage of the total Navaho population (which is about 65,000). This is probably because few Navahos are currently coming in very close contact with Anglo structure.

Of the catatonic schizophrenics, it would be of value to know more about the details of their admission. If they were referred from the reservation it probably meant that they were considered psychotic within the Navaho milieu; if, on the other hand, they were referred by agencies off the reservation (as was Bill), it would imply an evaluation derived from Anglo perspective. This will become a more poignant problem with increasing off-reservation movement of the Navaho people.

In addition to what this study may infer with respect to the Navaho Indians, it is hoped also that it may illustrate the need to consider the influence of cultural environment in any study of individual personality. The psychiatric approach usually concerns itself with the abnormal personality, and evaluates the individual according to concepts of what constitutes the normal personality. Too often these concepts are preconceived and stereotyped, giving very little consideration to the individual's cultural frame of reference. This factor naturally varies in proportion to the degree of the individual's acculturation.

The cultural factor seems to be particularly important in reconciling overt behavior with covert personality dynamics. This is often a difficult reconciliation even with patients of the general American cultural patterning, and becomes increasingly more difficult the farther removed the individual is from acculturation.

The need to consider emotional maladjustment with respect to cultural factors has long been recognized. It has, however, been somewhat of an academic acknowledgement which demands greater practical application on the clinical level.

Orientals Are Stoic

André M. Tao-Kim-Hai

In this article the author presents his view of what proper behavior should be for both himself and staff in a hospital setting. Some factors that helped shape his attitudes toward medicine are also presented. On a broader level the article deals with the basic issue of the importance of understanding different cultural behavior in the provision of services to different peoples. Discussion can be extended to the subject of stereotyping. The relevance of stereotyping is immediately apparent from the title of the piece. It is emphasized throughout the article with such examples as the staff's reference to the patient's food preferences, religion, pain, and nationality. Even well-intended people can unknowingly insult others. In an intercultural encounter it can be expected that insults will be greater in both quantity and intensity. This article also affords a nice opportunity to discuss the difference between generalizing about people and stereotyping them. We should, in fact, be reminded of this distinction in the reading of a number of the other articles presented in this collection. The processes of generalizing and stereotyping can be seen to have both positive and negative features with regard to the assimilating and sorting of information.

The most peaceful moments of my first stay in an American hospital came just after my operation. Bandaged, half doped, faintly aching, I lay flat on my back between smooth, clean sheets and hazily reflected that nothing is more annoying than a fresh incision with fresh stitches in one's abdomen except, of course, two fresh incisions with fresh stitches in one's abdomen. The thought, for some reason, made me chuckle, and the chuckle made me more than intellectually aware of the incisions—the result of that morning's operation for double hernia. But even pain did not quite touch me, and in the euphoria of ether intoxication I felt at one with the whole world, whose center for me was this New York hospital. I did not expect then that only a few days later I would commit there the most unpardonable sin for an Oriental (I am Vietnamese)—that of losing face through one's own bad behavior. But lose face I did, and to this day I wonder whether my shame was caused by the hypersensitivity of an ethnic minority group reduced to one specimen, or by my secret desire not to be treated as a foreigner in my wife's native land, or by my old, ill-suppressed Oriental prejudice against being openly pushed around by women, or simply by the fact that I had never been a hospital patient before and was hopelessly unprepared for the efficient, cold-blooded, and frequently, it seemed, nonsensical routines that are so familiar and so irritating to most convalescents. I still don't know, in short, whether my behavior was a display of just indignation or a childish tantrum.

I had a nurse, of course, after my operation—a woman whose white hair was ineffectually covered by a ridiculously small white bonnet, and who fluttered around my little private room with concentrated energy and, I am sure, efficiency. Despite a few minor differences, she reminded me of a Sister of Charity whom I had known twenty-eight years earlier in the Vietnamese town of Soctrang. My brother and I referred to this nun between ourselves as the *ange de charité*—a cliché we employed with no hint of irony because we knew she worked without salary and because the two huge, triangular white wings of her coif flapped over her shoulders angelically whenever she moved. On her flat chest she wore a black wooden cross with a worn metal Christ on it, and from her belt swung a long, heavy rosary. She was gentle and cheerful, as we imagined angels to be, although she sang in a French strongly tinged with a Marseille accent, which we somehow felt was not the true tone of angels. Did my New York nurse speak French? I was too weak in the hours following the operation to find out, and too weak even to try to identify her accent, which might have been that of Brooklyn. She was plump and there was none of the selfless gentleness of the nun about her. But a nurse is a nurse, I told myself, and therefore an angel. With this reassuring conclusion, I closed my eyes and sank back into the fog of ether, thinking about how poorly my childhood had prepared me for modern medical care.

I was born in a small village on the banks of a canal, among the rich rice fields of South Vietnam. According to local standards, my father was a wealthy man, for he owned over a hundred and twenty hectares of rice fields, and our family lived in an enclosure containing a tile-roofed master house and several thatch-roofed outbuildings for farm hands, domestic servants, water buffaloes, and agricultural implements. This was an inviting world for a young boy, and I enjoyed it in an active, almost headlong fashion, collecting a vast assortment of cuts and bumps along the way. Whenever I hurt myself I would cry to get my mother's attention. She would come at once to scold not me but the object that hurt me, and then would rub my bruise or wash my cut with rain water, as the case might be (we had no clinic in our village, and no arnica or mercurochrome in our household), and tell me to forget about it. Then she would carry me across the yard to my favorite old water buffalo, and I would have an extra ride on his back all around our compound, to inspect the sparrow nests under the eaves of our red tile roof, to pass in review the dwarf coconut palms along the wide ditches where our barges were moored, or to pick hibiscus flowers from the hedge that separated our compound from the communal canal. Or, if it was raining, my mother would lay me in a hammock and swing it gently with one foot while she sat in a wicker chair beside me and read me passages from ancient stories that were full of heroes who suffered with equanimity—including a general who had a broken arrowhead removed from one arm and the wound cleansed with rice alcohol while playing Chinese chess with his free hand.

My older brother was, in his small way, another example to me. If he had a toothache, he would hold a spoonful of rice alcohol in his mouth—a Vietnamese remedy based on the principle of fighting pain with fire—without whimpering. He would even challenge me, in sign language, to one of the innumerable games Vietnamese children have played for generations, and leering at me derisively over his mouthful of fire, beat me, no matter what the game. The fact that he was incapable of comment or small talk only added to his importance.

After my father's death, in 1910, my education fell temporarily to my mother and to one or another of her younger brothers. Maternal Uncle Number Three was a true scholar, whose philosophy was based on a mingling of native tradition, Taoism, Confucianism, and Buddhism. Along with my letters, he taught me our fundamental Vietnamese beliefs—among them the concept of man's three souls. The Superior Man, he often told me, pays little attention to his vegetative soul, restrains his animal soul under all circumstances, and strives to develop his spiritual soul as much as possible, in order to distinguish himself from cabbages, eggplants, coconut palms, cats, dogs, pigs, and water buffaloes. This uncle had a vegetative soul plagued by a number of minor tropical diseases—malaria and various skin eruptions—but he sternly refused to take notice of its sufferings. He classified his internal troubles into two categories—those caused by an excess of internal heat, to be treated with rhinoceros horn, and those caused by a deficiency of internal heat, to be treated with ginger. The first medicine is prepared by patiently rubbing a rhinoceros horn—from which the rhinoceros has been detached, of course—across the rough inner surface of an earthenware bowl containing cold water. When the water becomes milky, you drink it until your fever subsides. The second remedy is no more than a hot infusion of fresh ginger sweetened with rock sugar. You drink it until you feel warmer, which is very soon. My uncle had no quarrel with other local medicinal products, such as deer antler, dried bumblebees, tiger bones, ginseng, orange peel, and mint, but he saw no reason to complicate his life with them when he had a rhinoceros horn stored in a tin box and ginger growing in his own yard. As for surgical operations, he considered them sins against filial piety. Were they not mutilations of one's body, which was a precious gift from one's parents and not to be tampered with under any circumstances?

The concessions he did make to illness were rare and grudging. He bore his skin diseases without even scratching. He would drink rhinoceros-horn water and bathe himself with it from time to time, although he expected no rapid results. My mother used to bathe our mangy dogs in creosote diluted with water, and she urged my uncle to try the same cure for his skin troubles. "Of course, it must hurt a little," she said, "but it does the dogs a lot of good. You, Little Brother, have the same vegetative soul that dogs have, so why don't you try it?"

Little Brother resented this reminder of the least of his three souls. He was also an adult Vietnamese and only human, and was therefore suspicious of the creosote because it came in a bottle with a French label. But to prove to his elder sister that he did not shy away from pain he bathed himself once or twice with her dog medicine, proving simultaneously that it did not hasten the purging of his blood.

Malaria made him more cooperative with his vegetative soul. In some uncanny fashion, he knew when he was about to have a malarial seizure, and he would prepare his mat and his concoctions beforehand. As soon as he started to feel the chill, he would drink the ginger, lie down on his mat, and shake lamentably. After a time, the chill would pass, and there would be a little lull. Then the fever would seize him, and he would drink rhinoceros-horn water and perspire profusely for a while—a long while, it seemed to me. When the fever subsided he would sit up, give me a quizzical smile, half of apology and half of pride, and prepare himself a pot of Chinese tea while smoking one of the conical cigarettes he made out of black Vietnamese tobacco and the same coarse white paper I made kites with.

When I went off to a boarding school run by a group of Christian Brothers, I encountered another way of dealing with physical miseries. The *très cher Frère Infirmier* in charge of the school's infirmary was a fat man with a big red beard, and big blue eyes made bigger by thick lenses, who spoke French and Vietnamese with a Breton accent and who believed in Western medicine and Christian purgatory. Armed with a bottle of iodine and an applicator, he could make the smallest wound feel like a major abscess, and he classified our cuts and bruises as deserving, according to their size, one hundred days, two hundred days, or three hundred days of deliverance from purgatory, provided the patient offered his pain as a sacrifice to the Almighty and did not cry or whimper. Any rise in body temperature—checked with the *cher Frère's* oral thermometer—was followed by the administration of castor oil. The patients stood at attention in a row, and the *Frère Infirmier,* a huge bottle of castor oil in one hand and a teaspoon in the other, passed slowly down the line like a fatherly colonel, explaining to neophytes that they would receive three spoonfuls of the stuff, each worth one hundred days' remission from purgatory if the medicine was bravely offered to God. Sometimes a spoonful of castor oil, through no fault of the recipient, refused to stay down. The *Infirmier* would continue his distribution as though nothing unusual had happened, but he would keep the unfortunate boy after the others had been dismissed, to console him for his medicinal and spiritual loss.

As I lay now on my hard hospital bed and tried to remember the exact appearance of the *Infirmier's* face, my half-closed eyes were struck by a strong electric light switched on over my head. Another face, tanned and kind, seemed to be floating above me. I made an effort to focus on it, and recognized it as that of my surgeon. Behind him was a group of internes.

"How're you doing?" the surgeon asked me in a gentle voice.

"I'm doing all right, Doctor," I answered.

He uncovered me by pulling down the sheet and pulling up my hospital gown. My belly was warm, his fingers were cold, and at the best of times I am ticklish. The result was that I winced, and my face must have shown an inexplicable hilarity. The internes converged on me, watching me seriously. The cold fingers poked; I wiggled and giggled involuntarily. The soft voice asked "Does it hurt?" I answered "No," partly because my flesh was still numb and partly to reassure him that my wiggling was not due to pain. The internes looked on with intense gravity, from which I surmised that I was a rare sort of hospital patient, to be observed with special attention. The examination went on like this for some time, until at last the surgeon covered me again and departed with his solemn retinue.

I had full confidence in my surgeon and liked him, although many of our earlier encounters had been marked by this same kind of foolish misunderstanding. I must admit that our first meeting, in 1948, I had disliked him. I had joined the United Nations staff in New York in 1946. Two years later, at the conclusion of a routine physical examination—the U.N. had its own clinic and its own staff of doctors giving regular physical checkups to all members of its Secretariat—a charming French-speaking woman doctor told me that she wanted me to see the specialist on hernia. "Just to make sure, you know," she added reassuringly. That was how I met my surgeon. He was nine years younger then, still under thirty, and perhaps a little less gentle than he is now. I was far from patient with him, not because of my youth, since I was already forty-three, but because I spoke little English and he knew no French. When he asked me to uncover my middle, I started to explain to him in my slow English that I had never noticed anything wrong.

He cut me short with an impatient "Yes, but—" and plunged a long, firm finger into me. "Cough!" he commanded. I didn't feel like coughing, but I tried to oblige. "Louder!" he snapped. I did my best. He poked harder, and I began to giggle.

"There's nothing to laugh about," he said, and my blood pressure rose several points. After all, I was much older than he (in Vietnam he would have had to call me *ông,* which literally means "grandfather"), and we were of equal rank in the U.N. But my limited English prevented me from making a properly acid retort.

After a few more pokes, the doctor straightened up and asked, "How long have you had this double hernia?"

His tone was an accusation, as if I had known of the hernia all along and had willfully concealed it on my medical questionnaire. But again my English wouldn't come, and I could only answer him with a phrase I had learned from comic strips—"I dunno."

"Why don't you know?" he fired at me.

Nobody had asked me such a question since the days when I was a *soldat de deuxième classe* in the French Army. Sensing my rising temper at last, he tried to make me feel at ease. "You must be a real tough guy," he said.

This was no better. I had heard the epithet "tough guy," but I had always translated it to myself as *"mauvais garçon."* Again he must have seen my anger and incomprehension, because he modified his statement. "You don't pay much attention to minor pains, do you?"

After that, we got along better. He told me that there was no hurry about an operation, but I must come to him for an examination at least once a year. So for the next seven years I dutifully reported to his office, where he would poke and I would jump, and the operation would again be postponed, because, he told me, it was only the beginnings of a hernia. Last year, however, I informed him of my decision to retire from the U.N. and move to Hawaii, and he said that the time had come for surgery. I was not getting any younger, he told me, and I might not find such good hospital facilities away from New York. My wife voted with the doctor, and I reluctantly agreed. I did not then know what was in store for me.

One afternoon late last winter, I presented myself at the hospital, where my wife and I waited patiently and endlessly for a nurse in the admitting office to grant me an audience. At last she produced questionnaires and began to ask me a series of questions that reminded me of my first encounter with the Gestapo, in Marseille in 1943. My difficulties started with the very first questions: "What's your first name? What's your last name?"

Being intellectually scrupulous, I wanted clarification on what she meant by first and last. "First is what comes first. Last is what comes last," the bureaucrat-nurse said with infinite weariness.

My trouble was that we tradition-bound Vietnamese have been more reluctant than the Chinese to Westernize our way of writing our names, even when we live in a Western country, by reversing our usual order of family name first and given name last. My Vietnamese name is Tao-Kim-Hai, the family name, Tao, coming first. But when I became a French citizen in 1929, I was required by law to add a Western given name in front of my old name. Thus my full name, André Marie Tao-Kim-Hai, now contains two first names first, then my family name, and then two first names *last.* After much explanation on my part and bored impatience on the nurse's part, my names were written down, but I reduced the name Marie to the initial M, in order to avoid confusing the nurse as to my sex.

"Country of birth?"

This was easy, or so I thought, and I answered without hesitation, "Vietnam."

The young lady held her pen poised but refused to write. "Never heard of it," she said, as if I had just invented a new country.

Vietnam is not a new country. Its first king is thought to have died in the year 2879 B.C. Perhaps an American lady, even a professional and educated lady, cannot be expected to know Vietnamese ancient history, because the name of the country has changed several times. But how about Bao-Dai, Ho Chi Minh, Ngo Dinh Diêm, Saigon, Hanoi, and Diên-Biên-Phu?

"Is it in China?" the nurse asked.

Now, that is a question calculated to drive any Vietnamese wild. The Vietnamese respect China as the seat of a very honorable culture, but they cannot forget the thousand years of war between China and Vietnam. Historically, ethnically, geographically, and politically the lady was wrong, but I drew a deep breath and held my temper. It took a long time, but eventually the nurse passed me, not *cum laude,* and turned me over to a male attendant, who turned me over to a cashier to pay in advance for private nurses. Finally, I was allowed to go to my room.

The room was small but comfortable and well located, with a balcony and a view over the city. When my sister-in-law was in the Soctrang hospital in 1929, she had a whole suite to herself on the ground floor, surrounded by a hedge of blooming hibiscus. Here in New York there was no blooming hibiscus but a hedge of dirty buildings, with a few skyscrapers in the background. Nevertheless, my room cost at least twenty times as much as the suite in the Soctrang hospital and at least twice as much as the room I had occupied in the Waldorf-Astoria in 1945. At that price, I decided, I could expect good service, some comfort, and a certain measure of privacy. I changed my business suit for pajamas and a robe, said goodbye to my wife, and eased myself comfortably into the one armchair and started to read.

The door opened suddenly and a voice boomed "Hi, André!" It was a Catholic priest, plump and jovial, complete with prayer book and stole. "How about Confession and Communion?"

I had told the admitting nurse expressly that although I was a Catholic, I did not want a priest, but here he was. He seemed a bit disappointed when I told him that it was not to be a serious operation, that I expected to survive, and that, anyway, I did not take death as seriously as many other Christians do. I tried to talk religion with him, but he did not seem particularly interested, and left after a few minutes.

Almost immediately, another man came in. He pointed an accusing finger at me and said with what I took to be a Middle European accent, "You have tuberculosis. You have venereal disease. You have—" There was not the slightest interrogative inflection in his voice.

"Who are you?" I interrupted.

"The anesthetist," he answered.

"Parlez-vous français?"

"Oui," he said, and resumed *"Vous avez la tuberculose. Vous avez des maladies vénériennes. Vous avez—"* as affirmatively as ever.

During the first afternoon in the hospital, many other unexpected and unknown visitors came in, always without knocking, without introducing themselves, and without stating their business—except for the man who came to rent me a television set. I was both annoyed and amused, assuming, rightly or wrongly, that all this was the normal routine of an American hospital.

There is nothing to report about the next morning, except that a man came in to prepare me for the operation and a nurse popped in to give me a hypodermic, the significance of which I did not realize until I woke in the afternoon and discovered the incisions in my abdomen.

That evening, when I was fast asleep, somebody again turned on the light above my head. I looked at my watch and found that it was a few minutes after ten. Two young male internes and a young woman interne were sitting in chairs tilted back against the wall and looking at me. I recognized them as having been in the group that had visited me with the surgeon that afternoon. They smiled at me and I smiled back at them. We talked. One interne said that he had been surprised when I giggled during the surgeon's examination in the afternoon. "Orientals are stoic," he stated sententiously.

I decided that by "stoic" he meant tough, in the way my surgeon meant it when he said I was a tough guy, and I took it to be a compliment. But I wondered about "Orientals" and asked him for his interpretation of the word.

"Chinese, of course," he said.

I asked him if he thought the whole Orient—whatever geographical limits he gave to that word—was peopled by Chinese. To my astonishment, he said that he took it for granted that I was Chinese, and anyway, all yellow people were the same. I asked him if he thought all white people were the same. I saw that he was embarrassed, and I was aware that it was I who was embarrassing him. I tried to put him at ease—as if I were a host in this room, and not a man who had just had an operation and was hoping to be allowed to sleep—with the story of my adventure with some Canadian broadcasters.

A few years back, I told the interne, I had received a telephone call from Ottawa inviting me to go there as the guest of the Canadian Radiodiffusion and read a few pages of French text for a film sound track.

"Don't any of you in Canada speak French any more?" I asked.

"Yes, but we want somebody from the Orient to do it."

"What's the text?" I asked.

But it was a long-distance call, and they didn't want to go into details. I was glad to visit Canada at somebody else's expense and get paid for it besides. I flew to Ottawa, had an excellent French lunch, and was shown the film, which was about India, and I read their text aloud into a microphone. I read it in my own French accent, which had grown out of twenty-two years' residence in France, out of my study of French diction, and out of several years spent as an habitué of the Club du Faubourg, where Parisian orators discuss everything from Paul Valéry to colonialism. When I finished my recording, despair was on the faces of my Canadian hosts. I sensed that I was a complete failure, and said I was sorry.

A French-Canadian said, *"Mais c'est de la Comédie-Française!* Couldn't you read French with an Oriental accent?"

"Which Oriental accent?" I replied. I explained that I did not know any of the dozens of languages spoken in India, any more than I knew Japanese or Chinese or Laotian or Cambodian or Malay or Siamese or Burmese, or whatever languages they speak in Afghanistan, Tibet, and Inner and Outer Mongolia. All I knew was Vietnamese, and my Vietnamese friends had told me that I spoke Vietnamese with an American accent, whatever that might be.

At the end of this story, the internes dropped the subject of race and tackled me on Oriental religions. I had a hard time explaining to them that neither Taoism nor Confucianism nor Buddhism is a religion in the Western sense of the word. They shrugged, and one of them said, "Tell us about Oriental food." But here again I had to say that I could find no common denominator for a Japanese *sukiyaki,* a Korean *pulgogi,* a Indonesian *nasi goreng,* a Siamese *mee kraub,* and an Indian curry. And so they left. They had not been unkind, but I had a feeling that they were disappointed by my inability to give them any general ideas and unhappy because they were no longer sure of the general ideas they had had.

My real troubles started the next morning. Around five, a nurse came into my room and propped both doors wide open. I had never been awakened so early in my life except once in Oxford, where an English maid woke me before dawn to serve me early-morning tea. Here, in the New York hospital, my nurse served me an early-morning thermometer, without asking my consent or cooperation. I resolved to be patient, however, and tried, unsuccessfully, to go back to sleep. Around seven o'clock, I thought it was late enough to ask for a special favor, and I rang. Ten minutes later, a nurse in her late twenties whom I had never seen before came in. Before I had time to ask her please to bring me a cup of coffee or anything hot, and kindly to close the door when leaving, she shouted at me, "Whatsa matta, boy?"

I was nonplussed by the rudeness of her tone and her vocabulary, but I managed to lodge my double request. "Breakfast at eight-thirty," she snapped, and went out immediately—without closing the door.

She went out so fast that I had no time to formulate an appropriate reply. The word "boy" had stung me more than the nurse's tone and manner. I did remember that before my American father-in-law died, my mother-in-law used to explain his occasional absence from their cottage in Florida by saying "He must be out bowling with the boys"—by which she meant a group of gentlemen who were in their seventies. But I also could not forget my personal knowledge that the French in their colonies use the word "boy" to mean "servant." They even call a female servant a "boyesse." Suddenly angry, I wanted to ring for the nurse again and explain all this to her, but then I remembered my conversation with the internes and decided to live up to their high opinion of the stoicism of Orientals.

Around eight-thirty, several nurses invaded my room, all shockingly healthy and cheerful, and chattering like parakeets. I heard a jumble of overlapping greetings and questions, such as "Hi, boy!" "How do you feel this morning, sweetie?" "He looks wonderful!" "Where did you get this beautiful silk robe?" "Here's your breakfast." "Don't you like coffee? You prefer Chinese tea?" and "Soft-boiled eggs—no chop suey here!" I was confused, and I couldn't sort out the questions fast enough to answer any of them. Then a couple of male attendants walked into the crowded room, one of them shouting at me in Chinese, *"Ni hau ma? Ni hau pu hau?"* When I did not answer, he added, "You Chinese? What dialect you speak? . . . No Chinese? Jap?" The other attendant turned on the television, which responded with a blurred image and a blare of sound.

Suddenly my surgeon came in and the nurses and attendants became silent at once and filed out of the room. Gently he examined me. When he was through, he asked, "How do you feel?"

"Physically, as good as possible," I answered. "Mentally, not so good."

"Why?"

I explained to him that I had the impression of being a rare animal in a zoo. In fact, I added, this was worse than a zoo, because in a zoo the public is not supposed to excite the animals. The surgeon tried to cheer me up, telling me that there was a lack of privacy and social amenities in almost all hospitals. He went as far as to explain the psychology of nurses and hospital workers, who tend to become insensitive because they, fully clothed and able-bodied, habitually deal with more or less helpless patients who are stripped of their business suits and their vertical dignity.

This reasoning cheered me slightly, and I pondered over it later, when a nurse came to wash me. Her method was without consideration or kindness but efficient and thorough. No wonder nurses have a superiority complex, I reasoned as she rubbed my back, and no wonder I feel inferior, being babied like this. I quoted Spinoza to myself. "An emotion which is a passion ceases to be a passion as soon as we form a clear and distinct idea thereof."

But matters did not improve in the succeeding days. I was a "boy," I was a dumb Oriental. I was addressed in what sounded like pidgin English. I heard allusions to what the hospital staff thought of as Oriental ways and Oriental foods. Even my American wife was not spared rudeness, vexation, and humiliation. Although she had an M.A. in Greek before many of the nurses were born, these young ladies took it for granted that the wife of such a strange man could not amount to much. Several times I nearly exploded, but my wife, who can always guess my mood with accuracy, succeeded in calming me. I tried to remember my Maternal Uncle Number Three's teaching about the Superior Man. It was not my job, I told myself, to enlighten the hospital staff about world tolerance or the sensitiveness of one normal Oriental. My job was to restrain my animal, emotional soul and allow my physical, vegetative soul the best possible chance to heal my two incisions.

The moment of drama came unexpectedly. Its protagonist—the external, visible, and immediate cause—was a nurse, but as I think back on it, I realize she was no protagonist at all but only the last straw. Try as I may, I cannot even recall exactly what I said to her, or why I said it. I only remember her reply. "*I* am the supervisor," she said. "*I* am the head nurse here. *I* know my work and I know people like you!"

Jumping hastily and unnecessarily out of bed and fumbling with the telephone, I shouted to the operator, "I want my surgeon! I want him immediately!" Then I raved confusedly, incoherently, childishly, ridiculously. I don't remember most of what I said; I remember only that the hand grasping the telephone shook and that my legs would barely hold me up. The nurse herself did not seem to trust her eyes; it must have been a scene she was not used to. I shouted at her, "I am a patient! I'm not a nurse! I'm not under your supervision!"

The surgeon came, and I poured out to him all my bitterness as a patient in general and as an Oriental patient in particular. In a loud, shrill tone I told him that a hospital should take care not only of the physical welfare of its patients but of their mental welfare as well, and that nurses should treat their patients as human beings, whatever their race, sex, religion, and state of health. In the middle of my ravings, I again saw the nurse staring at me, her eyes wide open, her mouth slightly ajar, and her arms hanging foolishly down. "If you have nothing to do, get out of here!" I shouted at her. "Get out of here!"

Abruptly, my excitation and exhilaration subsided, and I felt ashamed of myself. I was also angry—angry with myself, with all the nurses on my floor, with the whole hospital, with the entire United States of America, and with all the human stupidity in the world. The surgeon had listened to me in silence. When I had calmed down, he quietly asked me, "Would you like to change floors?"

His gentle suggestion made my anger flare up again, and I cried out, louder than necessary, that I would not retreat. Suddenly finding myself in command of the English language, I said that I wanted to stand my ground and fight it out, to shout back at those who shouted at me, to be sarcastic when I met sarcasm, and to make myself either respected or hated as a patient and as an Oriental.

Gently the doctor eased himself out, and my wife came in. She told me that I had been wrong. I knew she was right, but I shouted at her, too, angrier than ever. She left. I was alone for a long, long time. A feeling of shame overcame me—only shame, nothing more.

Someone knocked at my door—a thing I wasn't used to any more—and I managed a "Come in." A young nurse with red hair appeared with a tray. "Your dinner, sir," she said without any emphasis. It was the natural thing for her to say, but I felt embarrassed, as if I were being shown a special treatment that I did not deserve. Guardedly I smiled at her and thanked her. I readied myself for dinner, cooperating eagerly as she set up the collapsible table. I pointed out to her a box of liqueur chocolates from Holland and invited her to help herself. She did so with grace. I asked her if she spoke French, and—miracle!—she did. She spoke it with a Canadian accent, but it was French all the same. I felt like kissing her then and there, just as I had felt like kissing the first girl I saw in the Free Zone of France after I left Frontstalag 152 in the Occupied Zone, in 1941. In both cases, however, I did not feel that I had won a battle.

From that day on, all the nurses I encountered treated me decently, finishing all their sentences with "sir"—even their supervisor, who reappeared discreetly the next day. I knew that I had behaved badly, that I had not been even faintly civilized, and that I had reacted in sheer animal passion. But I did not know how to apologize to the head nurse without embarrassing her. To make up for my inability to formulate an adequate apology, I cooperated with all the nurses and attendants beyond the call of a patient's duty. I took my own temperature. I took my own bath, sitting on the edge of the tub in my bathroom. I ate all my breakfast, although the eggs were never the way I liked them and the coffee was too American and too weak. I shared my gifts of candy and cookies with all the nurses. My guilt, nevertheless, lingered on, and I wondered if the head nurse now tolerated me as a spoiled and incurably ill-bred boy beyond redemption, whether she hated me or possibly even admired me for my outburst, whether future patients in this hospital would profit or suffer from my wild explosion, and whether Orientals would be received here from now on with special attentions or would not be admitted at all. These were some of the questions I was left with as a result of my first experience in a hospital, and I am afraid that I will not find satisfactory answers to them even after my scars fade and are forgotten.

Voodoo Illness in the Black Population

Loudell F. Snow

There are very few articles that focus primarily on perceptions of "scientific" medical services within the black community. This selection by Loudell Snow allows for discussion of several important points. (While Snow's focus is on certain segments of the population and their particular folk medical beliefs, there is also the important recognition that scientific medicine is utilized as well.) This point is often under-emphasized in researchers' fascination with practices that are "different." Snow, on the other hand, stresses the importance of examining the specific interaction between physician and client in order to determine why modern scientific medicine is perceived as unsatisfying. The point is made that both systems leave something to be desired. It is suggested that an examination not only of medical systems but also of people's self-image and world view might provide some answers. The author also provides a view of the collaboration between scientific and folk medical practitioners that is different from the traditional approach espoused in the anthropological literature. Readers interested in the state of health in the black community and the available services might begin with such works as those by Seham (1973); Parker and Kleiner (1966); Snow (1977); and Norman (1969), especially the chapter by Elam entitled, "What Does the Ghetto Want From Medicine?" Of equal importance in Norman's book is the statement that, economically and socially, "the Ghetto is not the homogeneous neighborhood that many think it to be." The "myth of the melting pot," both at the inter- and intracultural levels, becomes a relevant topic for discussion at this point. Harrison and Harrison (1971) also present information on the "Black Experience and White Health Care" through a view of tradition and history as well as through an examination of the response of blacks to available health-care services. Another work, though not as readily available, is that by Harrison (1967), which describes the health aspect of the lives of blacks living in Washington, D.C. The field of medical geography provides yet another perspective in an analysis of the distribution of medical services. For an introduction to the medical-geography perspective see Shannon and Dever (1974).

In the United States belief in witchcraft in the etiology of disease has been reported among a number of groups, including black Americans. It indicates a medical belief system which parallels that of modern scientific medicine, and individuals can and do use both. Informants often state that doctors do not *understand* witchcraft and cannot cure its effects. They may go on to say that the more a bewitched person goes to a doctor the worse the illness will become. This assures that there will be individuals with special powers in the community to whom the victim can turn for help. Acceptance of this premise serves healers of both persuasions: the root doctor whose livelihood depends on the belief that doctors cannot deal with witchcraft *and* the health professional who rationalizes that patients will not come in for treatment if they feel that their illness is supernatural in origin. In actual fact this is not what occurs: the majority of people who believe that their health problem is the result of evil magic—or who come to believe so—go to a doctor first. All too often this encounter is unsatisfactory in some way and we need to establish how and why—we need to know what the patient was told. Once the patient moves out of the professional into the folk system, of course, this is impossible to determine.

It is imperative, therefore, that the physician *know* about witchcraft beliefs and what symptoms are most likely to be interpreted as indicative of such activity, to preclude (a) incorrectly diagnosing an individual as mentally ill, (b) giving advice which frightens of confuses a patient into thinking an illness *is* "unnatural" in origin, or (c) inaugurating symptomatic treatment which does not reach the underlying stress. Clearly this is an area where cooperation between social scientist and medical scientist can be useful.

Terms used for witchcraft include *voodoo, a fix, a hex,* and *working roots.* An analysis of the ethnographic literature and the growing number of reports of such illnesses in medical journals is revealing as to who hexes whom, how, and why. The most common scenario involves a triangular social relationship in which two people are vying for control of a third. They are in the victim's immediate social group, moreover—friends or lovers, husbands or wives, parents, in-laws, siblings, or children. Those people from whom you expect support are also those who may be doing things to manipulate your behavior.

Why? — To attract a person to you, to prevent a loved one from leaving you, to remove a rival from the scene. Poor self-image and low self-esteem are implicit, the feeling that one is so unlovable, so weak, so without personal resources that magical means must be employed to get what you want and to keep it.

Given the personnel and the motive, how is it done? — Most commonly by "poison," a substance administered in the victim's food or drink. This too underscores the closeness of the relationships involved: not everyone has access to your food. There is resultant anxiety over eating: any bit of food, any sip of coffee, any swallow of beer may contain an ingredient aimed at robbing the individual of free will. The fact that there *are* people from whom you can buy the magical ingredients makes the fear concrete. Here is an advertisement from a Florida newspaper:

You don't have to go out of town to get what you want—I have what you want and need right here—I have traveled all the way to Africa and Haiti to get special roots that will control anything—Roots that will make a man or woman do what you want them to do.

The symptoms which may be attributed to such manipulation can be divided into two broad categories, behavioral and gastrointestinal. Any actions seen as being "crazy" are questionable, and most reports in the clinical literature are in psychiatric journals. There is the added fear that a hexed individual may not even realize that he or she is behaving strangely and therefore not know where to seek help:

"Well, I've heard people . . . could put stuff in your food, or they could come to your house and put something down for you. Yeah, I hear talk of it. Yeah, I hear about a few people, someone have control of 'em. They *do* act rather peculiar, they doesn't act normal or sensible. Well, for instance I've heard of men fixin' their wives and wives fixin' their husbands, stuff like that, you know. Well, if this *happens* to you, they say you would be the last person to suspect; anyone could tell you and you wouldn't believe it. I don't know why, but I hate the thought of a person takin' control of you if they want to" (Snow, 1974).

Gastrointestinal symptoms in this context are understandable because of the emphasis on something being introduced into the food or drink: loss of appetite, food that doesn't taste right, a bad taste in the mouth, nausea and vomiting, pain in the stomach, diarrhea or unexplained weight loss may be viewed with unease until they are explained. Chronicity or uniqueness of symptoms may also contribute to the fear that all is not well—an illness that is not responding to treatment may eventually be seen as the result of witchcraft, or a symptom seen as being very peculiar may be viewed as "unnatural" at the outset. Here are some examples of how a constellation of events comes to be seen as witchcraft, keeping in mind a personal conflict, a presumed motive, an opportunity, and a health problem. The first four are from my own data:

Case 1. Lansing, Michigan. A middle-aged man develops a rash "only where it shows," that is, on his hands, face, and neck. He goes to a physician, who tells him that it is not contagious and gives him a prescription for some ointment. Two weeks later the rash has not gone away—the failure of the doctor's medicine plus the fact that the symptom was seen as being highly unusual results in a root doctor being called in from Chicago (that's a 450-mile house call!). He makes a diagnosis of witchcraft and blames the victim's girl friend for putting something in his food. A fee of $250 is charged and a bottle of "jinx-removing" lotion is provided.

Case 2. Tucson, Arizona. A middle-aged man is in a minor car wreck and is taken to a hospital emergency room. He is uninjured but routine tests show blood in his urine. The doctor says that this has nothing to do with the accident. A minor surgical procedure produces a gelatinous mass about the size of a half dollar. The patient believes that a baby octopus has been removed from his bladder. He recalls that a few days earlier he was having a drink with a woman when her boy friend walked in. He decides that the other man became jealous and placed a dried octopus egg in his beer which subsequently hatched out in his bladder.

Case 3. Flint, Michigan. A man is running around with other women and his wife goes to her mother-in-law for advice. In this case the older woman—the victim's own mother—is a root doctor. She gives her daughter-in-law something to put in her son's food which will make him vomit if he looks at another woman. He develops nausea and vomiting and goes to a physician who can find no reason for his symptoms. When they persist his mother informs him of what she has done and admonishes him to behave himself. He tests it out and sure enough becomes severely nauseated at a girl friend's home. He now believes in the charm and knows that he is bound to his wife forever.

Case 4. Lansing, Michigan. A woman decides to visit her ex-husband in North Carolina. Soon after her return she begins to "act crazy" and she is taken from one doctor to another but they fail to help her. Her skin begins to darken and this frightening symptom leads her family to seek out a root doctor in Detroit. The root doctor says that she has been hexed by something which the former husband put in her food and that the darkening skin represents "the poison working in her system." It is predicted that on the way home the victim's car will run over a black snake which represents the evil charm—she is advised to give away a certain amount of money in small coins and to give her house a thorough cleaning. Coincidentally a snake *is* run over on the way back to Lansing—the money is given away, the house cleaned, and the woman is now reported cured.

What is missing in all of these accounts is both what transpired when the patient was in the doctor's office from the doctor's point of view and the nature of the transaction between the patient and the folk healer.

In contrast, here is an account of such a case from the professional aspect (Cappanari *et al.,* 1975); the physical manifestations of the illness were known but it took the near-death of the patient and three years' time to piece the story together. In summary, a nineteen-year-old woman enjoys excellent health until her marriage, when she soon becomes pregnant and things begin "to go downhill." Her mother-in-law is a "bad lady who cast(s) spells" and does not like her; she tells her her baby will be born dead. The baby *is* born dead at full term and the same day the patient develops abdominal pain, nausea, vomiting, and diarrhea. Four months later the persistence of these symptoms leads to rehospitalization and a diagnosis of regional enteritis. Therapy of corticosteroids, sulfonamides, and isoniazid is begun. Six months later the patient and her husband separate; on one occasion he has said that "he didn't want to leave, but something had power over him and was making him do it."

A year after the birth of the infant the patient is again hospitalized because of continued weight loss. She is tube fed, corticosteroids are increased, and she is released at a weight of 105 pounds (in contrast to her normal weight of 140 to 150 pounds). Eight more months pass and as medical efforts at relieving symptoms have failed, the patient goes to a "gypsy" who explains the mother-in-law has hexed her with poisoned cake. The gypsy refers her to another healer who prescribes a gallon of medicine. The girl tries to drink it but it makes the nausea and vomiting worse. The husband serves her with divorce papers saying, "I must do this . . . I'm under another power, and besides you will die in January anyway."

This awful prophecy is unfortunately reinforced by a physician who tells her that she will always have her disease—regional enteritis—and that it will eventually kill her. In January (three years after her marriage and the month in which it is predicted she will die) her weight has fallen to 72 pounds, she is rehospitalized and a psychiatric opinion requested. The patient is described as depressed but not anxious or psychotic. She states, "I don't know if I'm going to die in January or not, but I believe my stomach trouble is caused by her spell." The psychiatric consultant calls in a minister said to be involved with a local voodoo cult. He tells her that the hex is all in her head and reads biblical passages concerning the casting out of devils. She enters a hypnoid-like state from which she emerges stating that she feels better. Her physical condition makes tube feeding necessary and she gains weight. Her spirits improve greatly after February when she has outlived the death prophecy: she then observes that her hex was never real, that she has had regional enteritis all along, and concludes, "Anybody can be fooled."

In this case the resolution of many of her problems might have come many months sooner had the health care team *known* about witchcraft beliefs and had they recognized that everything that happened to her pointed to such a deed. Sensitizing physicians to such beliefs is the simplest part of the problem, however—such information *is* being made available both in the clinical literature and in undergraduate medical education. But while this makes it easier to diagnose magical illness it does not really solve the question of how to help the patient. Perhaps many anthropologists would at this point suggest that a root doctor be called in to administer therapy or at least to collaborate in therapeutic efforts; this is in fact sometimes done with reported success.

I submit that this may be a risky business and should be carefully thought out beforehand. On a practical level we must admit that we do not really know how such healers operate; the evidence we have is fragmentary. We *do* know some things that should be taken into consideration before making such a referral, however: (a) The fee for removing a spell may be hundreds of dollars; even when the healer is a caring and conscientious person the patient is still left with a world view which will allow the same thing to happen in the next stressful situation. (b) Not all such healers *are* caring and conscientious: any who wish to prey on the fears of others can advertise that they are a "seventh son" or were "born with a veil." They may then diagnose and treat illness entirely by mail—the victim may spend a sizable sum of money on a bit of red flannel to wear somewhere on the body, be advised not to eat anyone else's cooking, and *still* be left with symptoms. (c) In a sort of reverse placebo effect, the healer may impress the patient that the treatment is powerful by administering toxic substances in order to produce dramatic physiologic reactions—examples are moth balls and carbon tetrachloride. (d) Many people fear the root doctor, who may have the reputation for being able to kill as well as cure, to put spells on as well as take then off; the presence of such an individual in a clinical setting implies tacit approval of such behavior on the part of the medical staff.

Finally, such a collaboration still does not address the underlying problem, a social system which allows so many people to have the kind of life experience contributing to low self-esteem, poor self-image, and a view of the world as a hostile and dangerous place. Until real social change comes about, any treatment of a witchcraft illness can only be symptomatic. At present such patients weave in and out of both health systems, ill served by both. Hopefully, the dialogue between the anthropologist and the health professional can at least help a little.

That Nigger's Crazy

Luisah Teish

The impact of racism on people's health has been well discussed in the literature. While this article can be used in that context, the discussion of drapetomania can also serve on a broader level to emphasize the arbitrary nature of illness designations. This "disease," first described by Dr. Samuel Cartwright in the *New Orleans Medical and Surgical Journal* (1851), apparently afflicted blacks only. Such labeling did not necessarily represent the prevailing medical ideology of the day—an exciting rebuttal appeared in the same journal several months later in which the author, James Smith (1852), argued effectively that one may not simply use the Greek word for a behavior and merely add a medical-sounding suffix to define a new disease. In this case *drapetes* means absconding, a flight, or a running away. Attaching this Greek root to the term *mania,* which implies craziness, created a new disease—the running-away disease suffered by black slaves. Such arbitrary labeling is still with us, as evidenced in the designation of mental illness (complete with institutionalization) for political dissidents in the Soviet Union. "Psychiatric epidemiology" is also well illustrated in the article "Startling Facts from the Census" in the *American Journal of Insanity* (Anonymous, 1851) (also reprinted by Szasz (1973) as "Madness and Blackness, 1840"). In that article we are shown that in 1840 the incidence of insanity and idiocy among blacks appeared to increase dramatically in the free states and as one went progressively north (1:14 in Maine as compared to 1:4310 in Louisiana). Perhaps these figures reflected an epidemic of drapetomania in the North? A careful and convincing rebuttal which dealt primarily with the quality of the statistics appeared in the same journal several months later (Jarvis, 1852). Unfortunately, such rebuttals rarely have the impact of the original treatises and are most often quickly forgotten. In the following article, Luisah Teish presents an angry view of the impact of racism on the form that medical diagnosis and treatment may take. For further information on drapetomania and a related "disease," dysaesthesia Aethiopis, Thomas Szasz's article "The Sane Slave" (1971) is highly recommended.

Reprinted by permission of the author and the *Madness Network News* (P.O. Box 684, San Francisco, California 94110). From *Madness Network News,* Vol. 3, No. 5, March 1976, p. 9.

One must be very careful how we accept the theories and treatments of psychiatrists. Basically psychiatry is about the business of making people behave in a way that is *respectable, acceptable,* and *controllable.* Little allowance is made for differences in cultural and survival factors. Once a label has been created they can then "treat" people for their "disorder" in any way they see fit. Most so-called "mental illnesses" are fabrications of the people who stand to benefit from having someone else submit to their way of thinking.

In 1851 a respected white physician, Dr. Samuel A. Cartwright, created a mental illness peculiar to Black people. The effort of the slave to gain his freedom by running away from the plantation, he said, was a symptom of a serious mental disease called *drapetomania.* Dr. Cartwright maintained that this hideous condition could be cured by recapturing the "patient," rubbing him down with oil and beating him into submission. Dr. Cartwright was known to be a liberal among his colleagues in New Orleans.

Less liberal but just as dangerous was the thesis of a Dr. John E. Lind. On May 20, 1916, Dr. Lind—a psychiatrist at St. Elizabeth's Hospital in Washington—read a paper to the Washington Psychoanalytical Society entitled "Phylogenetic Elements in the Psychoses of the Negro." Dr. Lind began his dissertation with a definition of his objects:

In using the word [Negro] in the title of this paper I mean of course the Negro as seen in the United States, the individual of whom it has been said that his father was a slave and his grandfather a cannibal. I have always found a difficulty in the current conception that the present-day African has reached levels only slightly inferior to the white race. This theory is held most extensively in regions where the Negro is infrequent and by persons having to do only occasionally with individuals of this race and then only with selected specimens.

Dr. Lind maintained that his view was "scientific":

The Negro, studied judiciously by those who are competent, appears to be at a much lower cultural level than the Caucasian. It is true that with his talent for mimicry, recalling to us in some measure our jungle cousins, he is able to present a remarkably exact, albeit superficial, representation of the white man. But no one who has associated with Negroes is willing to believe that this resemblance extends much below the surface.

Many of us will heave a sigh of relief that this is not 1916, but like Shockley and Jensen, these men have scientific "proof" to support their obscene racial garbage. Based on a series of no less than 32 "cases" of blacks incarcerated at Saint Elizabeth's Hospital, Dr. Lind summarized his view of "the psychology of the African," which was published [1917] in the *Psychoanalytic Review:*

The precocity of the children, the early onset of puberty, the failure to grasp subjective ideas, the strong sexual and herd instincts with the few inhibitions, the simple dream life, the easy reversion to savagery when deprived of the restraining influence of the whites (as in Haiti and Liberia), the tendency to seek expression in such rhythmic means as music and dancing, the low resistance to such toxins as syphilis and alcohol, the sway of superstition, all these and many other things betray the savage heart beneath the civilized exterior. Because he wears a Palm Beach suit instead of a string of cowries, carries a gold-headed cane instead of a spear, uses the telephone instead of beating the drum from hill to hill, and for the jungle path has substituted the pay-as-you-enter streetcar, his psychology is no less that of the African.

Beware! The labeling hasn't stopped; from "hostile," "aggressive," or "hyper-active" children being given Ritalin to "anti-social," "alienated," and "depressed" Black women being given shock, the story is the same. There is a label and a treatment for "the Black sickness." We know that if sanity is defined by white upper-middle class standards then we are in grave danger. It is very easy at this time, when Third World people are seeking their own identities, to say "That nigger's crazy. . . . *Lock him up.*"

Folk Diseases among Urban Mexican-Americans: Etiology, Symptoms, and Treatment

Cervando Martinez, Harry W. Martin

Martinez and Martin present a useful description of folk diseases in an urban setting. The article also touches on the important but often overlooked fact that members of various ethnic collectives are not restricted from possessing and acting on dual medical belief systems. The duality is indicated in the remark by the curandera who obeys her doctor's "orders." Utilization and acceptance of "modern" services is well presented by Karno and Edgerton (1969). In that article the authors also present a number of important factors which, they believe, explain the apparent underutilization of mental health facilities. Other authors who present somewhat differing views on this last subject are Torrey (1972) and Keefe, Carlos, and Padilla (1976). In addition to the well-known articles and books referred to in the following selection, the reader might also be interested in looking at Currier (1966) and Kiev (1968). There have been numerous studies dealing specifically with Mexican-Americans and health and the references presented in this book represent only some of the better-known selections. Readers could also be directed to the wealth of articles and books that focus on urban Latin Americans and their health.

Acculturation and assimilation of persons of Mexican origin in the Southwest has been slowed by various social mechanisms of the larger society which tend to keep these people separate, and by a tendency on their part to separate themselves from the larger community by living in *barrios*. One result of this sociocultural isolation is the preservation of many folk beliefs of Spanish and Hispanic-American origins. Most important among these from a medical point of view are the prescientific concepts of health and disease and the related practices.

Prominent among the disease concepts are *mal ojo* (evil eye), *empacho* (surfeit), *susto* (magical fright), *caída de mollera* (fallen fontanelle), and *mal puesto* (hex). Gillin [1948] gives a detailed account of *susto* in Guatemalan natives and draws parallels between folk and scientific (psychiatric) therapeutics. The existence of the first three concepts among Spanish-speaking Americans has been described by Saunders [1954:141–173]. Clark's work (1959:163–183] among Mexican-Americans in a California community led to a grouping of folk illnesses according to their presumed origins, i.e., disease originating from dislocated internal organs *(caída de mollera),* disease of magical origin *(mal ojo),* disease of emotional origin *(susto),* and a residual category containing *empacho.* Foster [1953] maintains that the concepts of *mal ojo* and *caída de mollera* stem from similar notions in Spain; *susto,* according to him, is indigenous to the new world. Rubel [1960] hypothesizes that belief in these illnesses persists because of a supportive relation to certain core values and behavior in the Mexican-American community, and in a later work, he describes the *susto* syndrome in terms of frustrated role expectations with this cultural group [1964].

Purpose of the Study

Although most reports on concepts of folk illness among Mexican-Americans directly or indirectly assert a widespread prevalence of belief in the notions, none provide data permitting estimates of how many people within a given population have knowledge of or subscribe to belief in them. This paper reports the results of an exploratory study designed for the following purposes: to determine the extent of knowledge about these concepts among Mexican-American women in a large Southwestern city; to obtain a detailed account of beliefs about etiology, symptomatology, and modes of treatment; to assess the extent to which acculturation diminishes knowledge about these concepts; and to determine if persons reporting knowledge of the illnesses resort to practitioners of scientific medicine for care, continue to resort to folk healers, or do both. This paper deals primarily with the first two aims.

Sample and Method

The sample consisted of 75 Mexican-American housewives living in a public housing project near the business district of the city. The subjects were interviewed in their homes with an interview schedule which was

designed following completion of several unstructured exploratory interviews. The respondents ranged in age from 18 to 84 with a median age of 39;
the group had a median of six years of schooling; eight had no formal education; 51 were born in the United States, and the rest were born in Mexico.

Findings

An overwhelming majority, more than 97 percent of the women interviewed, knew about each of the five diseases. Eighty-five percent had some
specific knowledge about symptoms and etiology of the *males,* except for
mal puesto; only two thirds were able to give information on the etiology
and symptoms of this disease. Similarly, 85 percent of the women reported
therapeutic measures for all the *males* except *mal puesto,* but only one third
could or would admit knowledge about its treatment. All but 5 percent of
the women reported one or more instances of these illnesses in themselves, a
family member, or in acquaintances. Reports of occurrence of the *males* in
immediate family members were employed as an index of belief in folk
maladies; no relationship appeared between this index and such characteristics as age, education, or place of birth. The only exception to this
general pattern occurred in connection with *mal puesto;* six of the eight
cases reported among immediate kin were cited by women under the median
age.

Mal ojo is an illness to which all children and adults with "light" blood
are susceptible. The blood is believed to be heated by electricity in a stronger
person's vision who looks at the afflicted admiringly or covetously but does
not touch him.

The "heating" of the blood produces the most often reported symptoms
of *ojo,* fever and vomiting. Crying and restlessness were reported by
one fourth of the sample, and in several interviews, an abnormality of the
eyes, such as inability to open the eyelids or an involuntary turning of the
eyes in different directions, was reported.

"Sweeping" the patient with an unbroken raw egg is considered the
treatment of choice for *ojo.* By "sweeping" *(barrer)* is meant both to pass
the egg over the body without touching, or to actually rub the body with the
egg. This is done in the sign of the cross or at random. Prayers recited
during the sweeping were reported in four fifths of the cases; such prayers
are recited in threes, e.g., three Ave Marias, *Padre Nuestros,* or Credos.
After sweeping, to extract the fever (heat) from the patient's body and
transmit it to the egg, the egg is broken and placed in a bowl of water. Three
crosses made from blessed palm or broomstraw are placed over the egg. The
bowl is then placed under the head of the patient's bed. During the night,
the egg is said to absorb the remaining fever and by morning it should be

"cooked"; according to some, one can see the "eye" on the yolk of the egg. The cooked egg is a sign that the patient had *ojo*.

A second mode of treatment reported by one fifth of the respondents is administered by the person who gave the "evil eye." The giver may simply touch the afflicted or he may give him a mouthful of water directly from his mouth. One woman commented that mouth-to-mouth treatment is now considered dangerous, although not disclaiming it, because of the risk of transmitting germs.

Empacho is caused by a bolus of poorly digested or uncooked food sticking to the wall of the stomach. This *mal* may occur in any age group or sex. The most frequently reported symptoms were lack of appetite, stomachache, diarrhea, and vomiting. Other symptoms include fever, crying and restlessness in children, and stomach discomfort.

The most often reported treatments for dislodging the bolus of food from the wall of the stomach were rubbing the stomach or rubbing the back, or more precisely, pinching the back. Attacking the bolus from the back involves grasping a fold of skin, pulling it up, and releasing it. This procedure is done with both hands and repeated three times until a telltale "pop" is heard signaling dislodgment of the *empacho*. Finally, a purgative or tea or both may be given. This part of the treatment is done in the morning before breakfast for three mornings. The tea may be made from *estafiate* (larkspur), *hojas de sen* (sena leaves), *manzanilla* (chamomile), or from ashes of the food that caused the *empacho*.

Caída de mollera, or fallen fontanelle, is believed to be caused by one of two things. In the first case, the child falls or is dropped and the blow is thought to cause the anterior fontanelle to cave in. There is also the belief that pulling the nipple out of the infant's mouth too vigorously causes the fontanelle to be sucked down into the palate. The fallen fontanelle results in a downward projection of the palate which inhibits the child's eating. The most commonly recognized symptom is the inability of the baby to grasp the nipple and feed; attempts to suckle are accompanied by slurping sounds and smacking lips. Other reported symptoms were crying, diarrhea, the fallen soft spot, sunken eyes, and vomiting.

Three treatments for *caída de mollera* were reported. These are usually done one at a time, but in some cases the first and second are done simultaneously. In the first, a finger is inserted in the child's mouth and the palate is pushed, supposedly back into place. The second treatment involves holding the child over a pan of water so that the tips of his hair barely touch the water. The third procedure is to apply a poultice, usually made from fresh soap shavings, to the depression. These procedures are not three necessary steps such that omission of one causes the treatment to fail. Rather, they are thought of simply as procedures that do the same thing; if all three are done, however, treatment is thought to be more effective.

According to the respondents, *susto* is usually the result of a traumatic experience which may be anything from witnessing a death to a simple scare at night. Children are more susceptible than adults and a group of individuals may develop symptoms at one time. For example, one woman reported that her entire family had *susto* after the drowning of one of her sons.

The most common symptom of *susto* is sudden desire to sleep, usually occurring around eleven in the morning. Accompanying symptoms may be anorexia, insomnia, hallucinations, weakness, and various painful sensations. A number of persons believed that untreated *susto* can lead to tuberculosis.

Treatment for *susto* involves "sweeping" the patient and reciting prayers in threes. The patient lies in a doorway wth the arms outstretched so that his body forms a cross, or he may lie on a cross drawn on the floor with a sheet over his body. Sweeping motions are made over him in the sign of the cross. This treatment is performed by a *curandera* (curer) or by a *señora*. (Two folk healers were mentioned by the respondents, *curanderas* and certain other women. Persons of the latter sort were usually identified as older female friends or relatives having knowledge of folk therapeutics. These persons were referred to simply as *señoras* by the respondents. For the lack of a better term, we follow this practice.) As the patient is being swept, three Ave Marias, Credos, or *Padre Nuestros* are repeated. The healer also calls out the patient's name saying, *"Vente, vente. No te quedes."* (Come on, come on. Don't stay behind.) The patient replies, *"Hay voy, hay voy."* (I'm coming, I'm coming.)

A tea of herbs may also be given, or the patient's face covered with a clean handkerchief and sprinkled with holy water. Another treatment is to spurt a mouthful of water or alcohol in the patient's face unexpectedly. One woman reported that she formerly jumped over her *susto* patients rather than sweeping them. With age, however, her arthritis forced her to resort to sweeping.

"Light" and "heavy" treatments for *susto* were also reported. The "heavy" treatment is for *susto pasado,* or old untreated cases, and includes sweeping, prayers, etc., as described above. A recently induced *susto, susto liviano,* requires the following "light treatment": crosses made from blessed palm are dipped in holy water and placed over parts of the patient's body to effect a cure.

Mal puesto literally means an evil or illness put on someone willfully by another. This putting of an evil or hex can be done either by a *curandera* or *bruja* (witch) upon request, or by any person knowing the intricacies of witchcraft. The hex, which may be given through food, a photograph, or by means of a small effigy of the victim, is usually prompted by jealousy. The disorder supposedly resulting from the hex is manifested in a variety of strange and, to the afflicted and his family, incomprehensible symptoms. In fact, the most common response to the question about symptoms was that a *mal* can be "different things." The symptoms most often reported were uncontrolled urination, sudden attacks of screaming, crying, and singing; in some instances, bodily exposure and convulsions occur. One respondent refused to describe symptoms she had witnessed in two of her acquaintances because they were too embarrassing for her to relate.

In contrast to the other illnesses, only one third of the informants reported knowledge of treatments for *mal puesto*. Among these, some reported that a special person had to give the treatment; others felt that the treatment could be performed at home by a family member; and some reported that either of these could be used. There was no consensus regarding who the special person should be, but *curanderas* were mentioned most frequently.

The treatment procedures requiring a special person were either not known or not divulged, except in one case in which the afflicted was given several medicinal enemas and was instructed to wear a bag of red cloth containing herbs. Treatments not requiring special persons included (1) making crosses at church by the afflicted, (2) making crosses on the arms with a mixture of chili powder and olive oil, (3) prayers, (4) burning incense, (5) herbs, and (6) massages.

Use of Folk Healers and Physicians

Persons most often resorted to for treatment of folk ailments were *señoras* and *curanderas;* in general, payment is not required for these services. The availability of these healers is indicated by the fact that one *curandera* and eight *señoras* were identified by one or more respondents as residents of the neighborhood. These nine persons were among those interviewed. A majority of the women were aware that *señoras* were in the immediate locale, and more than one half of them had been treated by a *señora* at some time during their life. Only one fifth reported knowledge of a *curandera* and a similar proportion admitted to having sought the services of such healers.

Four fifths of the respondents reported visits to physicians, and three fifths obtained health services from clinics operated by the local health department. For the most part, these services were for other medical reasons; relief for folk ailments is rarely sought from physicians; however, several women cited instances in which they or others had sought treatment from physicians without disclosing the folk diagnosis. After one or two days, the patients went or were taken to folk healers on the judgment that the medical treatment was either ineffective or too slow. When questioned about physicians' ability to treat folk disorders, two thirds felt that doctors do not know how to treat these problems because of a lack of knowledge, faith, or understanding. One fifth were of the opinion that doctors would treat them, but refuse to do so for the same reasons, i.e., lack of knowledge and faith.

Conclusion and Implications

The findings provide additional evidence that belief in folk illnesses and use of folk healers continue to be widespread among urbanized Mexican-Americans. Participation in the system of folk beliefs and curative practices by no means, however, precludes reliance upon physicians and use of medical services for health problems not defined by folk concepts. Thus, many Mexican-Americans participate in two insular systems of health beliefs and health care. A woman identified by many of the respondents as a *curandera* demonstrated this compartmentalized participation. At the close of the interview she said, "I have to go take a nap now. My doctor says I need plenty of rest, and I don't want to disobey his orders."

The insularity of these systems is doubtlessly maintained by numerous social and psychocultural factors. Some of these are fairly obvious. Mexican-American patients rarely reveal to physicians their folk medical beliefs and practices for fear of criticism or ridicule. On the other hand, such notions are alien to thought ways of physicians, perhaps to the point of being ridiculous. And, in addition to not being informed by their patients, many physicians have rarely heard of these concepts or are indifferent about their existence and related practices.

The empirical conditions to which the folk concepts refer can perhaps be easily fitted into the framework of modern medicine; for example, *mal puesto* and *susto* appear to have psychiatric implications. The first of these likely encompasses an assortment of disorders, e.g., schizophrenia, epilepsy, and organic brain lesions. The second may fit under such labels as anxiety reaction or reactive depression. The remaining three ailments are no doubt explicable in other medical terms. Regardless of what etiologic factors and diagnostic labels may be most appropriate, these concepts and related curative practices warrant serious medical interest. Medical care is inadequate to the extent that it ignores them.

Gypsy Culture and Health Care

Gwen Anderson, Bridget Tighe

Medical services are often designed to satisfy the needs of hospital personnel rather than those of patients. For example, patients can be made to wait but physicians may not. The following article provides useful general information on Gypsies and stresses the importance of the constant presence of family and friends in the therapeutic regimen. The benefits to the patient can often be seen to outweigh possible dangers. This point is made in many studies, usually of groups with a strong tradition of folk medicine. The same situation may exist at the individual level for the general American culture though it is not characteristic of it. Cogent points are also made with reference to the importance of trust in medical practitioners and an understanding of the lay-referral system. These last issues have proved to be important for the effective provision of services to many groups in the United States.

"Oh no, I didn't go to the hospital to have my babies. I just delivered them in the back of the trailer on the road." These were the words of a Gypsy woman we met while we were taking part in an interdisciplinary study of Gypsies' use of health care services.

Our research team included two medical sociologists, an anthropologist, a public health nursing faculty adviser, a first-year medical student, and ourselves, two graduate students in public health nursing. Our varied interests and abilities proved invaluable and were apparent as soon as we began to collect our preliminary data and review the literature.

Some preliminary data came through interviews with hospital receptionists, doctors, nurses, social workers, policemen, sociologists, and other community members. We were gradually able to piece together a picture of the ways in which the medical community and the general public viewed the Gypsies. Medical people said Gypsies were difficult to work with and unreliable, disregarded hospital regulations about visiting hours and numbers of visitors, were light-fingered with hospital equipment, unconcerned with follow-up care, and inclined to falsify names and addresses.

The public saw the Gypsies as a romantic lot of wanderers living by fortune-telling, selling flowers, lying, and stealing.

The literature, though sparse, provided further important background information. We learned that for many centuries Gypsies have consistently avoided being studied and understood by those outside their own culture and have prided themselves on giving the non-Gypsy (Gaje) as little accurate information as possible. Gypsies and their Romany language originally came from India. From there they have traveled to all parts of the world. They have a sophisticated communications system whereby Gypsy communities in any geographic area are in close contact with one another and pass along important information about health, welfare, and legal counsel.

We read of an old legend, which was later repeated by one of the Gypsies in our study, that "it was a Gypsy who stole a nail from Christ's foot at the crucifixion and was rewarded the eternal right for all Gypsies to steal without being caught and punished."

Data Collection

On the basis of this preliminary information, we all realized it would be impossible to conduct a typical sociological survey of a reasonably sized, random sample of the Gypsy population. The Gypsies were obviously not of a nature to respond to direct questioning from Gajes. Therefore, we developed a research/service plan based primarily on public health nursing visits (by the two graduate students) to Gypsy homes on referral from hospital outpatient departments.

This, however, was easier planned than done, as gaining entry into Gypsy homes was difficult; throughout the entire eight-month study period, we established satisfactory contact with only eight families. Initial home visits to families after hospital referrals led us to false, nonexistent, or recently vacated addresses with no forwarding addresses; phone numbers given the hospital by Gypsy patients also proved false.

We were thus forced to alter our approach and make our initial contacts at the hospital clinics where, fortunately and surprisingly, Gypsy patients faithfully returned for their scheduled appointments. Even so, we and the hospital staff had to do a lot off persuading to convince the patients and their ever-present families of the desirability of home nursing visits and of the need for correct addresses and phone numbers.

Weekly visits were then made at mutually agreed upon times (our Gypsies refused early morning appointments) in the late morning or afternoon. Some Gypsies would move or leave town temporarily, thus interrupting the visits. One family felt that public health nursing services were unnecessary and after three visits requested termination.

We were generally well received (although somewhat warily at first) and were ultimately able to be of service in giving home nursing care, health education, interpretations of medical treatment regimens, and in acting as mediators in Gypsy interactions with the rest of society. We were frequently offered food and drink and were occasionally honored by invitations to holiday or wedding festivities.

Interestingly, the cultural data that our research efforts uncovered were similar to data in the literature. We made many additional health observations, however, in our contact with the eight families. We categorized the observations into "family and social structure," and "Gypsy and societal interaction," and "Gypsy health attitudes."

Family and Social Structure

In the first category, which described the family and social structure, we found the Gypsies to be close knit regarding both their families and ethnic units. In all instances, we observed extended families consisting of up to 12 members each per residence, with additional friends and relatives coming and going at will. There was frequent communication among Gypsies via telephone and direct word-of-mouth at frequent informal and formal social gatherings. Our Gypsies loved parties and were encouraged in this by their religion, which recognizes numerous church holiday celebrations. One of the authors was invited to one of the many such religious holidays and was the only Gaje present. Approximately 90 Gypsies within a radius of 100 miles joined in the household singing and feasting on roast pig and spicy, hot, stuffed peppers. The entire party moved on within a few hours to yet another household party, and another, and another still, till the day's end.

This cultural solidarity appears to extend far beyond local or even state boundaries to an almost international awareness among Gypsies of other specific Gypsies in other cities or countries and of ways to reach one another. Gypsy children were discouraged from playing with Gaje children. This is an example of the conscious desire among Gypsies to protect their cultural identity and secrets from Gaje influence and curiosity.

Consequently, although somewhat influenced by the changing times, many Gypsy traditions remain. For example, we learned that Romany is, and is expected to remain, a language of Gypsies alone; that Gypsy law is determined by "the council" and has it own systems of reward and punishment; and that marriage to a Gaje is taboo. In the words of one Gypsy man, "you can never really know and trust a man until you live with him—unless perhaps he is someone like an M.D. whose background you can assume."

Interaction with the Society

Gypsy interaction with the society at large is greatly affected by their ethnocentricity, but there are other influences as well. One of these influences is the Gypsy wanderlust, which had taken most of our study families to many parts of the United States and had allowed them to settle down only when forced by illness to remain near medical facilities. Such mobility has greatly interfered with the school enrollment and education of Gypsy children who remain, like their parents, unable to read and write fluently, if at all. As a result of one Gypsy mother's inability to read the directions on a prescription, a topical wart removal preparation was generously applied to the body of her small child with resultant widespread second-degree burns. Our families had many welfare recipients (sign painters are not in demand) and they encountered many associated problems due to prejudices toward Gypsies, their misunderstanding of regulations, changing and false addresses, and written communication difficulties.

Health Attitudes

We found that Gypsy interactions with the health care system were not unlike those of other groups in the poverty culture, such as Indians, Puerto Ricans, blacks, and indigent whites. They, too are forced to manipulate the system to receive basic care and often suffer as a result of their lack of sophistication in obtaining the most from the limited facilities available to them. The Gypsies, however, possess a distinct advantage in their mobility, which allows them to shop around for services and in their access to the experiential learning of other Gypsies' past interactions with health care providers.

Our Gypsy families consistently showed a wariness of medical personnel and facilities, and they changed doctors frequently as a result of unfavorable experiences or recommendations from fellow Gypsies. The fact that a certain doctor or hospital had once cured a Gypsy was communicated via the extensive social networks for years after the event had occurred, so that new patients went to previously tested care givers. In one instance, a family traveled to cities in four states nearly halfway across the United States in a futile search for a medical cure for laryngeal cancer, their choices based solely on the Gypsy communication network recommendations.

Where care was satisfactory, the Gypsies remained and trust evolved. However, if a doctor changed medication without an explanation, or left a promise unfulfilled, or appeared too aloof or impatient, the Gypsies moved on to another doctor in another hospital.

Gypsy health attitudes seemed to fall into two categories: crisis care, which they use predominantly, and preventive and follow-up care, which they use poorly. In crisis situations, where immediate, observable need was present, we discovered a somewhat unrealistic overuse of emergency or clinic facilities. Health was highly valued by the Gypsies and, when illness struck, they demanded the best specialists and offered to pay any price. Whole families were in crisis over one sick member whom they accompanied to, and remained with at, the hospital in defiance of all visiting rules and regulations. Several Gypsies commended a particular hospital for relaxing its visiting hours for them or allowing the husband of a critically ill woman to sleep overnight in her room, or employing a private duty nurse who reported frequently on her patient's condition to the waiting Gypsy encampment in the hospital lobby.

We learned that many Gypsies were aggressively inquisitive, demanding explanations from many health personnel about a diagnosis or treatment. As a result they were surprisingly aware of medical problems relevant to themselves or family members.

A problem we encountered frequently among our families was hypertension and, when we made our weekly visits, not only did all family members gather around and ask to have their blood pressures taken, but friends and other relatives soon began dropping by.

Clinic follow-up appointments were well kept as long as the Gypsies perceived the need. However, when follow-up involved such severe alterations in life-styles as not sleeping late or omitting spicy, greasy foods, it was generally ineffective. One elderly Gypsy woman with diabetes carried all her various pills in one bottle inside her bra. Other Gypsy patients commonly added, omitted, or shared medications with family members. Surprisingly, for such a mobile culture, few families owned automobiles. Most depended on buses or car pools with friends or relatives for trips to hospitals or grocery stores.

Among stationary families, some children were immunized, but this was not so in the transient families. Except for one man who didn't know where to get one, there was no interest in physical examinations. Prenatal care was poor, and eyes went without glasses because of vanity.

Data Analysis

In analyzing our data, we identified numerous health problems, some uniquely Gypsy and some common to most minority groups in our society, but all with broad implications for medical and nursing care.

To the Gypsies, medicine was for curing, not preventing, disease. Serious problems, such as diabetes and high blood pressure, went undetected until far advanced. Consequently, treatment was often overwhelmingly lengthy and complicated, especially for people who desired immediate results, had limited understanding of disease physiology and pharmacology, and were inadequate in their command of the written English language. The result was mutual frustration and distrust among health personnel and patients as appointments were not kept, as treatment regimens were misunderstood and not explicitly followed, and as Gypsies moved from hospital to hospital in search of help and understanding. In the wake of such confusion, false addresses, and lack of interest in follow-up care, it was practically impossible from a hospital viewpoint to refer, follow-up, and transfer records.

Thus, because of their cultural uniqueness, Gypsies overused crisis health facilities and grossly underused preventive and follow-up care resources.

Recommendations

In general, when a Gypsy patient is admitted to a hospital, one way that a nursing care plan can take into consideration the high family-centeredness of the culture would be to have the patient assigned to a room as near the outside door as possible. This will minimize the disturbances caused by many visitors coming and going at odd hours and staying overnight. If possible, highly seasoned, high-fat foods should be included in the patient's diet. If a party can be arranged, it might do much for the patient's mood.

Two other cultural traits we found were a rather high degree of vanity about appearance, particularly facial features, and great female genital modesty. These traits have implications for the need for privacy and for emotional support when treatments are prescribed that involve, for instance, the use of eye glasses or female genitourinary procedures.

Special attention, too, should be given to communications and establishing rapport, particularly in view of the Gypsy distrust of the Gaje.

We concluded that Gypsies were not receiving good, comprehensive, health care partly because of their own cultural idiosyncrasies and partly because of inadequacies in the health care delivery system. This is not atypical of minority groups in our society, and once again points out the vital need for health care workers to recognize and incorporate cultural differences in the planning and delivery of comprehensive health care.

How Doctors Are Unfair to Women

William A. Nolen

"If ovaries were testicles there'd be a lot fewer of them removed." Nolen's article speaks well for itself. Additionally, some interesting issues are raised relating to the cross-cultural approach in viewing behavior. Many articles on health-care delivery to various cultural groups stress such points as the importance and role of modesty in the acceptance or rejection of services. What remains implicit in the recounting of such cases is the importance of modesty in our own culture. Indeed, an important function of cross-cultural comparisons is the clarification of problems in our own culture. While it was not Nolen's intention to be concerned with the nature of care received by men, he does, in his tone, imply that the stated issues apply only to women. Analogous situations that apply to men must be addressed as well; this acknowledgment allows for a broader view of the nature of services provided for all people. Regarding women, many of Nolen's observations, in all probability, are correct, and it is good that we are given the opportunity to examine them. The amount of available literature on women and society is vast. To sample the material that deals specifically with women and health and is also consonant with the following selection see Chesler (1972), Frankfort (1973), and Corea (1977).

Are doctors—men doctors, that is—male chauvinist pigs? We've been so labeled, certainly, dozens of times, and not only by the more vociferous members of the women's movement. Women who couldn't care less about becoming heads of state or playing pro football are griping about their doctors. A substantial percentage of the female sex thinks doctors are unfair to women.

Are they right? In a word, yes. Not all doctors are guilty, perhaps, but there is much too much truth for comfort in this accusation.

The obstetrician-gynecologist has, as you might expect, been the prime target for those women who are looking for chauvinistic tendencies in the medical profession. They haven't had to look very hard.

There are, for example, obstetricians who induce labor in most of their patients simply so that they (the doctors) won't have to get up at night; there are gynecologists who pass out birth-control pills as if they were peanuts, without fully informing their patients of the possible risks associated with oral contraceptives; there are gynecologists who do pelvic examinations with all the care they'd show if they were rummaging for a map in the glove compartment of their car. These doctors—not all, but certainly some—have frequently been inconsiderate of their patients and have occasionally victimized them.

But before the rest of us in the medical profession start throwing stones, we'd better take a good look at our own practices. Talk about living in glass houses!

Consider, for instance, the matter of the hysterectomy, an operation performed more commonly by the general surgeon than by the gynecologist. Even the most gung-ho member of the A.M.A. would probably concede that at least some of these operations are done for reasons that are without true merit: small, asymptomatic fibroids, for example, or pelvic "discomfort," or minimal bleeding that could be controlled by less drastic measures. There are surgeons who have a cavalier attitude toward hysterectomy. They consider the uterus an inessential, dispensable organ, and they're sometimes too quick in removing it. That, I'd say, is male chauvinism at its most flagrant.

A patient's ovaries are another favorite target of both gynecologists and general surgeons. There's a saying in surgical circles that "if ovaries were testicles, there'd be a lot fewer of them removed." I know that's true.

Often, particularly when repairing a recurrent hernia in a man, I'd like to remove the testicle on the affected side. With the testicle out of the way, and the spermatic cord that runs to it, it's much easier to make a strong, solid repair of the hernia. But only rarely do I ask a patient to agree to let me remove the testicle—and then only if he is around 80 years old. Even though I know that removing one testicle will not diminish a man's potency, virility, or fertility, I don't make the request. Instead, I work around the cord when I do my hernia repair—sometimes accept a less solid repair with a greater chance of recurrence—because I know from experience that it's the rare patient who will agree to removal of a testicle. The testicles are symbols of manhood and are parted with only under duress.

On the other hand, I've seen ovaries removed with a minimum of consideration for the patient. Often when a woman develops a cyst on her ovary—a benign growth, which is fairly common—it's possible to remove the cyst and leave the rest of the ovary in place. Possible, but a bit more difficult and time-consuming than simply removing the entire ovary. As long as there's a second, healthy ovary, too often surgeons take the easy course. Their reasoning is, "She'll still have one good ovary—why bother about fooling around with this one?" That too is flagrant male chauvinism and completely unjustifiable. But it happens with some frequency.

I don't want to get into the breast-cancer controversy all over again, but there's little doubt that male chauvinism has been partly responsible for the blind perpetuation of the radical mastectomy as the standard operation for cancer. A woman's breast is a symbol of femininity and extremely important to her. Doctors have always been aware of this, but until recently we haven't given this factor the consideration it deserves. About 90 percent of the doctors in this country—and about 95 percent of the surgeons—are men. We can be sure that if more members of the medical profession had been women, research into the results of more conservative operations for breast tumors—research that has started only recently—would have gotten under way years ago.

A final example of male chauvinism among doctors—perhaps the most important and widespread example of all—can be classified under the general heading of "protectionism." Because it *is* so widespread, and because most doctors aren't even aware that they're guilty of it, protectionism seems to me the most serious chauvinistic sin that medical men commit.

Here's what I mean by protectionism: If a man comes into my office bleeding from a stomach ulcer and I decide that he needs an operation, I'll spend 15 minutes, half an hour—all day if necessary—explaining to him what his problem is and how and why I propose to treat it. He's a man, and I feel he wants to know and has a right to know all the facts, worrisome as they may be. I feel an obligation to make certain he is fully informed.

On the other hand, if I see a woman patient who needs to have her gall-bladder removed, I'm inclined to take a paternal attitude. "Don't worry at all, Mrs. Smith," I'll tell her. "Just leave everything to me." Then, when she has left the office, I'll call her husband and explain everything to him.

This is medical protectionism: the doctor taking a paternal, protective attitude toward his women patients while at the same time treating his men patients as equals. When we doctors act in this fashion, we're not even aware that we're being chauvinistic. Our behavior is simply a reflection, in the medical field, of the protective—chauvinistic, if you will—male attitude that has always been part of society. Men fight the wars and earn the living; men protect women from cold and hunger. Just so, the male doctor shields his female patients from worries about sickness and death. It seems to most of us the natural thing to do.

But it's unfair—I acknowledge that—and it has to change. Women have as much right as men to know what's going on in their bodies, what the doctor proposes to do about it and why. That right is both moral and legal—not to mention human—and we doctors have to respect it. I know in the past that I've been guilty of this particular brand of chauvinism, and I'm trying very hard to change my ways.

Which brings me to a final comment and a piece of advice. Most doctors aren't guilty of male chauvinism for malicious reasons, but rather because of bad habits we developed before women began asserting their right to equal consideration, making us aware of the unfairness of our ingrained attitudes. Most of the things we do that can be labeled chauvinistic are done unintentionally; until recently, we had simply never given these matters any real thought.

So help us out. If your doctor treats you in a fashion that you consider demeaning, tell him about it. Don't let him treat you as a second-class citizen. If he's the kind of man he ought to be, he'll accept your criticism graciously.

And if he won't listen and learn, then find another doctor. There should be no place in the medical profession for the male chauvinist pig.

V

HEALTH BELIEF SYSTEMS

All peoples have belief systems that provide for their health needs. For decades, social and behavioral scientists have been collecting data that reflect the tremendous diversity in these systems. These systems, in turn, have been categorized in a variety of ways. Perhaps most commonly, a three-category scheme has been utilized—scientific, folk, and primitive.[1] Within any one of these categories the illnesses that are recognized have been variously classified as to cause and cure. In some schemes, illnesses may be divided into those which are natural or supernatural. As is the case for many classificatory systems, the boundaries are not clearly delineated. General distinctions can be made, however, to characterize each category. In *scientific* medicine, careful research using a variety of controls and statistical methods is essential, with accurate probability statements being one desired end. *Folk* medicine is often empirically sound medicine steeped in group tradition. *Primitive* medicine, often termed magical medicine, places an emphasis on cause and effect (as also does scientific medicine). However, in this realm the explanations exist in the world of the metaphysical, and while magic can never be rationally explained as such, it can be manipulated. These are but a sample of the features associated with the various medical systems. Yet there is not total acceptance of a single scheme; some authors lump folk and primitive medicine, claiming they are inseparable.

---

[1]This tripartite division of medical ideology and practice into scientific, folk, and primitive reflects one classification utilized by social scientists. It provides a useful (if ethnocentric) tool in ordering data on different cultures. It should by no means be assumed that people seeking treatment conceptualize in a manner consistent with this construct.

Medicine is, it seems, a mishmash of scientific, folk, and magical beliefs. In reality there are elements of folk medicine in all cultures and, as was stated earlier, the lines separating it from scientific medicine are not always clear. Nino Fidencio, a Northern Mexican folk curer of some renown, purposefully scoured the countryside collecting herbs with which he would then experiment. His empirical observations were perhaps lacking in scientific rigor, but many of his concoctions were effective. It must be noted that the Nino utilized spiritual techniques as well. Many scientific medical marvels derive, in fact, from empirically sound folk bases. Oliver Wendell Holmes sums up this fact well in the following quotation from his *Medical Essays* (Calder, 1962:9): "Medicine . . . learned from a monk how to use antimony, from a Jesuit how to cure agues, from a friar how to cut for stone, from a soldier how to treat gout, from a sailor how to keep off scurvy, from a postmaster how to sound the Eustachian tube, from a dairy-maid how to prevent smallpox, and from an old market woman how to catch the itch-insect. It borrowed acupuncture and the moxa from the Japanese heathen, and was taught the use of lobelia by the American savage."

There is also an element of magic in modern scientific medicine, though many prefer that it be subsumed into that category labeled "suggestion." *The Merck Manual,* for example, suggests hexing for removal of warts as especially effective for young people. *Hexing* is a pretty magical word. Similarly, doctors may be seen to invoke the supernatural each time they designate ℞ on a prescription. Ritchie Calder (1962:54) contends that the symbol does not stand for *recipe* as many would argue, and he prefers to trace the use of ℞ to Galen, who "advised his fellow physicians to sprinkle their writing with Egyptian symbols to impress their patients." According to Calder, ℞ derives from the "Eye of Horus" in roughly the following sequence:

EYES OF HORUS	ROMAN CORRUPTION	SHORTENED	MODIFIED TO SIGN OF ZEUS	RATIONALIZED BACK TO RECIPE

The importance and scope of suggestion have only recently been recognized. Suggestion is central to much of what Torrey presents with his four components of psychotherapy (see the introduction to Section IV). As subjects of serious scientific investigation, suggestion and the mental aspect of healing have barely been touched.

While social scientists are left to argue about how the systems should be catalogued, most people appear to have little difficulty in adapting or utilizing dual medical systems. Regarding the use of dual medical systems, the Navaho, for example, are depicted as being clear in their dividing illnesses into categories that call for treatment by specific specialists. There are those illnesses best treated by medical doctors (such as tuberculosis or appendicitis), those best treated by Navaho practitioners (such as lightening sickness and lizard illness), and those that can be treated by either type of practitioner (such as snakebite) (Adair and Deuschle 1970:11, 33). This division may, however, be a recent innovation useful for providing a place for scientific medicine within the Navaho belief system.

Folk medical beliefs influence the way in which people will interact with practitioners. Potential problems often derive from the basic conflicts in explanation of health processes. Problems may, of course, also derive from the social interaction itself (see Section III).

The articles in this section emphasize the similarities and differences in health care systems. Bernard Ortiz de Montellano provides a sample of the tremendous body of empirically sound folk medicine employed by the ancient Aztec. The majority of the medicines brought the desired results as dictated by Aztec beliefs regarding disease locus and causality.

The short news item on the root of the fagara tree illustrates the dynamics surrounding the process of innovation and modernization.

George Spindler presents information on the persistence of a folk medical tradition in a culture where the scientific tradition enjoys firm acceptance as well. The resultant blending makes very difficult any clear distinction between the two.

The final article, by Jay Haley, demonstrates how closely any therapy must articulate with the ethos of a society in order to be effective. Using his knowledge of what makes for successful treatment, Haley provides guidelines designed to insure failure in psychotherapy.

In a sense, much of what is scientific medicine is constantly becoming part of the folk medical domain (if one accepts the initial dichotomizing). This assimilation takes place in the sense that folk medicine is public or group medicine. It can be argued that demystifying scientific medicine is a good thing. While such an endeavor can have numerous benefits, it can also be argued that such a maneuver may be detrimental. For example, the placebo effect is increasingly undermined through too much honesty (honesty is, after all, an American ideal). Once again we are confronted with a number of ethical questions. Do we inform patients of everything (such as the fallibility of medicine and its practitioners) and in so doing hamstring medicine by weakening a powerful technique—suggestion? This question is not meant to suggest that being informed is necessarily antithetical to effective cure. But the question is a consideration.

If, as Shakespeare put it, "What's past is prologue," many important lessons yet remain to be learned from the folk medical world.

Empirical Aztec Medicine

Bernard Ortiz de Montellano

Many people have a tendency to equate folk medicine with superstitious belief and/or magic. This tendency is general in the United States. While it is not being suggested that all folk medicine is efficacious or empirically sound, a good deal of it is. (And concededly, modern scientific medicine is not always effective.) This article presents an interesting case where the bulk of the identifiable medicines appear to accomplish exactly what was intended by the people in question. Readers accordingly can begin to appreciate the cultural accomplishments of the ancient civilizations of the New World. Examples of empirically sound medicine can be found in many "primitive" and "folk" societies. Modern medicine is presented with the interesting task of attempting to merge sound scientific practice with sound folk practice in order to provide both acceptable and optimum services. For complementary information on Aztec drug use, see Ortiz de Montellano (1974/1975) and the tables and bibliography that accompany the following article as it appeared in *Science*.

The medicinal concepts of the Aztecs at the time of the Spanish Conquest were a mixture of magic, religion, and science. Disease could be attributed to a specific deity; for example, blisters and eye diseases were believed to be caused by Xipe Totec. Illness could also be attributed to the efforts of evil sorcerers. Treatment involved religion, magic, positive medical intervention, or a combination of these.

Studies of Aztec medicine have usually focused on the religious and magical characteristics of the treatment. Most of those dealing with the medicinal herbs used by Aztec physicians are out-of-date, sketchy, or simply translations of original Nahuatl texts. Hallucinogenic drugs, however, have been studied in more depth, and these studies have essentially confirmed the effects produced and the identity of the plants described in native sources.

The successful use of anthropological sources in the identification of potential hallucinogens suggested that it would be possible to use these sources, together with modern knowledge, to evaluate the effectiveness of other Aztec medicinal plants. This article deals with a number of medicinal plants which have been identified botanically and analyzed chemically. The chemical components are evaluated to determine whether they could produce the effects ascribed to the plant by the Aztec *ticitl* (physicians). A thorough review of hallucinogens has appeared recently, and this category of medicinal plants is not dealt with here.

Sources of Information

The oldest source of information on medicinal herbs available is an herbal written in Nahuatl by Martin de la Cruz in 1552 and translated into Latin by Juan Badiano. The herbal was prepared as a gift to King Charles I of Spain to obtain his goodwill for the Colegio de Santa Cruz de Tlatelolco, a school run by the Franciscans to train young Aztecs in Christianity, which was then under attack by other religious orders who felt that the Franciscans were too sympathetic to the old ways of the Indians.

Friar Bernardino de Sahagun, who arrived in Mexico in 1529, spent most of his life writing an encyclopedic work on the Aztecs. The information was developed through questionnaires submitted to informants. The questionnaires were answered and written down in Nahuatl by scribes. Three sets of data were developed: the first *(Primeros Memoriales)* at Tepepulco, the second *(Codex Matritense)* at Tlatelolco, and the most extensive *(Florentine Codex)* at Tenochtitlan. On the basis of these documents, Sahagun wrote a version in Spanish, *Historia General de las Cosas de Nueva Espana,* which was published after his death.

Francisco Hernandez, personal physician to Philip II of Spain, was sent to Mexico, where he spent the years between 1571 and 1577 gathering material on the plants, animals, and minerals of the New World. The material he gathered formed a basis for the work *Historia Natural de Nueva Espana.* This complete work was never published and was lost during the fire at the Escorial Palace. A truncated version by Reccho was published in 1651. Subsequent versions have been published, based on a rough draft found in Madrid a century later.

Francisco Ximenez, a Dominican friar, worked at the hospital in Huaxtepec. This was the site of an Aztec botanical garden and the repository of a copy of Hernandez's original work. In 1615 Ximenez published a version of Hernandez's work, which he augmented with material gathered in the course of his own practice.

All these sources have deficiencies for our purpose, because we are primarily interested in the pure native view about medicine. Hernandez had the views on disease which were current in Europe, and he fitted information given to him by native informants into the framework of this ideology. He classified plants by terms such as "warm," "cold," and "moist," but whether the natives used such classifications is debatable. He discussed therapeutic properties in terms of the Hippocratic doctrine of humors, although conflicts arise between European theory and Aztec practice. This contradictory evidence has led to much dispute concerning the origin of the present "hot-cold" folk theory of disease. Ximenez's work suffers from similar deficiencies.

Sahagun's work adheres much more closely to the information he obtained from the Aztecs. However, from internal evidence it seems that his informants were responding to a set of specific questions rather than to an open-ended question, and the facts elicited were thus influenced to an unknown extent by the Spanish 16th-century *weltanschauung* reflected in the questions. The Spanish version of Sahagun is not an exact or literal translation of the Nahuatl protocols, and thus the *Florentine Codex,* which was written in the language of the informants themselves, is more reliable.

The *Badianus Codex* should be the most authentic source of all, since it was both written and translated by natives, but it, too, presents some problems. There is internal evidence that the author had access to European herbals, and the vocabulary which Badiano was forced to use in Latin might not be the exact equivalent of the Nahuatl vocabulary. A further weakness may be that it is the work of a single author, and his theories may not have been as generally held as those espoused in the *Florentine Codex,* which was a collegial effort.

Methodology

The principal difficulty in this study is to correctly identify the plant mentioned in the sources. This is partly due to the practice of using the same Nahuatl name for obviously different plants. For example, there are 37 plants called *iztac-patli* (white medicine) and 21 called *cihuapatli* (women's medicine) in the work by Hernandez. Hernandez tried to clarify the situation by adding place names to the Aztec word. This system of nomenclature is probably due to Hernandez rather than to his native informants. The use of multiple names can result in the same plant being identified by different sources as belonging to different genera or families. An additional handicap is presented by descriptions which are not clear or illustrations which are not sufficient for an unambiguous identification. In an attempt to minimize this problem, I consider here only plants whose botanical identification is agreed on by at least three sources.

Even if the botanical identification is correct and the plant contains the proper chemical ingredients, the dosage given may be either excessive or insufficient. This question is more difficult because the amount of medicine to be taken is rarely stated or is given in an imprecise manner by the sources. In this article it is assumed that if the proper chemical substance is present, the dosage prescribed would be adequate to produce the desired result.

Although the religious or magic aspects of Aztec medicine have been greatly emphasized, much empirical research was done by Aztec doctors and their predecessors. The botanical gardens which so astonished the Spanish conquerors had been established as early as 1467 by Motecuhzoma I. These gardens were maintained primarily to provide the medical profession with raw materials for medicinal formulas and for experimentation. Beginning with Motecuhzoma I, the emperor's envoys had a mission to seek out additional species.

Evidence of the effectiveness of native medicine is given both by the comments of Spanish conquerors and by the quick adoption in European pharmacopoeias of sarsaparilla, palo santo, and sassafras, all of which are mentioned by Nicolas Monardes in the herbal which he wrote in 1565.

It would be inappropriate to judge the effectiveness of these drugs by modern medical standards or even by 16th-century European standards. The effectiveness should be evaluated in the context of the beliefs of the Aztec informants. For example, the Aztecs believed that fever was caused by interior heat, which could be eliminated by a diuretic, a purgative, or a digestive. If an herb they prescribed for fever, such as *totoncaxihuitl (Cassia occidentalis),* is in reality a purgative, then the herb should be considered to be an effective drug. Whether a purgative is also a fever reducer is not relevant for the purpose of evaluating the empirical investigative quality of Aztec medicine. The ability of the *ticitl* should be judged according to their view of the etiology of disease. If the plant recommended by Aztec medicine for a particular ailment contains chemicals which have been accounted therapeutic for that ailment within the last 70 to 80 years, then the empirical observation is even more successful.

["Table I. Some Aztec medicinal herbs" is omitted from this reprint.]

Evaluation of Therapeutic Effectiveness

No problem is presented if, in fact, the substance contains chemicals which produce the effects predicted by native sources. It is more difficult to evaluate negative evidence, that is, cases where reported plant constituents would not produce the effects claimed. There are three possible explanations for this: (i) the plant is ineffective; (ii) effective substances are present, but they have not been isolated because the plant has not been studied fully; and (iii) the botanical identification is not accurate.

Artemisia mexicana (effective). Thujone and thujyl alcohol are components of oil of wormwood, which was used formerly as a tonic and anthelmintic; santonin is an anthelmintic; and camphor is a mild irritant, stimulant, and colic reliever.

Bocconia frutescens (effective). Chelerythrine and sanguinarine are active local irritants. They have been used as expectorants. Water extracts of *B. frutescens* exhibit diuretic, anti-inflammatory, and antimicrobial activity.

Bromelia pinguin (effective). Pinguinain is a proteolytic enzyme with an antiedematous effect.

Carica papaya (effective). Papase is an enzyme which topically will remove clotted blood, purulent exudate, and necrotic tissue from surface wounds and ulcers. Therefore, it should be effective for rash. Internally, it is a protein digestant, and thus it is a digestive. Carpaine is said to slow the heart and depress the nervous system.

Casimiroa edulis (effective). Evaluation of this substance is more difficult since several extrapolations are needed. Histamine is a vasodilator but it is not active orally. *N,N*-Dimethyl histamine or casimiroidine might, however, be active orally. Fagarine has been used experimentally as an analog of quinidine to slow down and regularize heartbeats. This combination of ingredients should possess hypnotic and sleep-producing properties.

Cassia occidentalis or *Cassia alata* (effective). Chrysophanic acid and its glycosides are cathartic, and the reduction product chrysarobin is used topically for psoriasis and other chronic skin diseases.

Chenopodium graveolens (effective). Ascaridole is the main component of the anthelmintic oil of chenopodium. The oil is also a local intestinal tract irritant, which would be useful in dysentery. Volatile oil components would aid in restoring free breathing.

Euphorbia calyculata (effective). Externally, salicylic acid is an exfoliative and a fungicide insecticide. The latex from *Euphorbia* is a strong purgative and vesicant. This would be expected to be an effective remedy for skin infections and sores.

Helianthus annuus (not effective). It is not clear how the compounds found in sunflower seeds would relieve fever.

Liquidambar styraciflua (effective). The balsam storax obtained from *Liquidambar* is a stimulating expectorant and was used at one time for various catarrhs. Externally, as an ointment, it has been used as a parasiticide in scabies and other parasitic infections.

Montanoa tomentosa (possibly effective). This remedy, still used in folk medicine, is troublesome because the evidence is contradictory. There is wide agreement from native sources that *cihuapatli* is oxytocic, and there is wide agreement concerning its identity with *M. tomentosa.* The reported constituents would not a priori be oxytocic, and there is conflicting literature concerning its effectiveness.

Passiflora jorullensis (not effective). Carboline alkaloids are potent monoamine oxidase inhibitors and muscular relaxants. They have been used as psychic sedatives and anodynes. Monoamine oxidase inhibitors have been used against Parkinson's disease. Their usefulness as diuretics, diaphoretics, and remedies for poisons and snake bites is doubtful.

Perezia adnata (possibly effective). Gallic acid, being an astringent, might be useful in the treatment of sore throat by reducing inflammation of the membranes, but the other components do not explain the purgative and cathartic properties ascribed by native sources.

Persea americana (effective). Unsaturated heptadecatriols and their acetate esters act as antibiotics against gram-negative bacteria. They would be effective emollients against scars and sores.

Pithecolobium dulce (not effective.)

Plantago mexicana (effective). The *Plantago* seed is used as a cathartic. Polysaccharides are good bulk laxatives and cathartics.

Plumbago pulchella (effective). Plumbagin (methyljuglone) is active against bacteria, particularly staphylococcus, and thus might be effective against furuncles and acne. Since it is useful against urinary tract infections, it might be considered diuretic. It has a caustic effect externally.

Psidium guajava (not effective).

Rhamnus serrata (effective). Chrysophanic acid is a cathartic, as mentioned above under *Cassia.*

Salix lasiopelis (effective). Hydrolysis of salicin yields salicylic acid. Salts have been used internally as a urinary antiseptic, analgesic, and antipyretic. The acid is used externally as a local antiseptic and is fungicidal for chronic eczemas.

Schoenocaulon coulteri; Veratrum frigidum (effective). Veratrine is a mixture of cevadine, veratridine, cevadilline, and cevine. This mixture is extremely irritating to mucous membranes. Formerly it was used medicinally as a topical anodyne counterirritant. Cevine has been evaluated as an insecticide. These compounds are quite toxic and thus would be effective in killing mice. Extracts of *Schoenocaulon officinale* show a strong toxic action toward houseflies. Since the alkaloids in *Schoenocaulon* and *Veratrum* match the various claims made for *zozoyatic,* the identification of this plant as *Stenanthium frigidum* or *Zygadenus* sp. is placed in doubt.

Smilax aristolochiaefolia (possibly effective). The effectiveness of sarsaparilla is doubtful although it has been used formerly in chronic rheumatism, skin diseases, and syphilis.

Tagetes erecta (not effective). Alphaterthienyl is a nematicide, but otherwise the native predictions do not seem to be borne out.

Talauma mexicana (possibly effective). The compounds reported for this species would not a priori be active, but there are persistent clinical reports of digitalis-like activity.

Theobroma cacao (effective). Theobromine is a diuretic, stimulant, and smooth muscle dilator. Cacao butter is a mild cathartic and protects the gastrointestinal tract.

Summary and Conclusions

If Aztec medicinal herbs are evaluated by standards which take the etiology of disease prevailing at the time into account, the results are favorable. Of the 25 plants dealt with in this article, 16 would produce most of the effects claimed in native sources, 4 may possibly be active, and 5 do not seem to possess the activity claimed by native informants. Thus, in this sample, a majority of the remedies were found to be effective. More work is needed to determine whether this proportion would be found for the remaining several hundred medicinal plants mentioned in native sources. It is clear that although magic and religion were quite important in the Aztec treatment of disease, there was a strong empirical underpinning which has not received the attention it merits.

The Fagara Tree

United Press International/Star-Free Press

In addition to opening the way for discussion of various aspects of sickle cell anemia, this article also presents us with an empirically sound example of folk medicine. There have been reports that tooth decay for some peoples in the world has increased dramatically. While diet, no doubt, can be implicated to some degree, some researchers have linked the increase to a change from traditional techniques of oral hygiene to the modern scientific methods.

We are additionally presented with an example of the process of innovation and discovery in action. Perhaps a warning can be derived from this chance discovery of a potential cure. Without the proper training, researchers would not have recognized the possible alternative uses for the fagara root. One cannot help but wonder about how many cures have been overlooked because there was no one present to recognize them. A plea here is for recognizing the importance of the interdisciplinary approach to research and design of health care services. Readers interested in the innovative process should begin with Barnett's classic work (1953).

New York (UPI)—The root of a tree which Africans use as a toothbrush may provide the cure for sickle cell anemia, the blood disease that affects 50,000 black Americans, according to a noted researcher.

Professor Koji Nakanishi, head of a research team at Columbia University, said Friday a synthetic chemical produced from the plant has converted diseased sickle-shaped blood cells back into healthy ones in test-tube experiments.

"We are very cautious about saying we have a cure because we don't have any clinical results—that is, no human patients have been given the drug," said Nakanishi, an organic chemist. "But this is the most promising treatment for sickle cell I've seen so far."

Sickle cell anemia is a genetically carried disease usually fatal to victims, who are almost exclusively blacks or persons of Mediterranean descent.

"Normal red blood cells are round," Nakanishi said. "But in some people, mostly blacks, the cells are deformed into sickle shapes when they do heavy exercise. The deformed cells cannot pass through the blood vessels and the vessels become clotted."

The current research began by mistake, Nakanishi said, when Dr. Donald Ekong of the University of Ibadan, Nigeria decided to see why the fagara, a commonly found shrub tree in African countries, made such a good toothbrush.

"Africans use the root of the tree and cut it so it becomes brushlike and use it as a toothbrush," Nakanishi said.

"So Dr. Ekong thought if it had properties which keep the teeth from decaying, it might be antibacterial. He began testing it on a medium of blood, and the fagara root began changing the shape of sickled red blood into healthy round ones.

"This is how he became interested in its possibilities as a cure for sickle cell."

The Columbia research team found a new method for duplicating the fagara's chemical properties synthetically, so it would be available in large quantities without the tree. The product is known as DBA.

"We made a radioactive version of DBA and began testing its effect on hemoglobin, the major part of blood which is attacked by sickle," Nakanishi said.

"If it does the same thing in tests on humans that it did in the test tube—in other words rearrange the sickle cells back into round cells—it could be the cure we're looking for.

"So far we've only tested the synthetic for acute toxicity," Nakanishi said. "It's proven nontoxic in the short run, but there's no guarantee that it won't have long term effects if it's given to patients over a period of years."

Volksheilkunde

George D. Spindler

At places in this book the terms "scientific" and "folk" have been used as though they were clearly distinguishable. In this selection, Spindler specifically states that the distinction between "sound" medicine and "ritual" or "magical" medicine is not so easy to make. It should, of course, be remembered that much of what is ritual in any system of medicine may have therapeutic value. It can be shown, however, that folk and scientific medicines have more in common than ritual therapeutic efficacy alone. For example, many scientific medicaments clearly work. Folk medicines (from which many scientific medicines are derived) are also seen to be empirically sound (witness Aztec medicine). It is perhaps wise to note that both scientific and folk medicine benefit from the fact that most people stricken with minor ailments will usually recover regardless of the treatment received. Note also the numerous questions about these systems of medicine that can affect the attitudes toward treatment: for example, how esoteric is medical knowledge, to what extent is the community involved in the therapeutic process, how active or passive is the patient in the healing process, and how explicit and pervasive is ritual in the therapeutic regimen? The following article, describing the maintenance of a traditional medical system, serves also to illustrate an aspect of German culture and world-view, the utilization of dual systems of medicine, and the fact that all peoples have folk medical beliefs. A sampling of studies on folk medical beliefs for different "Western" peoples includes Withers (1946), Kourennoff (1970), Hand (1976), and *MD* (1958). There is also a wealth of popular books advocating one or another system of folk healing.

Cultural definitions of disease, its detection and cure, constitute a particularly fertile area for the proliferation and maintenance of self-verifying beliefs, for health and illness are intimately linked with personal and communal survival, and are areas of belief and behavior where anxiety is omnipresent. It is this area which we will now consider. Volksheilkunde—"folk healing"—is present in some form in most homes in Burgbach. Some of Volksheilkunde is physiologically as well as psychologically effective. Volksheilkunde beliefs are, however, self-verifying without external, controlled evidence, simply because most people with minor, and many with major, diseases or hurts recover with or without treatment. Volksheilkunde also has contributed to the maintenance of other cultural subsystems, as do all self-verifying beliefs and ritualized behaviors. Volksheilkunde is imbedded in the family, which, as we have seen, is a particularly significant social unit in Burgbach, as elsewhere in Germany.

Various forms of Volksheilkunde are represented not only at the informal level of ordinary household remedies passed on from parent to child, but also in remedies sold in *Drogerien* (stores resembling drugstores but not selling prescriptions) as well as in remedies for disease syndromes described in textbooks approved by the State Ministry of Education for use in the Grundschule. There is a very substantial literature on Volksheilkunde in its various forms that ranges all the way from technical, seemingly scientific treatises, to a useful book to have around the house called *Unser Hausfreund* (Roff 1956).

It is difficult for Americans to understand Volksheilkunde. Many Americans use home remedies and nearly all use aspirin or something similar for almost every conceivable psychological or physiological complaint. Volsheilkunde in its most complete form, however, goes far beyond this. It is a set of attitudes and beliefs that is supported not only by folk in the most remote village, but also to some extent by professional medical personnel. Volksheilkunde is not merely a survival from the past, although it contains many elements from the past. It is a living pattern. It contains within its total range not only concepts and behaviors that are probably medically effective, but also many that seem to be heavily ritualized. These are not mutually exclusive categories, for ritual behaviors often have decisive psychosomatic effects. The borderline between what is pragmatically valid and what is magical belief or ritualized behavior, particularly in medical practice, is extremely difficult to ascertain. We can define this shadowy area better by describing a sample of Volksheilkunde beliefs and remedies. We will consider common home remedies, therapeutic bathing, and Heilkräuter-tee (healing tea.)

Common Home Remedies

Among the twenty-five women interviewed in Burgbach representing the major life styles and social aggregates described in the last chapter, the following remedies were commonly used at home.

Toothache: hold a warm clay-filled sack on the stricken area; bite on cloves; chew hard black bread; use hot compresses; use schnapps-saturated cotton wads; put clove oil on the sore spot; put clove oil on a cotton wad stuffed into the cavity.

Infection and fever: drink a lot of water and other liquids, drink camomile and peppermint teas; drink Lindenblüten tea; wrap the calves of the leg or the entire upper part of the body with compresses soaked in a water-and-vinegar solution; wrap infected areas with compresses of sour milk or pig lard.

Headaches: wrap the head with a compress soaked with water, vinegar, and milk; drink various teas; take a cool foot bath.

Sneezing and coughing: drink honey and cognac mixed together with hot water and lemon; wear a flannel cloth with camphor on the chest; use a vaporizer to which vinegar has been added; inhale camomile-tea steam and drink hot camomile tea; rub oil and fat compresses on the chest; drink onion juice with brown sugar, or drink radish juice with brown sugar; take a steam bath with the addition of camomile tea or eucalyptus oil; drink hot malt wine; drink lemon juice; use a sweat cure.

Insomnia: drink Baldrian tea; eat onions which have been boiled in milk immediately before retiring; drink a mixture of cold milk and honey; place the bed with the feet toward the south and the head toward the north; sleep with the head higher than the feet.

Stomach aches, cramps, and heartburn: drink various cognacs and schnapps; eat zwieback; drink Baldrian and bloodroot teas; drink peppermint tea and put warm cloths on the stomach.

Constipation: eat sour milk or cottage cheese; eat apples and drink apple juice; chew tobacco and swallow the juice; sit in a tub of warm water; use suppositories, particularly in the form of a small splinter of soap; drink honey and water on an empty stomach; eat raw sauerkraut; use any one of a number of medicinal herb teas *(Kräuterteen).*

Burns: use salad oils as a dressing; use butter or codliver oil and bind with muslin; make a paste of vegetable oil and potato meal; cover with the white of a fresh egg; use a compress soaked with one of several teas.

Diarrhea: eat zwieback and drink cold red wine; fast and then drink black teas and zwieback; chew and swallow charcoal; eat oatmeal; drink hot chocolate cooked with water instead of milk; drink a raw egg mixed with cognac; drink a number of herbs mixed together and steeped, including Kamillenblüten and Anis.

Worms: eat garlic and onions or raw carrots; take honey, use an enema of salt and soap water; drink mineral water with pumpkin or gourd seeds; drink hot milk; use one of several teas recommended for worms.

It is quite impossible to separate out precisely what is "sound" medical practice and what is ritualized or magical practice in these remedies. There is a mixture of physiologically relevant and irrelevant. For our purposes it is not important that this separation be made. Irrespective of their medical efficacy or lack of it, these remedies will be used without objective evidence of their efficacy. They are self-sustaining beliefs as applied by the people who use them. They all provide something for the members of the household to do for someone who is stricken with minor illness or hurts. The probability that the patient will recover, regardless of what is done, is high. Therefore almost any practice that is not downright harmful is validated. Even harmful practices, to the extent that they do not result in the death of the patient, may be validated by eventual recovery, temporary remission of symptoms or partial recovery.

We do not mean to imply that in the homes where these remedies are used professional medical help is not called for or employed. Nearly all German families are covered by health insurance programs, and in a community like Burgbach medical help is relatively easily available. The women interviewed pointed out that the conditions treated were all minor. They said that when a serious condition developed, medical help is always used. They pointed out further that there was no necessary contradiction between the use of professional medical help and the use of home remedies of this type.

Therapeutic Bathing

Therapeutic bathing is widely used in Germany both in standard medical practice and in home treatment of minor illnesses or chronic, nonacute conditions not requiring hospitalization. It is also featured in many curing spas scattered throughout the Black Forest and other vacation areas.

Among the twenty-five Burgbach women interviewed on health practices as well as thirty other households in which relevant inquiries were made in the context of other studies, therapeutic bathing in some form was used, even if it meant no more than taking a hot bath with the addition of one of several aromatic solutions that are readily available on the market. Some baths that appeared to be heavily ritualized are used rather infrequently but are known by nearly all persons interviewed.

In general, therapeutic bathing is regarded as an aid to nature in the disposal of body poisons, as a means of strengthening nerves, arousing appetite, improving digestion, and enlivening circulation and metabolism. The baths are of several types.

Sitzbad: a simple tub bath (in which one sits) which achieves maximum results with the coldest possible water.

Mud bath: the same as Sitzbad but with approximately one kilogram (2.2 lbs.) of silt mixed in with the water.

The Luftlichtbad: the body is sprinkled with water and then the bather runs around naked breathing deeply.

The Reibebad: the bather sits on a small bench in the tub, dips a towel into cold water and vigorously rubs the body from the pit of the stomach down. The feet must be kept dry.

Dampfbad: steam from boiling hay blossoms, oats, straw, or zinnia is directed upon the afflicted part of the body and the part is covered with a saturated cloth to hinder evaporation.

Bettdampfbad: the naked patient is wrapped in a sheet which has been immersed in lukewarm water. He or she is covered with wool blankets, and hot water bottles are places on the armpits and feet. After sweating for one or two hours the patient is washed with cool water.

Ganzwaschung: one begins by washing the right foot and then the left foot, continuing on up to the hips on the foresides of the legs, followed by the backsides. After this, the upper body is washed starting with the right arm and followed by the left arm and continuing to the left breast, downwards to the stomach, then up the right side to the breast, followed in turn by the side parts of the body, and finally the back. Some authorities recommend no drying with towels

Many additives to the various warm and cold baths may be used. Hay flowers are believed to stimulate the skin and to relieve arthritis, rheumatism, and lung congestion. When added to bath water spruce needles, or one of the many commercial preparations of similar character, through their aroma, it is believed, work to calm the nervous system and stimulate blood circulation and metabolism. Oak bark is useful as an additive for various skin diseases, hemorrhoids, and tuberculosis of the lymph glands. Camomile is added to the bath to treat colds with fever, eczema, wounds, hemorrhoids, blisters, and various infections and abdominal complaints. Bran makes the skin soft when added to bath water and is used for skin diseases, eczema, and psoriasis. Mustard is one the the strongest stimulants and is used for grippe, bronchitis, lung inflammation, headache, and congestion of any kind. Very often these substances are taken in the context of a *Wechselbad.* This kind of bath begins with a few minutes of warm to fairly hot water and ends with several seconds in cold water. This is believed to have a beneficial and stimulating effect on circulation.

The same general remarks can be made about therapeutic bathing as can be made about home remedies. It is clear that variation in the temperature of bath water, including sweating, and probably even the vapors from the various herbs added to the bath water have physiological effects which may, indeed, be beneficial in the treatment of certain conditions and for certain patients. They may also, it is assumed, be harmful in the treatment of certain conditions. For persons not seriously debilitated by illness, they probably induce a general feeling of well being. In any event, they are again something that one can do about one's condition or for someone else in the family.

All of the baths, even those that do have definite beneficial physiological effect, involve ritual elements which in themselves create psychoemotional states which may be further effective in producing satisfactions only tangentially or not at all related to curing specific ailments. The highly ritualized baths, such as the complex Ganzwaschung, must produce these benefits entirely through the ritual process itself.

Heilkräuter-tee

Heilkräuter-tee (tea from medicinal herbs) is widely used in Germany on a very casual basis for the treatment of practically any minor condition and as an aid to recovery from more serious ones. Nearly every Drogerie in the Remstal area sells a wide variety of such teas. *Apotheken*[1] sell medicinal herbs as teas as well as prescription and pharmaceutical products, including aspirin and other common household drugs that do not require professional supervision for their use in the United States. There are few households which do not use medicinal herb teas. Most people simply assume that they are beneficial and useful, though people in the highest educational levels tend to be more skeptical about any home remedies, therapeutic baths, or herbal teas. The reading books of the third and fourth grade in the Grundschule, however, contain several pages describing and listing specific herbal teas and their presumed effect. Many students reported that they were offered teas by the families they were observing whenever they had a headache or if they professed to be coming down with a cold, or suffering with a mild stomach disorder, or from general malaise.

There are at least eighty domestic medicinal herbs which can be used alone or mixed to form *Komplex Kräuter* (mixtures of medicinal herbs). The six listed below are the most commonly used, according to local *Drogisten*.

Anis (anis seed) stimulates action of digestive organs, brings relief from asthma, and is good for colic in children.

Fenchel (fennel) is good for coughs and asthma, strengthens nerves in the stomach and intestines, and is good as an eye wash and to strengthen the optic nerve.

Kamille (camomile) helps relieve almost any form of stomach pains, spasms, or cramps, especially when mixed with peppermint tea; calms nerves, and when dissolved in bath water helps arrest inflammation or reduce swelling; also used as a hair dressing and bleaching and darkening hair.

Linde (lime tree blossom) is good for colds, stomach cramps, and in general for soothing, tranquilizing effects, and, in solution, useful as a skin cleanser.

Minze (mint or peppermint) is especially good for the stimulation of the kidneys, helps weak hearts, soothes the restless and worried, and should be taken every day.

---

[1]It should be clear that there is no precise equivalent to the American drugstore in Germany. The Drogerie comes closest because everything from toothpaste to film may be sold in them, but only Apotheken have prescription counters—and many medicines, such as aspirin, require prescriptions.

Salbei (sage) strengthens stomach and intestinal walls, helps remove blockages in the liver and gall passages, is good as a gargle against throat irritation, and helps reduce "night-sweating."

There are also a very large number of commercially prepared tea complexes made up of mixes of several of the eighty common domestic herbs used for teas and labeled according to the body part or organ or the type of disease for which they are believed effective. Some of these sold most frequently in local Remstal Drogerien are listed below.

Abführ-Tee: helps clean intestines, ridding them of digestive wastes and preventing constipation, also recommended for hemorrhoids.

8-Blüten-Tee (Schlaf-und-Nerven-Tee): this eight blossom sleep-and-nerve tea regulates sleep and calms and strengthens the nerves.

Blutkreislauf-Tee: this tea for improving circulation of the blood is believed to be good for arteriosclerosis and high blood pressure; it cleans and freshens the blood and should be a daily drink for the middle-aged and aged.

Blutreinigungs-Tee: this blood-cleansing and disinfecting tea should be taken every year in the spring and fall. The "herbal hormones" in the tea are believed to effect the removal of waste materials that occur as a result of chemical changes in the body and also to relieve general tiredness that is a result of "impure" blood.

Bronchial-Tee: this tea helps to relieve inflammation of the air passages and relieves in the elimination of phlegm.

Diabetiker-Tee: in general, recommended as a supplement to the doctor's care in the treatment of diabetic patients.

Entfettungs-Tee or *Schlankheits-Tee:* this weight-reducing tea works to withdraw the excess fat from the intestinal tract into the bowels, preventing its disposition in the form of fat on the body.

Harnsäure-Tee: this so-called uric acid tea is recommended for people with arthritis and rheumatism as it is believed to prevent the formation of uric acid crystals that form in the joints and cause pain.

Nerven-Tee für Frauen: this nerve tea is believed to be especially beneficial for women and particularly young women during menstruation and in general helps dissipate the accompanying disturbances such as headache, backache, and a general sick feeling.

Nieren-und-Blasen Tee: this kidney and bladder tea stimulates the regularity of the kidneys and strengthens them, dissolves salt in the urine, and prevents a buildup of stones and grit in the kidneys.

There are thirty commonly used Komplex Kräuter-Teesonten packaged by any one of several companies and available on the shelves of the Drogerie.

It is impossible to assess the specific medicinal claims made in support of the use of these many different herbal teas. Since all of them contain chemical substances found in nature, they may have some physiological effect. However, the actual amount of any such substances consumed, except by the most avid of tea drinkers, must be minute.

No one interviewed denied all efficacy to the Heilkräuter-Tee. They are used by families of all income and education levels, though not to the same extent in all families. Even the families of three interviewed doctors used teas rather extensively, and all three doctors indicated that they often recommended tea as a part of their treatment. Heilkräuter-Tee is also served in hospitals with meals, and many dentists prescribe camomile tea for patients who have had dental work.

Whatever their medical effect, there are substantial ritual elements in tea drinking. Many of the remedies such as the "blood-cleaning" tea are taken at only certain times of the year as an almost ceremonial seasonal observance. Other teas are consumed only at certain times of the day or only after or before certain meals or in association with certain foods. Even the association of specific teas with specific disorders may be considered ritualistic in character. Preparation of the various teas also involves considerable ritual. Some insist that the tea must be boiled with the water and then strained. Others say that the water must be boiled first and then poured on the tea, and some will never boil the water but rather let the tea steep in cool water overnight. Each method of preparation has its separate justification. these are self-verifying beliefs and ritualized behaviors that constitute an elaboration of means to an empirically unknown end. The ritual elements may indeed be the most important contribution to the assumed effect of the teas just as is the ritual of the therapeutic bath. The ritualized means produce the satisfaction. And again, the teas, like all forms of Volksheilkunde, make some kind of action possible from within the household to protect and succor its members.

General Attitudes toward Health and Disease

The people of Burgbach and the surrounding vicinity are very concerned about health and bodily functions. What one eats and drinks is considered important as well as how much exercise one gets and how much fresh air one breathes. Natural foods and natural exercise are considered good and beneficial to general health and well-being. Whereas Americans tend to be weight conscious, the people of Burgbach seem to be "health and nature" conscious. Attitudes toward disease and the treatment of illness and injury also seem to be quite different in the two cultural contexts. To the American student fresh from the aspirin-seltzer-antihistamine-antibiotic complex, not only the ordinary citizens of Burgbach but also German medical personnel seem very cautious about treatment of illness or injury. American students in Germany often complain that they "get nothing" from doctors they go to with ordinary ailments or even with what seems to them a serious condition such as flu. Some students who have suffered broken limbs or other bodily injury have complained that the period of confinement to bed and to a hospital is much longer than they would have had to endure at home. Be that as it may, it is true that the medical personnel interviewed expressed doubts about the desirability of heavy treatment such as the prescription of antibiotics, except when they were absolutely necessary, and indicated that all such radical interventions in the natural functioning of the body constituted a severe physiological jolt. They felt that more natural ways of recovering were more desirable.

An emphasis upon nature and natural processes underlies many of the specific values and practices expressed in Volksheilkunde. As the author of one of the books that many families keep in the house for ready reference wrote, "He who trusts nature has not built on sand" (Roff 1956). Or consider the following comment from an advertising brochure from the Burgbach Fruit Juice Manufacturing Plant.

> Out of nature continually comes much that is good. We all need a natural way of life. Only a very few people are still directly bound to nature. Only a few still work in the air and sun and live correctly. . . .
> It is certain—we are all caught up in the spider web of modern civilization and cannot live as exceptions to this life. We nevertheless have the opportunity to live more naturally without leaving the job and losing time. We may introduce into our bodies materials which come out of the great store of power in nature. Doctors and scientists have firmly established that through the use of apples, elimination problems as well as liver and kidney disorders are favorably influenced.
> We may not measure the worth of nutritional stuffs alone according to calories, proteins, vitamins, and other materials, but must also note the harmonious order in which they are contained in the means of nourishment.
> Nature created structures in the organs of plants which have a definite purpose. . . .

This orientation toward nature and natural processes runs deep in the culture of the Remstal and probably deep in German culture as a whole. People keep plants in the living and dining rooms as they are thought to contribute to the purity of the air. People take walks in high places in the forest on the ridges or through the vineyards in order to get the fresh wind and better air.

This generalized orientation is reinforced by a "school" of medicine that has been practiced in Europe and to some extent in North America for some time—the homeopathic school. The fundamental precept of this school is that recovery from illness must be through the natural processes of the body, and that the function of medication should be to stimulate these processes. Surgery or strong drugs such as antibiotics should only be taken in case of emergency when the body appears incapable of healing itself, or with the aid of natural medications in small doses. Drugs may be administered but only in infinitesimally small amounts to trigger natural bodily functions.

The homeopathic orientation certainly cannot be said to dominate modern German medical practice, but some of the continuity between medical practice and Volksheilkunde may be in part due to the influence of this school of medical practice. In any event, there seems to be an internally coherent pattern that includes some parts of contemporary medical practice as well as folk belief and practice. However, the coherence of the pattern neither validates nor challenges the validity of either folk or professional medical practice.

The culture pattern we are considering here is demonstrated by the results of an interview with one family. The male head of the house is a lawyer. Both he and his wife are university educated and are sophisticated people. The doctor is not called in this household until it is clear that the illness is beyond the ability of ordinary household treatment to handle. Frau Kahn, as we will call her, says that she likes to use natural cures. Rest, a good bath, and some tea are about all that one needs for most illnesses since the body cures itself. If one of the children is feeling a bit low, she will give him or her one of the several teas that she uses habitually and tells the child to lie down. If it looks as if a cold is developing, camomile tea will be taken because it loosens the bronchial tubes and allows drainage, Frau Kahn says. If there is a sore throat, gargling with hot lemon juice and honey or hot salt water is recommended, and if there is a stomachache involved, a warm towel is placed on the stomach and one drinks camomile or peppermint tea or both. Above all, one must stay in bed and keep warm and avoid all chilling. Even if a fever may appear, the use of antiobiotics is not anticipated. Frau Kahn says that the body builds up resistance to antibiotics and that when they are really needed, they no longer help. She says that even aspirin is too harsh and is unnecessary. If it looks as if there is a serious case of grippe, or one of the several common childhood diseases, the doctor will be called. Usually the doctor, according to Frau Kahn, recommends more tea, more rest, sweating, and staying in bed until all symptoms disappear. As the patient recovers from either the common cold or the childhood diseases, he or she will continue to get warm tea but also may choose from any combination of possibilities from the many *Säfte*—apple juice, grape juice, orange juice, currant juice, carrot juice, and so on—with or without mineral water.

Families with less education and with a life style closer to that of the more traditional Weingärtner-Bauer culture differ from the family just described mainly in the greater extent to which home remedies are used, the high degree of specificity concerning the relationship between treatment, disease, and cure, and reliance upon what appears to be a great amount of ritualization of the kind described in previous sections. The goal is the same—life and health. The Volksheilkunde remedies are rituals that produce auxiliary satisfactions and are self-sustaining because they do.

Final Comments on Volksheilkunde

Cultural continuity is the theme of this chapter. We are concerned with some of the ways in which there is continuity with the past in Burgbach (and Remstal) culture and with some of the processes that support this continuity. In the first section we dealt with the reaffirmation of identity expressed in the yearly Kirbefest. In this section we have discussed Volksheilkunde, a cultural complex centering upon disease and its cures. The widespread use of Volksheilkunde in Remstal homes is a direct expression of cultural persistence. Volksheilkunde is of very long standing, reaching well back in time to the Middle Ages and in forms specifically represented in the present pattern. This complex of attitudes and values, beliefs and practices, as we have seen, is related to an orientation toward nature and natural life processes that extends beyond folk or professional medical practice into other patterns and sectors of behavior. The general orientation toward nature and health and the specific health practices support each other and in so doing, constitute a significant process of cultural continuity.

We may look tentatively beyond these direct relationships to some indirect functions of the Volksheilkunde. These practices make possible the treatment of minor illness and injury in the home and family that therefore provide a sense of security that reinforces the familial orientation we have already discussed. Volksheilkunde is another way in which the family insulates and protects the individual from the threatening world outside. Familial values thus strengthened may in turn support a relatively conservative cultural orientation in the midst of an urbanizing, modernizing environment, providing that the family and its child-training environment are slower to adapt to changed conditions than other institutions and practices, or if the family transmits and reinforces values that are incongruent with full social participation in the outside world. We have some evidence that the values of parents of children in our elementary school sample are culturally conservative. Dahrendorf (1967) also argues that the familial, private values in German society are a block to full scale public participation and the taking of responsibility for public values, and that the family has precedence over the school.

Whatever its indirect functions, it appears that Volksheilkunde is becoming weaker. Drogisten who have been in the business for more than twenty years said that the decline in the use of medicinal herbal tea was substantial, particularly during the last ten years. All cultural persistence is, however, relative to varying rates of change. As seen from the American observers' point of view, the survival of Volksheilkunde is more impressive than its decline.

Lastly, we should take note of the fact that we have not been discussing a culture pattern limited to Burgbach, the Remstal, Baden-Württemberg, southern Germany, or even to Europe. Volksheilkunde is found in some form throughout Europe and, in attenuated form, in America as well. It should also be clear that we are not taking the supercilious position that American attitudes toward health and disease are less ritualized or more sophisticated than German attitudes or Burgbach attitudes. The American who goes to the doctor with a severe cold, demanding an antibiotic for a "virus" may be thinking magically. He may well be less sophisticated in his reasoning than the user of Volksheilkunde who has a clear rationale in mind about the relationship between illness, treatment, and bodily processes. Ritual elements are present in all medical practice, folk or professional. The important point in our analysis is that a whole system of beliefs and practices concering health and disease, a very basic area of human thinking and behavior, has survived in a complex form and constitutes a major cultural continuity in the community we are studying. It has survived partly because it is ritualized and self-verifying. That it helps validate the family, home, and parental care as an indirect function may also be significant.

The Art of Being a Failure as a Therapist

Jay Haley

Psychotherapists in all societies enjoy success. E. Fuller Torrey (1972) argues that such therapists in homogeneous folk societies may be even more effective than their counterparts in the more complex hetero-geneous societies such as the United States. In any case, there will be success to the extent that practitioners make their application of the four components of psychotherapy (see the introduction to Section IV) meaningful within their cultural milieu.

Jay Haley in the following article has suggested measures which will insure *failure* in therapy. Of course, in describing how to fail, Haley is essentially identifying the dynamics of therapy and the elements funda-mental to therapeutic success. Perhaps a thirteenth point could be added to his "twelve steps to failure": Since fifty to seventy percent of the patients on waiting list control groups appear not to seek treatment and actually "recover" despite lack of such "treatment," it would be advisable to insure that patients never be given the opportunity to wait lest they be lost to the therapist's plan for failure and, instead, be doomed to probable recovery. The list of "Five B's Which Guarantee Dynamic Failure" could be expanded with a sixth—Be Prompt.

What has been lacking in the field of therapy is a theory of failure. Many clinicians have merely assumed that any psychotherapist could fail it he wished. Recent studies of the outcome of therapy, however, indicate that spontaneous improvement of patients is far more extensive than was previously realized. There is a consistent finding that between fifty and seventy percent of patients on waiting list control groups not only do not wish treatment after the waiting list period but have really recovered from their emotional problems—despite the previous theories which did not consider this possible. Assuming that these findings hold up in further studies, a therapist who is incompetent and does no more than sit in silence and scratch himself will have at least a fifty percent success rate with his patients. How then can a therapist be a failure?

The problem is not a hopeless one. We might merely accept the fact that a therapist will succeed with half his patients and do what we can to provide a theory which will help him fail consistently with the other half. However, we could also risk being more adventurous. Trends in the field suggest the problem can be approached in a deeper way by devising procedures for keeping those patients from improving who would ordinarily spontaneously do so. Obviously, merely doing nothing will not achieve this end. We must create a program with the proper ideological framework and provide systematic training over a period of years if we expect a therapist to fail consistently.

An outline will be offered here of a series of steps to increase the chance of failure of any therapist. This presentation is not meant to be comprehensive, but it includes the major factors which experience in the field has shown to be essential and which can be put into practice even by therapists who are not specially talented.

1. The central pathway to failure is based upon a nucleus of ideas which, if used in combination, make success as a failure almost inevitable.

Step A: Insist that the problem which brings the patient into therapy is not important. Dismiss it as merely a "symptom" and shift the conversation elsewhere. In this way a therapist never learns to examine what is really distressing a patient.

Step B: Refuse to directly treat the presenting problem. Offer some rationale, such as the idea that symptoms have "roots," to avoid treating the problem the patient is paying his money to recover from. In this way the odds increase that the patient will not recover, and future generations of therapists can remain ignorant of the specific skills needed to get people over their problems.

Step C: Insist that if a presenting problem is relieved, something worse will develop. This myth makes it proper not to know what to do about symptoms and will even encourage patients to cooperate by developing a fear of recovery.

Given these three steps, it seems obvious that any psychotherapist will be incapacitated, whatever his natural talent. He will not take seriously the problem the patient brings, he will not try to change that, and he will fear that successful relief of the problem is disastrous.

One might think that this nucleus of ideas alone would make any therapist a failure, but the wiser heads in the field have recognized that other steps are necessary.

2. It is particularly important to confuse diagnosis and therapy. A therapist can sound expert and be scientific without ever risking a success with

treatment if he uses a diagnostic language which makes it impossible for him to think of therapeutic operations. For example, one can say that a patient is passive-aggressive, or that he has deep-seated dependency needs, or that he has a weak ego, or that he is impulse-ridden. No therapeutic interventions can be formulated with this kind of language. For more examples of how to phrase a diagnosis so that a therapist is incapacitated, the reader is referred to *The American Psychiatric Association Diagnostic Manual.*

3. Put the emphasis upon a single method of treatment no matter how diverse the problems which enter the office. Patients who won't behave properly according to the method should be defined as untreatable and abandoned. Once a single method has proven consistently ineffective, it should never be given up. Those people who attempt variations must be sharply condemned as improperly trained and ignorant of the true nature of the human personality and its disorders. If necessary, a person who attempts variations can be called a latent layman.

4. Have no theory, or an ambiguous and untestable one, of what a therapist should do to bring about therapeutic change. However, make it clear that it is untherapeutic to give a patient directives for changing—he might follow them and change. Just imply that change happens spontaneously when therapists and patients behave according to the proper forms. As part of the general confusion that is necessary, it is helpful to define therapy as a procedure for finding out what is wrong with a person and how he got that way. With that emphasis, ideas about what to do to bring about change will not develop in an unpredictable manner. One should also insist that change be defined as a shift of something in the interior of a patient so that it remains outside the range of observation and is uninvestigable. With the focus upon the "underlying disorder" (which should be sharply distinguished from the "overlying disorder"), questions about the unsavory aspects of the relationship between therapist and patient need not arise, nor is it necessary to include unimportant people, such as the patient's intimates, in the question of change.

Should student therapists who are not yet properly trained insist upon some instruction about how to cause change, and if a frown about their unresolved problems does not quiet them, it might be necessary to offer some sort of ambiguous and general idea which is untestable. One can say, for example, that the therapeutic job is to bring the unconscious into consciousness. In this way the therapy task is defined as transforming a hypothetical entity into another hypothetical entity and so there is no possibility that precision in therapeutic technique might develop. Part of this approach requires helping the patient "see" things about himself, particularly in relation to past traumas, and this involves no risk of change. The fundamental rule is to emphasize "insight" and "affect expression" to student therapists as causes of change so they can feel something is happening in the session without hazarding success. If some of the advanced students insist on more high-class technical knowledge about therapy, a cloudy discussion of "working through the transference" is useful. This not only provides young therapists with an intellectual catharsis but it gives them a chance to make transference interpretations and so have something to do.

5. Insist that only years of therapy will really change a patient.

This step brings us to more specific things to do about those patients who might spontaneously recover without treatment. If they can be persuaded that they have not really recovered but have merely fled into health, it is possible to help them back to ill health by holding them in long-term treatment. (One can always claim that only long-term treatment can really cure a patient so that he will never ever have a problem the remainder of his life). Fortunately the field of therapy has no theory of overdosage, and so a skillful therapist can keep a patient from improving for as long as ten years without protest from his colleagues, no matter how jealous. Those therapists who try for twenty years should be congratulated on their courage but thought of as foolhardy unless they live in New York.

6. As a further step to restrain patients who might spontaneously improve, it is important to offer warnings about the fragile nature of people and insist they might suffer psychotic breaks or turn to drink if they improve. When "underlying pathology" becomes the most common term in every clinic and consulting room, everyone will avoid taking action to help patients recover and patients will even restrain themselves if they begin to make it on their own. Long-term treatment can then crystallize them into therapeutic failures. If patients seem to improve even in long-term therapy, they can be distracted by being put into group therapy.

7. As a further step to restrain patients who might spontaneously improve, the therapist should focus upon the patient's past.

8. As yet another step with that aim, the therapist should interpret what is most unsavory about the patient to arouse his guilt so that he will remain in treatment to resolve the guilt.

9. Perhaps the most important rule is to ignore the real world that patients live in and publicize the vital importance of their infancy, inner dynamics, and fantasy life. This will effectively prevent either therapists or patients from attempting to make changes in their families, friends, schools, neighborhoods, or treatment milieus. Naturally they cannot recover if their situation does not change, and so one guarantees failure while being paid to listen to interesting fantasies. Talking about dreams is a good way to pass the time, and so is experimenting with responses to different kinds of pills.

10. Avoid the poor because they will insist upon results and cannot be distracted with insightful conversations. Also avoid the schizophrenic unless he is well drugged and securely locked up in a psychiatric penitentiary. If a therapist deals with a schizophrenic at the interface of family and society, both therapist and patient risk recovery.

11. A continuing refusal to define the goals of therapy is essential. If a therapist sets goals, someone is likely to raise a question whether they have been achieved. At that point the idea of evaluating results arises in its most virulent form. If it becomes necessary to define a goal, the phrasing should be unclear, ambiguous, and so esoteric that anyone who thinks about determining if the goal has been achieved will lose heart and turn to a less confused field of endeavor, like existentialism.

12. Finally, it cannot be emphasized enough that it is absolutely necessary to avoid evaluating the results of therapy. If outcome is examined, there is a natural tendency for people not fully trained to discard approaches which are not effective and to elaborate those which are. Only by keeping results a mystery and avoiding any systematic followup of patients can one ensure that therapeutic technique will not improve and the writings of the past will not be questioned. To be human is to err, and inevitably a few deviant individuals in the profession will attempt evaluation studies. They should be promptly condemned and their character questioned. Such people should be called superficial in their understanding of what therapy really is, oversimple in their emphasis upon symptoms rather than depth personality problems, and artificial in their approach to human life. Routinely they should be eliminated from respectable institutions and cut off from research funds. As a last resort they can be put in psychoanalytic treatment or shot.

This program of twelve steps to failure—sometimes called the daily dozen of the clinical field—is obviously not beyond the skill of the average well-trained psychotherapist. Nor would putting this program more fully into action require any major changes in the clinical ideology or practice taught in our better universities. The program would be helped if there was a positive term to describe it, and the word "dynamic" is recommended because it has a swinging sound which should appeal to the younger generation. The program could be called the therapy which expresses the basic principles of dynamic psychiatry, dynamic psychology, and dynamic social work. On the wall of every institute training therapists, there can be a motto known as *The Five B's Which Guarantee Dynamic Failure:*

Be Passive
Be Inactive
Be Reflective
Be Silent
Beware

A Note on Readings

Books providing overviews of the various fields include those by Simmons and Wolff (1954), King (1962), Kiev (1972), Opler (1967), Frank (1974), Mechanic (1968), MacGregor (1960), and Seward (1972). Most of the books remaining to be mentioned are collections of articles.

Collections with a generally anthropological perspective include those by Paul (1955), Galdston (1963), Lynch (1969), Landy (1977), and Logan and Hunt (1978).

Of a more sociological nature are the works by Apple (1960), Scott and Volkart (1966), Spitzer and Denzin (1968), Jaco (1958), and Freeman, Levine, and Reader (1963).

Several works concentrate primarily on mental health. Included are those by Opler (1959), Kiev (1964), de Reuck and Porter (1965), Finney (1969), and Plog and Edgerton (1969).

A sizeable number of books are directed to the nursing profession while reflecting a basic anthropological or sociological approach. Works by Brink (1976) and Skipper and Leonard (1965) are examples of this approach.

Ethnicity is the focus for numerous other collections and readers are directed to such works as those by Leslie (1976), Bullough and Bullough (1972), Adair and Deuschle (1970), Spicer (1977), and Danielson (1978).

There are, additionally, several professional journals which specialize in the type of material that is of present concern (e.g. *Social Science in Medicine,* the *Journal of Health and Social Behavior,* and *Culture, Medicine, and Psychiatry).* In addition, relevant articles appear in numerous journals representing many fields. Useful sources of bibliographic references include Polgar (1962), Scotch (1963), Freeman, Levine, and Reader (1963), and Landy (1977).

It is assumed that the curious reader will wish to examine the bibliographies of those articles contained in the collections cited above.

This listing should by no means be deemed complete. Many of these works also cut across disciplinary lines and are therefore difficult to place in any specific field. Furthermore, authors of many works like these are sometimes identified with a discipline different from the one that encompasses the contents of their respective books.

References

Adair, John, and Kurt W. Deuschle. 1970. *The People's Health: Medicine and Anthropology in a Navajo Community.* New York: Appleton-Century-Crofts.

American Institute of Architects, Committee on Hospitals and Health. 1960. "Report." *Journal of the American Institute of Architects.*

Anonymous. 1851. "Startling Facts from the Census." *American Journal of Insanity* 8(2):153–155.

Anonymous. 1968. Folk saying (dating to the 15th century or earlier). In *Familiar Medical Quotations,* M.B. Strauss, ed. Boston: Little, Brown, and Co.

Apple, Dorrian, ed. 1960. *Sociological Studies of Health and Sickness: A Source Book for the Health Profession.* New York: McGraw-Hill Book Company.

Baker, A., R. L. Davies, and P. Sivadon. 1959. *Psychiatric Services and Architecture.* Geneva: World Health Organization.

Barnett, Homer G. 1953. *Innovation: The Basis of Culture Change.* New York: McGraw-Hill Book Company.

Barnouw, V. 1950. "Acculturation and Personality among the Wisconsin Chippewa." *American Anthropologist,* Memoir No. 72, Vol. 52.

Bates, B. 1970. "Doctor and Nurse: Changing Roles and Relations." *New England Journal of Medicine* 283:129–134 (July 16).

Bates, Marston. 1959. "The Ecology of Health," in *Medicine and Anthropology,* Iago Galdston, ed. New York: International Universities Press.

Beeson, P. B., and Walsh McDermott, eds. 1971. *Cecil-Loeb Textbook of Medicine,* 13th edition. Philadelphia: W. B. Saunders Company, pp. 609–655, 947–1138, 1883–1913.

Beland, I. L. 1970. *Clinical Nursing: Pathophysiological and Psychosocial Approaches,* 2d ed. New York: Macmillan Company, pp. 358–463.

Birdwhistell, R. L. 1952. *Introduction to Kinesics.* Washington, D.C.: Foreign Service Institute, U.S. Department of State.

Brink, Pamela J., ed. 1976. *Transcultural Nursing: A Book of Readings.* Englewood Cliffs, N.J.: Prentice-Hall.

Bullough, Bonnie, and Vern Bullough, eds. 1971. *New Directions for Nurses.* New York: Springer Publishing Company, Inc.

_____. 1972. *Poverty, Ethnic Identity, and Health Care.* New York: Appleton-Century-Crofts, Meredith Corp.

Calder, Ritchie. 1962. *Medicine and Man: The Story of the Art and Science of Healing.* New York: Signet Books, New American Library.

Calhoun, J. B. 1961. *A Behavioral Sink.* (Manuscript.)

Cappanari, Stephen C., Bruce Rau, Harry S. Abram, and Denton C. Buchanan. 1975. "Voodoo in the General Hospital: A Case of Hexing and Regional Enteritis." *Journal of the American Medical Association* 232:938-940.

Cartwright, Frederick F., and Michael D. Biddiss. 1972. *Disease and History: The Influence of Disease in Shaping the Great Events of History.* New York: Thomas Y. Crowell Co.

Cartwright, Samuel A. 1851. "Report on the Diseases and Physical Peculiarities of the Negro Race." *New Orleans Medical and Surgical Journal* 8:228-237.

Cassel, John. 1955. "A Comprehensive Health Program among South African Zulus." In *Health, Culture and Community,* Benjamin Paul, ed. New York: Russell Sage Foundation.

Cassem, Ned H. 1973. "What You Can Do for Dying Patients." *Medical Dimensions* (Oct.) 29-34.

Chesler, Phyllis. *Women and Madness.* New York: Avon Books.

Chombart de Lauwe, Paul Henry, ed. 1959a. *Famille et Habitation.* Paris: Editions du Centre de la Recherche Scientifique.

_____. "Le milieu social et l'étude sociologique des cas individuels." *Informations Sociales* 2:41-54.

Clark, Margaret. 1959. *Health in the Mexican-American Culture.* Berkeley and Los Angeles: University of California Press.

Clark, Marie W. 1967. "Vanishing Vagabonds: the American Gypsies." *Texas Quarterly* 10:204-210 (Summer).

Clinicopathologic Conference Case Presentation (BCH # 469861), 1967. *Johns Hopkins Medical Journal* 120:186-199.

Clebert, J. P. 1969. *The Gypsies.* Baltimore: Penguin Books.

Cohen, Albert. 1955. *Delinquent Boys: The Culture of the Gang.* Glencoe: Free Press.

Corea, Gena. 1977. *The Hidden Malpractice: How American Medicine Treats Women as Patients and Professionals.* New York: William Morrow and Company.

Currier, Richard L. 1966. "The Hot-Cold Syndrome and Symbolic Balance in Mexican and Spanish Folk Medicine." *Ethnology* 5:251-363.

Dahrendorf, Ralf. 1967. *Society and Democracy in Germany.* New York: Doubleday and Company.

Danielson, Larry. 1978. *Studies in Folklore and Ethnicity.* Los Angeles: California Folklore Society.

Davie, J., and T. Freeman. 1961. "Disturbances of Perception and Consciousness in Schizophrenic States." *British Journal of Medical Psychology.*

Deasy, Leila C. 1956. "Socio Economic Status and Participation in the Poliomyelitis Vaccine Trial." *American Sociological Review* 21:185-191.

de Reuck, A. V. S., and Ruth Porter, eds. 1965. *Transcultural Psychiatry* (CIBA Foundation Symposium). Boston: Little, Brown and Company.

Devereux, George. 1950. *Reality and Dream.* New York: International Universities Press.

Dowling, Harry F., and David Sakow. 1952. "Time Spent by Internists on Adult Health Education and Preventive Medicine." *Journal of the American Medical Association* 149:628–631 (June 14).

Dubos, René. 1959. *Mirage of Health.* New York: Harper and Row.

————. 1965. *Man Adapting.* New Haven: Yale University Press.

Duff, Raymond S., and August B. Hollingshead. 1968. *Sickness and Society.* New York: Harper and Row.

Ehrenreich, Barbara, and John Ehrenreich. 1970. *The American Health Empire: Power, Profits and Politics.* New York: Vintage Books.

Ellis, Albert, 1951. *The Folklore of Sex.* New York: C. Boni.

Erasmus, Charles J. 1952. "Changing Folk Beliefs and the Relativity of Empirical Knowledge." *Southwestern Journal of Anthropology* 8:411–428.

Finney, Joseph C., ed. 1969. *Culture Change, Mental Health and Poverty.* Lexington: University Press of Kentucky.

Foster, George M. 1952. "Relationships between Theoretical and Applied Anthropology: A Public Health Program Analysis." *Human Organization* 11(3):5–16 (Fall).

————. 1953. Relationships between Spanish and Spanish-American Folk Medicine. *Journal of American Folklore* 66:210–217 (July).

Foulkes, Edward F. 1972. *The Arctic Hysterias of the North Alaskan Eskimo.* Anthropological Studies No. 10, American Anthropological Association.

Frank, Jerome D. 1974. *Persuasion and Healing: A Comparative Study of Psychotherapy,* rev. ed., New York: Schocken Books.

Frank, L. K. 1958. *Creating a Life Space.* (Manuscript.)

Frankel, Barbara. 1970. *Childbirth in the Ghetto: Folk Beliefs of Negro Women in a North Philadelphia Hospital Ward.* M.A. thesis, Temple University.

Frankfort, Ellen. 1973. *Vaginal Politics.* New York: Bantam Books.

Freeman, Howard E., Sol Levine, and Leo G. Reader, eds. 1963. *Handbook of Medical Sociology.* Englewood Cliffs, N.J.: Prentice-Hall.

Freemon, Frank R., and Frank T. Drake. 1967. "Abnormal Emotional Reactions to Hospitalization Jeopardizing Medical Treatment." *Psychosomatics* 8:150–155.

Galdston, Iago, ed. 1963. *Man's Image in Medicine and Anthropology.* New York: International Universities Press.

Garn, Stanely M. 1962. *Human Races.* Springfield, Illinois: Charles C. Thomas.

Gillian, John P. 1948. "Magical Fright." *Psychiatry* 11:387–400 (Nov.).

Glasser, Ronald. 1976. *The Greatest Battle.* New York: Random House.

Green, Arnold W. 1946. "The Middle-Class Male Child and Neurosis." *American Sociological Review* 11:31–41.

Grey, Alan. 1949. *Relationships between Social Status and Psychological Characteristics of Psychiatric Patients.* Ph.D. dissertation, University of Chicago.

Hall, Edward T. 1955. "The Anthropology of Manners." *Scientific American* 192:85–89.

_____ . 1960. "The Language of Space." *Landscape Magazine.* Fall. Reprinted: *Journal of the American Institute of Architects,* February, 1961.

_____ . 1969. *The Hidden Dimension.* New York: Anchor Books, Doubleday and Company.

Hallowell, A. Irving. 1963. "Ojibwa World View and Disease." In *Man's Image in Medicine and Anthropology,* Iago Galdston, ed. New York: International Universities Press.

Hand, Wayland D., ed. 1976. *American Folk Medicine: A Symposium.* Publications of the U.C.L.A. Center for the Study of Comparative Folklore and Mythology. Berkeley and Los Angeles: University of California Press.

Harrison, Dorothy Doyle Watts. 1967. *Cultural, Social, and Psychological Factors Affecting the Acceptance of Modern Medicine in an American Subculture.* Ph.D. dissertation, Catholic University of America.

Harrison, Ira E., and Diana S. Harrison. 1971. "The Black Family Experience and Health Behavior," In *Health and The Family,* Charles Crawford, ed. New York: Macmillan Company.

Henry, W. 1947. "The Thematic Apperception Technique in the Study of Culture-Personality Relations." *Genetic Psychology Monographs* 35:3–135.

Hill, G. L., et. al. 1977. "Malnutrition in Surgical Patients: An Unrecognized Problem." *The Lancet* pp. 689–692 (March 26).

Hollingshead, August B., and Frederick C. Redlich. 1958. *Social Class and Mental Illness.* New York: John Wiley and Sons.

Howard, J., and N. Byl. 1971. "Pitfalls in interdisciplinary teaching." *Journal of Medical Education* 46:772–781 (Sept.).

Hughes, Charles, and John M. Hunter. 1970. "Disease and Development in Africa." *Social Science in Medicine* 3:443–493. Also in *Custom Made: Introductory Readings for Cultural Anthropology,* Charles Hughes, ed. 1972. Chicago: Rand McNally Publishing Co.

Isumi, K. 1957. "An Analysis for the Design of Hospital Quarters for the Neuropsychiatric Patients." *Mental Hospitals* (April Architectural Supplement.).

Jaco, E. Gertly, ed. 1958. *Patients, Physicians and Illness: Sourcebook in Behavioral Science and Medicine.* Glencoe, Ill.: Free Press.

Jarvis, E. 1852. "Insanity Among the Colored Population of the Free States." *American Journal of Insanity* 8:268–282 (Jan.).

Kalish, Richard A., and David K. Reynolds. 1976. *Death and Ethnicity: A Psychocultural Study.* Los Angeles: Ethel Percy Andrus Gerontology Center/University of Southern California Press.

Karno, Marvin, and Robert B. Edgerton. 1969. "Perception of Mental Illness in a Mexican-American Community." *Archives of General Psychiatry* 20:233–238 (February).

Keefe, Susan E., Manuel L. Carlos, and Amado M. Padilla. 1976. "The Mexican-American Extended Family: A Mental Health Resource." A paper presented at the Southwestern Anthropological Association Meeting in San Francisco, April 14–18.

Kesey, Ken. 1962. *One Flew Over the Cuckoo's Nest.* New York: Signet Books/New American Library.

Kiev, Ari, ed. 1964. *Magic, Faith, and Healing: Studies in Primitive Psychiatry Today.* New York: Free Press.

————. 1968. *Curanderismo: Mexican-American Folk Psychiatry.* New York: Free Press.

————. 1972. *Transcultural Psychiatry.* New York: Free Press.

Kimball, Chase P. 1970. "A Case of Pseudocyesis Caused by 'Roots.' " *American Journal of Obstetrics and Gynecology* 107:801–803.

King, Stanley. 1962. *Perceptions of Illness and Medical Practice.* New York: Russell Sage Foundation.

Kira, Alexander. 1966. *The Bathroom: Criteria for Design.* Ithaca: Cornell University Press.

Kling, V. 1959. "Space: a Fundamental Concept in Design in Psychiatric Architecture." In *Psychiatric Architecture.* C. Goshen, ed. Washington, D.C.: American Psychiatric Association, pp. 21–22.

Kluckhohn, C. 1947. "The Influence of Psychiatry on Anthropology in America during the Past One Hundred Years." In *One Hundred Years of American Psychiatry,* J. K. Hall, G. Zilboorg, and H. Bunker, eds. New York: Columbia University Press, pp. 589–617.

Kluckhohn, D., and D. Leighton. 1948. *Children of the People.* Cambridge, Mass.: Harvard University Press.

Kniep-Hardy, Mary, and Margaret A. Burkhardt. 1977. "Nursing the Navajo." *American Journal of Nursing* 77:95–96 (January).

Koos, Earl Loman. 1954. *The Health of Regionville.* New York: Columbia University Press.

Kourennoff, Paul M. 1970. *Russian Folk Medicine.* London: W. H. Allen and Company, Ltd.

Kübler-Ross, Elisabeth. 1969. *On Death and Dying.* New York: Macmillan Publishing Company.

Kunnes, Richard. 1971. *Your Money or Your Life: Rx for the Medical Market Place.* New York: Dodd, Mead and Company.

Landy, David, ed. 1977. *Culture, Disease, and Healing: Studies in Medical Anthropology.* New York: Macmillan Publishing Company.

Langness, L. L. *Other Fields, Other Grasshoppers.* Philadelphia: J. B. Lippincott Company.

Leininger, M. 1971. "This I believe . . . about interdisciplinary education for the future." *Nursing Outlook* 19:787–791 (Dec.).

Leslie, Charles, ed. 1976. *Asian Medical Systems.* Berkeley: University of California Press.

Levin, P., and E. Berne. 1972. "Games Nurses Play." *American Journal of Nursing* 72:483–487 (March).

Lewin, K., 1958. *A Dynamic Theory of Personality.* New York: McGraw-Hill Book Company.

Lind, John E. 1917. "Phylogenetic Elements in the Psychosis of the Negro." *Psychoanalytic Review* 4:303–332.

Linton, Ralph. 1936. *The Study of Man.* New York: D. Appleton-Century Co.

Logan, Michael H., and Edward E. Hunt, Jr., eds. 1978. *Health and the Human Condition: Perspectives on Medical Anthropology.* North Scituate, Mass.: Duxbury Press.

Los Angeles Times. 1974. Article on Homosexuality as a Mental Disorder. April 9.

Lynch, L. Riddick, ed. 1969. *The Cross-Cultural Approach to Health Behavior.* Madison, N.J.: Fairleigh Dickinson University Press.

Lynden, Patricia. 1967. "Last holdouts." *Atlantic* 220:42–46 (Aug.)

MacGregor, Francis C. 1960 *Social Science in Nursing: Application for the Improvement of Patient Care.* New York: Russell Sage Foundation.

McNeill, William H. 1976. *Plagues and People.* Garden City, N.Y.: Anchor/Doubleday.

Maduro, Reynaldo. 1975. "Hoodoo Possession in San Francisco." *Ethos* 3:424–447.

Malinowski, Bronislaw. 1948. *Magic, Science, and Religion.* Glencoe: Free Press.

Marriott, McKim. 1955. "Western Medicine in a Village of Northern India." In *Health, Culture, and Community: Case Studies of Public Reactions to Health Programs,* Benjamin Paul, ed. New York: Russell Sage Foundation.

MD. 1958. "Homely Medicine." *MD,* pp. 102–108 (Nov.).

Mead, Margaret. 1955. *Cultural Patterns and Technical Change.* New York: Mentor Books, New American Library, Inc.

Mechanic, David. 1968. *Medical Sociology.* New York: Free Press.

Michaelson, Mike. 1972. "Can a 'Root Doctor' Actually Put a Hex on or Is It All a Great Put-on?" *Today's Health,* pp. 39–42 (March).

Moholy-Nagy, L. 1949. *The New Vision.* New York: Wittenborn, Schultz.

Montagu, Ashley, ed. 1964. *The Concept of Race.* New York: Free Press.

Murdock, George P. 1949. *Social Structure.* New York: Macmillan Company.

NDES. 1976. *Neurological Disease Epidemiologic Study: Summary.* Division of Epidemiology in cooperation with U.C.L.A. Department of Neurology (January).

Nelson, Harry. 1973. "Multiple Sclerosis: A Link to Geography?" *Los Angeles Times,* July 16, Part I, p. 16.

Newsweek. 1973. "A Farewell to Flatulence." *Newseek,* July 9.

Norman, John C. 1969. *Medicine in the Ghetto.* New York: Appleton-Century-Crofts.

Opler, Marvin, ed. 1959. *Culture and Mental Health.* New York: Macmillan Company.

———. 1967. *Culture and Social Psychiatry.* New York: Atherton Press.

Ortiz de Montellano, Bernard. 1974/1975. "Aztec Medicine: Empirical Drug Use." *Ethnomedizin* 3(3/4):249.

Osmond, H., 1957. "Function as the Basis of Psychiatric Ward Design." *Mental Hospitals* (April Architectural Supplement), pp. 23–29.

———. 1959. "The Historical and Sociological Development of Mental Hospitals." In *Psychiatric Architecture,* C. Goshen, ed. Washington, D.C.: American Psychiatric Association, pp. 7–9.

Paffenbarger, Ralph S., and James Watt. 1953. "Poliomyelitis in Hidalgo County, Texas, 1948: Epidemiological Observations." *The American Journal of Hygiene* 58:269–287.

Parker, Seymour, and Robert J. Kleiner, eds. 1966. *Mental Illness in the Urban Negro Community.* New York: Free Press.

Paul, Benjamin D. 1953. "The Cultural Context of Health Education."*Symposium Proceedings.* Pittsburgh: Pittsburgh School of Social Work.

_____ , ed. 1955. *Health, Culture, and Community: Case Studies of Public Reactions to Health Programs.* New York: Russell Sage Foundation.

Payne, Thelma Dobbins. 1970. *Behavioral Responses of Japanese Patients to Illness, Birth, Accidents, Surgery, and Death.* M.A. thesis, California State University, Los Angeles.

Petrello, Judith. 1976. "Your Patients Hear You, but Do They Understand?" *RN Magazine,* pp. 37–39 (Feb.)

Plog, Stanley C., and Robert Edgerton, eds. 1969. *Changing Perspectives in Mental Illness.* New York: Holt, Rinehart and Winston.

Polgar, Steven. 1962. "Health and Human Behavior: Areas of Interest Common to The Social and Medical Sciences." *Current Anthropology* 3:159–205.

Pratt, Lois and Margaret Mudd. 1956. "Patients' Medical Care Expectations as Influenced by Patient-Physician Interaction." Paper read at American Sociological Society Meetings, Sept. 7.

Primeaux, Martha. 1977. "Caring for the American Indian Patient." *American Journal of Nursing.* 77:91–94 (Jan.).

Reader, George, Lois Pratt, and Margaret Mudd. 1957. "Clinic Patients' Expectations of Medical Care." *Modern Hospital* 89:1 (July).

Redlich, F. C., A. B. Hollingshead, and E. Bellis. 1955. "Social Class Differences in Attitudes toward Psychiatry." *American Journal of Orthopsychiatry,* 25:60–70.

Rocereto, LaVerne P. 1973. "Root Work and the Root Doctor." *Nursing Forum* 12:414–427.

Roff, Adolf. 1958. *Unser Hausfreund.* Lorch: Karl Rohm Verlag.

Rosebury, Theodor. 1969. *Life on Man.* New York: Viking Press.

_____ . 1971. *Microbes and Morals: The Strange Story of Venereal Disease.* New York: Viking Press.

Rosenblatt, Paul C., R. Patricia Walsh, and Douglas A. Jackson. 1976. *Grief and Mourning in Cross-Cultural Perspective.* New Haven: Human Relations Area Files (HRAF) Press.

Rosenhan, D. L. 1973. "On Being Sane in Insane Places." *Science* 179:250–258.

Roueche, Berton. 1947. *Eleven Blue Men.* New York: Berkley Publishing Company.

Rubel, Arthur J. 1960. "Concepts of Disease in Mexican-American Culture." *American Anthropologist* 62:795–814 (Oct.).

_____ . 1964. "The Epidemiology of a Folk Illness: Susto in Hispanic America." *Ethnology* 3:268–283 (July).

Sagarin, Edward. 1962. *The Anatomy of Dirty Words.* New York: Lyle Stuart.

Saunders, Lyle. 1954. *Cultural Difference and Medical Care: The Case of the Spanish-Speaking People of the Southwest.* New York: Russell Sage Foundation.

_____ . 1972. "Healing Ways in the Spanish Southwest." In *Readings in Anthropology,* Jesse D. Jennings and E. Adamson Hoebel, eds., New York: McGraw-Hill Book Company. Also in Jaco (1958).

Scotch, Norman. 1960. "A Preliminary Report on the Relation of Sociocultural Factors to Hypertension Among the Zulu." *Annals, New York Academy of Sciences* 84:1000–1009.

_____. 1963. "Medical Anthropology." In *Biennial Review of Anthropology,* B. J. Siegel, ed. Stanford: Stanford University Press.

Scott, Clarissa S. 1974. "Health and Healing Practices among Five Ethnic Groups in Miami, Florida." *Public Health Reports* 89:524–532.

Scott, W. Richard, and Edmund H. Volkart. 1966. *Medical Care: Readings in the Sociology of Medical Institutions.* New York: John Wiley and Sons.

Searles, H. 1960. *The Nonhuman Environment.* New York: International Universities Press.

Seham, Max. 1973. *Blacks and American Medical Care.* Minneapolis: University of Minnesota Press.

Seligmann, Arthur, Neva McGrath, and Lois Pratt. 1957. "Level of Medical Information among Clinic Patients." *Journal of Chronic Diseases* 6(5):497–509.

Selye, Hans. 1956. *The Stress of Life.* New York: McGraw-Hill Book Company.

Seward, Georgene. 1972. *Psychotherapy and Culture Conflict in Community Health.* New York: Ronald Press.

Shannon, Gary W., and G. E. Dever. 1974. *Health Care Delivery: Spatial Perspectives.* New York: McGraw-Hill Book Company.

Shryock, R. H. 1947. *The Development of Modern Medicine: An Interpretation of the Social and Scientific Factors Involved.* New York: Alfred A. Knopf.

Simmons, Leo W., and Harold G. Wolff. 1954. *Social Science in Medicine.* New York: Russell Sage Foundation.

Simmons, Ozzie E. 1953. *The Health Center of San Miguel: An Analysis of a Public Health Program in Chile.* Santiago: Institute of Inter-American Affairs.

_____. 1955. "The Clinical Team in a Chilean Health Center." In *Health, Culture, and Community: Case Studies of Public Reactions to Health Programs,* Benjamin Paul, ed. New York: Russell Sage Foundation.

_____. 1955a. "Popular and Modern Medicine in Mestizo Communities of Coastal Peru and Chile." *Journal of American Folklore,* 68:57–71.

Sivadon, P. n.d. *Techniques of Socio-therapy.* (Manuscript.)

Skipper, James K., and Robert C. Leonard. 1965. *Social Interaction and Patient Care.* Philadelphia: J. B. Lippincott Company.

Smith, Aileen M., and W. Eugene Smith. 1975. *Minamata: Words and Photographs.* New York: Holt, Rinehart and Winston.

Smith, D. W., and C. Gips. 1963. *Care of the Adult Patient.* Philadelphia: J. B. Lippincott Company, pp. 363–392, 598–641.

Snell, John E. 1967. "Hypnosis in the Treatment of the 'Hexed' Patient." *American Journal of Psychiatry* 124:3:311–316.

Snow, C. P. 1964. *The Two Cultures: A Second Look.* Cambridge, England: Cambridge University Press.

Snow, Loudell. 1973. " 'I Was Born Just Exactly with the Gift': An Interview with a Voodoo Practitioner." *Journal of American Folklore* 86:272–281.

_____. 1974. "Folk Medical Beliefs and Their Implications for Care of Patients." *Annals of Internal Medicine* 81:82–96.

_____ . 1977. "Popular Medicine in a Black Neighborhood." In *Ethnic Medicine in the Southwest,* Edward H. Spicer, ed. Tucson: University of Arizona Press.

Sollenberger, H. 1951-1955. *Orientation Lectures Given to Point IV Technicians Attending the Foreign Service Institute.* Washington, D.C.: U.S. Department of State.

Sommer, R. 1959. "Studies in Personal Space." *Sociometry* 22:247-260.

_____ . 1961. "Leadership and Group Geography." *Sociometry* 24:99-109.

Sommer, R., and Ross, H. 1958. "Social Interaction on a Geriatric Ward." *International Journal of Social Psychiatry* 4:128-133.

Sommer, R., and Whitney, G. 1961. "Design for Friendship." *The Canadian Architect.*

Spicer, Edward D., ed. 1977. *Ethnic Medicine in the Southwest.* Tucson: University of Arizona Press.

Spitzer, Stephan P., and Norman K. Denzin. 1968. *The Mental Patient: Studies in The Sociology of Deviance.* New York: McGraw-Hill Book Company.

Stein, Leonard I. 1968. "The Doctor-Nurse Game." *American Journal of Nursing* 68:101-105 (Jan.).

Steiner, George. 1967. *Language and Silence.* New York: Atheneum.

Sullivan, Harry Stack. 1947. *Conceptions of Modern Psychiatry.* Washington, D.C.: William Alanson White Foundation.

_____ . 1954. *The Psychiatric Interview,* New York: W. W. Norton and Company.

Szasz, Thomas S. 1960. "The Myth of Mental Illness." *The American Psychologist* 15:113-118 (Feb.).

_____ . 1961. *The Myth of Mental Illness.* New York: Harper and Row.

_____ . 1970. *Ideology and Insanity.* Garden City, N.Y.: Anchor Books/ Doubleday and Company.

_____ . 1971. "The Sane Slave: An Historical Note on the Use of Medical Diagnosis as Justificatory Rhetoric." *American Journal of Psychotherapy* 25(2) (April).

_____ . ed. 1973. *The Age of Madness.* Garden City, N.Y.: Anchor Books/Doubleday and Company.

Taylor, Carol. 1970. *In Horizontal Orbit: Hospitals and the Cult of Efficiency.* New York: Holt, Rinehart, and Winston.

Tinling, David C. 1967. "Voodoo, Root Work, and Medicine." *Psychosomatic Medicine* 29:483-490.

Torrey, E. Fuller. 1972. *The Mind Game.* New York: Bantam Books.

_____ . 1974. *The Death of Psychiatry.* Radnor, Pa.: Chilton Book Company.

United States Navy. 1959. *Preliminary Report on Shelter Occupancy Test* 3-17 (USN Roh-TR-418). U.S. Naval Radiological Laboratory.

Wagley, Charles. 1968. *The Latin American Tradition.* New York: Columbia University Press.

Warren, Kenneth S. 1974. "Precarious Odyssey of an Unconquered Parasite." *Natural History,* pp. 46-53 (May).

Watson, James D. 1968. *The Double Helix.* New York: Signet Books/New American Library.

Webb, Julie Yvonne. 1971. "Louisiana Voodoo and Superstitions Related to Health." *Health Reports* 86:4:291–301.

Weckowitz, T. I. 1957. "Notes on Perceptual World of Schizophrenic Patients." *Mental Hospitals,* pp. 23–24. (April Architectural Supplement).

Weed, L. L. 1970. *Medical Records, Medical Education and Patient Care.* Cleveland: Press of Case Western Reserve University.

Wellin, Edward. 1955. "Water Boiling in a Peruvian Town." In *Health, Culture, and Community: Case Studies of Public Reactions to Health Programs,* Benjamin Paul, ed. New York: Russell Sage Foundation.

Whitten, Norman E. 1962. "Contemporary Patterns of Malign Occultism among Negroes in North Carolina." *Journal of American Folklore* 75:311–325.

Winick, C., and Holt, H. 1961. "Seating Positions as Non-verbal Communication in Group Analysis." *Psychiatry* 24:171–182.

Winslow, David J. 1969. "Bishop E. E. Everett and Some Aspects of Occultism and Folk Religion in Negro Philadelphia." *Keystone Folklore Quarterly* 14:2:59–80.

Wintrob, Ronald. 1972. "Hexes, Roots, Snake Eggs? MD vs. Occult." *Medical Opinion* 1:7:55–61.

———. 1973. "The Influence of Others: Witchcraft and Rootwork as Explanations of Behavior Disturbances." *Journal of Nervous and Mental Disease* 156:318–326.

Wintrob, Ronald, Robert A. Fox, and Ellen O'Brien. 1971. "Rootwork Beliefs and Psychiatric Disorder among Blacks in a Northern United States City." Paper presented at the V World Congress of Psychiatry, Mexico City, December, 1971.

Withers, Carol. 1946. "Folklore of a Small Town." *Transactions of the New York Academy of Sciences,* Series II 8:234–251. Also in *Medical Care: Readings in the Sociology of Medical Institutions,* W. Richard Scott and Edmund H. Volkart, eds. New York: John Wiley and Sons, 1966.

Wittreich, W. F., M. Grace, and K. Radcliffe, Jr. 1961. "Three Experiments in Selective Perceptual Distortion." In *Explorations in Transactional Psychology,* F. Kilpatrick, ed. New York: New York University Press.

Woodbury, M. A. 1958. *Ward Dynamics and the Formation of a Therapeutic Group.* Rockville, Md.: Chestnut Lodge Symposium. (Mimeograph)

Yoors, Jan. 1967. *Gypsies.* New York: Simon and Schuster.

Zinsser, Hans. 1935. *Rats, Lice and History.* Boston: Little, Brown and Company.

Zola, Irving K. 1966. "Culture and Symptoms: An Analysis of Patients' Presenting Complaints." *American Sociological Review* 31:615–630.